How to Master the Spoken Word

Edwin Lawrence Godkin

How to Master the Spoken Word

ISBN: 978-1-64799-204-0

PREFACE

This work aims to show how to breathe correctly, produce voice properly, put the meaning into words by aid of inflection, emphasis, and the tones of the voice; how to improve the memory, acquire fluency of speech, control an audience, construct speeches, and in every way become competent to think on one's feet and express thought vocally in an entertaining, convincing, and moving manner. It is intended as a text-book to aid in making students proficient in the art of vocal expression. It aims to cover the field exhaustively, dealing in a comprehensive manner with all subjects pertaining to the construction and the delivery of speeches.

There are so many books treating of the subject of oratory that there would appear scant room for another, but as they all treat mainly of the way to speak, and only give general instructions as to how to speak, there is, in the author's opinion, a wide field for a book that explicitly shows not only what a person should employ in order to become a ready and effective speaker but also gives specific instructions as the employment of those means.

This book is intended to take the place of the living teacher wherever the services of a thoroughly competent one cannot be secured, or where the student desires to work in the privacy of his own room, and the aim of the author is to make it more practical and of greater value than any of the so-called "Personal Correspondence Courses" now being exploited, and for which exorbitant fees are charged. It may, however, be used to equal advantage by the teacher in the class room as a text-book.

No vague instructions such as, "speak in a clear ringing voice," "use expressive language," "mean what you say," etc., will be given; but in their place will be found directions as to how to gain a good voice, how to acquire the power of explaining by the tones of the voice the meaning of the spoken words, how to secure a delivery that will carry conviction to the listener, and how to construct speeches. In short, this book aims not only to tell the essentials of oratory but also to show the way in which they may be acquired. It contains the complete course in oratorical training as given in the Lawrence School of New York. Finally, the book is presented as a vade mecum that will pilot the would-be orator to success.

Edwin G. Lawrence

FOREWORD

Vital are the questions now confronting man the world over; but particularly are those questions important to Americans, because the United States of America is looked upon as the pioneer country of the world in all matters pertaining to man's emancipation from the injustice of ages, and that young country is expected to blaze a trail through the unsolved realm of progress along which the older nations may travel till they reach the plain of universal justice and liberty.

Among the problems now confronting the people are those of finance, labor, religion, conservation of natural resources, and civic justice. The questions are here, but where are the orators capable of making those questions clear to the masses? Where are the men to solve those problems? Some there are who are nobly responding to the demands of the times, but they are too few successfully to grapple with the task.

It is claimed that this is the age of the printing-press and that the necessity for orators no longer exists. This is surely not a valid claim. The newspaper is doing its work, and in many cases is doing it nobly, but it can never take the place of the human voice. An article may be printed in a paper having a circulation running into the hundreds of thousands, and yet the article will be read by only a small percentage of those into whose hands the paper falls; and out of this percentage a still smaller percentage will be influenced by the printed word. The speaker, on the other hand, addresses an audience of only a few thousand, but of that number, if the speaker is deserving of the name, he will influence a majority. Suppose he convinces and persuades only one hundred, the one hundred are so thoroughly brought into accord with the speaker that they go out into the world and, by word of mouth, bring ten times their number to the same way of thinking. By this means all great movements have flourished. John the Baptist, with the spoken word, prepared the way and made straight the path; Jesus of Nazareth taught by spoken symbols only; Paul of Tarsus carried Christianity into Greece and Rome by means of speech; Peter the Hermit enthused the Crusaders by his spoken utterances; Martin Luther brought about a reformation by his speech before the Diet of Worms; Patrick Henry aroused his countrymen by his eloquence; Daniel O'Connell accomplished Catholic emancipation in Great Britain by means of presenting the cause of religious liberty to friend and foe in the shape of the spoken word; Daniel Webster expounded the Constitution orally; William Lloyd Garrison, Wendell Phillips and Abraham Lincoln pleaded for the enslaved negro by word of mouth; and La Follette, Bryan, and Roosevelt are expressing the thoughts of the people of today by means of man's greatest attribute—speech.

Therefore, if any would take part in the glorious work of advancing the progress of the world, let him fit himself to discuss by word of mouth the great problems now confronting humanity.

THE VALUE OF ELOQUENCE

Faith cometh by hearing.

—St. Paul, Romans X:17

It is not enough to speak, but to speak true.

—Shakespeare

Mend your speech a little

Lest it may mar your fortunes.

—Shakespeare

The power of utterance should be included by all in their plans of self-culture.

—William Ellery Channing

He is an orator that can make me think as he thinks and feel as he feels.

—Daniel Webster

A vessel is known by its sound whether it be cracked or not; so men are proved by their speeches, whether they be wise or foolish.

—Demosthenes

I advocate in its full intent and for every reason of humanity, of patriotism, of religion, a more thorough culture of oratory.

—Henry Ward Beecher

Eloquence has a client which, before all, it must save or make triumph. It matters little whether this client be a man, a people, or an idea.

—Victor Cousin

It is to this early speaking practice in the great art of all arts, oratory, that I am indebted for the primary and leading impulses that stimulated me forward.

—Henry Clay

Ninety-nine men in every hundred in the crowded professions will probably never rise above mediocrity because the training of the voice is entirely neglected and considered of no importance.

—William E. Gladstone

He who does not use a gift, loses it; the man who does not use his voice or limbs, loses power over them, and becomes disqualified for the state of life to which he is called.

—Cardinal Newman

I recognize but one mental acquisition as an essential part of the education of a lady or gentleman, namely, an accurate and refined use of the mother-tongue.

—Charles W. Eliot

Extemporaneous speaking should be practiced and cultivated. It is the lawyer's avenue to the public. However able and faithful he may be in other respects, people are slow to bring him business if he cannot make a speech.

—Abraham Lincoln

The cultivated voice is like an orchestra. It ranges high, intermediate or low, unconsciously to him who uses it, and men listen, unaware that they have been bewitched out of their weariness by the charms of a voice not artificial, but made by assiduous training to be his second nature.

—Henry Ward Beecher

Men forget what they read; some do not read at all. They do not, however, forget when they are told by a vigorous speaker who means what he says.

—John Oliver Hobbes (Mrs. Craigie)

For who can suppose amid the great multitude of students, the utmost abundance of masters, the most eminent geniuses among men, the infinite variety of causes, the most ample rewards offered to eloquence, there is any other reason to be found for the small number of orators than the incredible magnitude and difficulty of the art?

—Cicero

CONTENTS

CHAPTER I

THE MAKING OF ORATORY

THE MEANS EMPLOYED BY GREAT ORATORS

The question is often asked, How can I become a public speaker? This might be aptly answered by putting another question, How did other men become public speakers? because by a careful study of the means they employed, others may become equally proficient. From the beginning of oratory down to the present day orators have made their effects in composition and delivery by the selfsame means, and if men of today will apply themselves to a mastery of those means with perseverance and intelligence equal to that of the men of the past, there is no reason why they should not meet with equal proficiency.

Let us go back to Gorgias, the Greek rhetorician and teacher of oratory, who was born about the year 483 b. c., and study the manner of his workmanship.

In his speech "The Encomium on Helen," he arranges his words in masterly style, making use of all the forms of construction that we possess at this time. He employs the series, the contrasts (single, double, and triple), the conditional, the negative, the positive, and, in fact, all the known forms of arranging words so as to make them best express the orator's meaning. Here is an effective concluding series he uses: "A city is adorned by good citizenship, the body by beauty, the soul by wisdom, acts by virtue, and speech by truthfulness," and he follows this sentence with the following one: "But the opposites of these virtues are a disgrace." Note how effective he makes the first thought by immediately contrasting it with one that rivets the attention to the graces of good citizenship, beauty, wisdom, virtue, and truthfulness, by stating that the reverse of these things are disgraces. Then follows a series of contrasts: "Man and woman, word and deed, city and government" which, he says, "we ought to praise," and then qualifies this positive with the conditional, "if praiseworthy," and then makes a strong contrast by stating, "and blame" which he qualifies by adding the conditional "if blameworthy." He then makes a statement very strong by employing a double contrast, "For it is equally wrong and stupid to censure what is commendable, and to commend what is censurable." After this clear reasoning comes another statement: "Now I conceive it to be my duty in the interest of justice to confute the slanders of Helen, the memory of whose misfortunes has been kept alive by the writings of the poets and the fame of her name." He ends his statement with this strong concluding series, "I propose, therefore, by argument to exonerate her from the charge of infamy, to convince her accusers of their error, and remove their ignorance by a revelation of the truth." Now read the entire paragraph:

A city is adorned by good citizenship, the body by beauty, the soul by wisdom, acts by virtue, and speech by truthfulness. But the opposites of these virtues are a disgrace. Man and woman, word and deed, city and government we ought to praise if praiseworthy, and blame if blameworthy. For it is equally wrong and stupid to censure what is commendable, and to commend what is censurable. Now I conceive it to be my duty in the interest of justice to confute the slanders of Helen, the memory of whose misfortunes has been kept alive by the writings of the poets and the fame of her name. I propose, therefore, by argument to exonerate her from the charge of infamy, to convince her accusers of their error, and to remove their ignorance by a revelation of the truth.

This is a masterly passage, clear in its statement, logical in its argument, and sound in its conclusion, making a splendid model for a student of oratory to follow. True, the mere faculty of arranging words will not constitute an orator, but it is one of the essentials that go to the making of one; and this power of arranging words, and the capacity for electing the appropriate theme, and judgment in adopting the proper delivery are the principal means that men have possessed in all times for the making of orators. It is essential that the arts of construction and composition should be diligently studied by speakers, for it is as impossible to have oratory without men who understand the rules of composition as it is to have orators without oratory. Matter that is to be spoken must not merely be well written, it must be constructed according to the rules of oratory in order that it may sound well. Literature is to be read, oratory is to be spoken; consequently words intended to be spoken must be arranged in such a manner as to make them more effective when uttered by the living voice than when they are set in dead type; and this can only be done by gaining a mastery of the rules of oratory and applying them correctly. We are now dealing with the creation of oratory; later, we will consider the making of orators. The example of Gorgias' oratory cited here gives a clear illustration of the effective use of words, and in order to emphasize this important point of the value of words according to their location, other examples follow.

William H. Seward in his "Plea for the Union" uses this sentence:

If the constellation is to be broken up, the stars, whether scattered widely apart or grouped in smaller clusters, will thenceforth shed forth feeble, glimmering, and lurid lights.

He opens with a conditional phrase, "If the constellation is to be broken up" and then commences his statement with "the stars" which he interrupts to interject the parenthetical phrase "whether scattered

2

widely apart or grouped in smaller clusters," goes back to his main thought with the words "will thenceforth shed forth feeble, glimmering, and lurid lights." "Feeble, glimmering, and lurid" constitute a commencing series qualifying "lights," and thus is brought about an effective close to a well-knit sentence.

Another well-arranged sentence for cumulative force is the following from the same speech:

After Washington, and the inflexible Adams, Henry, and the fearless Hamilton, Jefferson, and the majestic Clay, Webster, and the acute Calhoun, Jackson, the modest Taylor, and Scott, who rises in greatness under the burden of years, and Franklin, and Fulton, and Whitney, and Morse, have all performed their parts, let the curtain fall.

In long sentences, such as this, care should be exercised properly to group the members composing it, otherwise the force will be lost on account of a confusion of ideas. In this sentence there are three groups: Washington, Adams, Henry, Hamilton, and Jefferson constituting the first; Clay, Webster, Calhoun, Jackson, Taylor, and Scott the second; Franklin, Fulton, Whitney, and Morse the third. These, with the phrase "have all performed their parts," constitute a commencing series, the sense being completed by "let the curtain fall."

In his address, "The American Scholar," delivered at Cambridge, Mass., August 31, 1837, Ralph Waldo Emerson employed these words:

The theory of books is noble. The scholar of the first age received into him the world around; brooded thereon; gave it the new arrangement of his own mind and uttered it again. It came into him, life; it went out from him, truth. It came to him, short-lived actions; it went out from him, immortal thoughts. It came to him, business; it went from him, poetry. It was dead fact; now, it is quick thought. It can stand and it can go. It now endures, it now flies, it now inspires. Precisely in proportion to the depth of mind from which it issued, so high does it soar, so long does it sing.

This powerful passage is effective mainly because of the masterful arrangement of the words. Emerson opens with the positive statement that "The theory of books is noble." He follows this with the concluding series, "The scholar of the first age received into him the world around; brooded thereon; gave it the new arrangement of his own mind and uttered it again." Then comes the double contrast, "It came into him, life; it went out from him, truth." This is followed by a triple contrast, "It came to him, short-lived actions; it went out from him, immortal thoughts." Then comes another double contrast, "It came to him, business; it went from him, poetry." Then another triple contrast is used, "It was dead fact; now, it is quick thought." Then comes the positive statement that "It can stand and it can go." A concluding series then follows, "It now endures, it now flies, it now inspires," and the paragraph ends with the conditional phrase and the concluding phrases, "Precisely in proportion to the depth of mind from which it issued, so high does it soar, so long does it sing," the concluding clause containing the double contrast, "so high does it soar, so long does it sing." Few paragraphs of like length contain so much thought as does this one of Emerson's, and the immensity of thought could be placed in such a small space only because of the skilful disposition of the words, the meaning being made clear by the clever placing of one word against another word, one idea against another idea. The sentences are short, and while they may not be particularly beautiful, they are exceedingly strong.

In Lincoln's Second Inaugural Address is this telling sentence:

To strengthen, perpetuate, and extend this interest [slavery] was the object for which the insurgents would rend the Union, even by war; while the government claimed no right to do more than to restrict the territorial enlargement of it.

The words "strengthen, perpetuate, and extend" are a commencing series because they act on the word "interest." Slavery was the object for which the insurgents would separate the Union, even by going to the extreme of making war; while the Federal Government claimed merely the right to prevent its spreading into the territories. What makes this sentence so clear and so forceful is the manner in which the contrast is brought out regarding the acts of the insurgents and the claims of the Government.

One of the most expressive and best constructed sentences in English literature is the following from Lincoln's Gettysburg Address:

The world will little note nor long remember what we say here, but it can never forget what they did here.

This is a triple opposition, "The world will little note nor long remember" being contrasted with "but it can never forget," "we" with "they," and "say" with "did."

Another beautiful specimen of construction is the last paragraph of Lincoln's Second Inaugural Address:

With malice toward none; with charity for all; with firmness in the right, as God gives us to see the right—let us strive on to finish the work we are in: to bind up the nation's wounds; to care for him who shall have borne the battle, and for his widow and his orphan; to do all which may achieve and cherish a just and lasting peace among ourselves, and with all nations.

Had Lincoln merely said "with malice toward none" it would not have meant half so much as it does with the words "with charity for all" added. This example emphasizes the force of contrast, for by stating the positive "with charity for all" as well as the negative "with malice toward none," he makes his expressed thought clear, strong, and comprehensive, clinching the subject and leaving no possible loophole for a misunderstanding to creep in. "With firmness in the right" is fittingly qualified by "as God gives us to see the right," and the thought is splendidly closed with "let us strive on to finish the work we are in."

4

Then by means of a concluding series he states what this work is that we should strive to finish, and he concludes with the general summing up, "to do all which may achieve and cherish a just and lasting peace among ourselves, and with all nations."

Daniel Webster, in his address on the occasion of the laying of the corner-stone of Bunker Hill Monument, used this sentence:

Human beings are composed, not of reason only, but of imagination also, and sentiment; and that is neither wasted nor misapplied which is appropriated to the purpose of giving right direction to sentiment, and opening proper springs of feeling in the heart.

The orator states that reason is a portion of the composition out of which human beings are made, but that it is not the only ingredient; that imagination is a part also, as is sentiment, and that nothing is either wasted or misapplied which is used in rightly directing feeling, and freeing the heart of all obstructions in order that its emotions may come forth. In doing this, Webster uses the qualified negative "not of reason only," meaning, of course, that human beings are composed of reason, but stating that they are not composed "only" of reason, but of reason, imagination, and sentiment, and then, by means of two negatives, "neither" and "nor," he states that whatever is used for the object of rightly directing sentiment is not wasted and not misapplied.

In the same address, he says:

If, indeed, there be anything in local association fit to affect the mind of man, we need not strive to repress the emotions which agitate us here. We are among the sepulchers of our fathers. We are on ground distinguished by their valor, their constancy, and the shedding of their blood.

The first phrase is conditional, the balance of the sentence is negative. The orator ably opens with a condition because he is sure of all his listeners subscribing to it, and then he says that if there is anything of a local nature that is proper to act sufficiently on man's mind as to make an impression on it, then certainly we, standing over the graves of our fathers, and on the very ground that drank their blood, shed in the cause of liberty, should not be ashamed to give expression to the emotions these associations cause us to feel. In constructing these three sentences Webster uses a conditional clause and a concluding one, and two positive sentences, the last one consisting of a concluding series. The last sentence is much stronger and better as a series of three members than it would be as a sentence containing but one. It is far better to weld together the three facts that the ground was distinguished by their valor, their constancy, and the shedding of their blood, than it would be to state merely that it was distinguished by their valor.

Here is another of Webster's grand and expressive periods:

On this question of principle, while actual suffering was yet far off, they raised their flag against a power, to which, for purposes of foreign conquest and subjugation, Rome, in the height of her glory, is not to be compared—a power which has dotted over the surface of the whole globe with her possessions and military posts, whose morning drumbeat, following the sun, and keeping company with the hours, circles the earth with one continuous and unbroken strain of the martial airs of England.

This is a long sentence but a strong one and it is constructed so as to bring to the mind of the listener the picture which the speaker possessed. Notice that if the parenthetical phrases, which aid so much in picturing the scene, were omitted, the sentence would not be more than half its present size, but the vividness of the picture would disappear with the curtailing of the sentence. Here is the main idea: "On this question of principle they raised their flag against a power to which Rome is not to be compared—a power which has dotted over the surface of the whole globe with her possessions and military posts, whose morning drumbeat circles the earth with one continuous and unbroken strain of the martial airs of England." This example is cited to show that what are called loose sentences are necessary to beauty of expression and vivid picturing. Notice how the parenthetical clauses amplify and explain the thought—"while actual suffering was yet far off," "for purposes of foreign conquest and subjugation," "in the height of her glory," "following the sun, and keeping company with the hours." Without these coloring clauses the sentence would be strong, but it would lose much of its beauty.

Let us examine here an extract from the oratory of the ancients. Demosthenes, in his speech, "Against the Law of Leptines," delivered in 355 b. c., uses this language:

If now you condemn the law, as we advise, the deserving will have their rights from you; and if there be any underserving party, as I grant there may be, such a one, besides being deprived of his honor, will suffer what penalty you think proper according to the amended statute, while the commonwealth will appear faithful, just, true to all men. Should you decide in its favor, which I trust you will not, the good will be wronged on account of the bad, the underserving will be the cause of misfortune to others, and suffer no punishment themselves, while the commonwealth (contrary to what I said just now) will be universally esteemed faithless, envious, base. It is not meet, O Athenians, that for so foul a reproach you should reject fair and honorable advantages. Remember, each of you individually will share in the reputation of your common judgment. It is plain to the bystanders and to all men that in the court Leptines is contending with us, but in the mind of each of you jurymen generosity is arrayed against envy, justice against iniquity, all that is virtuous against all that is base.

The above is a literal translation of a portion of a speech that was delivered more than twenty-two centuries ago, and yet, in its construction, it does not differ in any material manner from a well constructed speech of today. Notice the conditional, "If now you condemn the law," followed by the parenthetical, "as we advise," and the concluding, "the deserving will have their rights from you," and compare the passage with any modern expression of a like nature. They will be found to correspond in every manner so far as the construction is concerned. Examine the extract in its entirety and you will see that a skilful use is made of negatives, positives, parentheses, conditionals, oppositions, series, and all the many forms of arranging words for an effective conveyance of thought which are possessed by speakers of the present time. In the manner of its construction, this extract from the speech of Demosthenes does not differ from the speeches of Seward, Webster, Emerson, and Lincoln which are here quoted, as they all depend for their effectiveness on the proper use of the rules of apposition, opposition, series, inflection, and emphasis; and all students of oratory are urged to study closely the chapters of this book which are devoted to these subjects.

Coming down to our own day, we find in the utterances of Roosevelt, Taft, Bryan, Watterson, La Follette, and many others the selfsame means of construction as were employed by Gorgias, Demosthenes, and Cicero. Theodore Roosevelt, in his address delivered at Chicago, April 10, 1899, used this forceful language:

As it is with the individual, so it is with the nation. It is a base untruth to say that happy is that nation that has no history. Thrice happy is the nation that has a glorious history. Far better is it to dare mighty things, to win glorious triumphs, even though checkered by failure, than to take rank with those poor spirits who neither enjoy much nor suffer much, because they live in the gray twilight that knows neither victory nor defeat.

Col. Roosevelt first compares the individual with the nation. He then employs an emphatic contradiction, following it with a short positive sentence. Then comes an effective contrast, separated to allow the use of a parenthetical phrase which amplifies the statement, and the end is a picture drawn with a few words—"because they live in the gray twilight that knows neither victory nor defeat."

William H. Taft, speaking at the unveiling of Lincoln's statue at Frankfort, Kentucky, on November 8, 1911, summed up the character of Abraham Lincoln in these well-chosen words:

With his love of truth, the supreme trait of his intellect, accompanied by a conscience that insisted on the right as he knew it, with a great heart full of tenderness, we have the combination that made Lincoln one of the two greatest Americans.

President Taft uses a commencing series and a parenthetical clause for conveying his thought. The series consists of three phrases: "With his love of truth," "accompanied by a conscience that insisted on the right as he knew it," and "with a great heart full of tenderness," the sense being completed by "we have the combination that made Lincoln one of the two greatest Americans." The phrase, "the supreme trait of his intellect," is parenthetical.

Col. Henry Watterson, on the same occasion, spoke thus:

Called like one of old, within a handful of years he rose at a supreme moment to supreme command, fulfilled the law of his being, and passed from the scene an exhalation of the dawn of freedom. We may still hear his cheery voice bidding us to be of good heart, sure that "right makes might," entreating us to pursue "with firmness in the right as God gives us to see the right."

Here we have the thought expressed by means of a concluding series of four members, and two positive statements reënforced by two quotations from Lincoln's Cooper Union Speech.

WORD-PICTURES

Besides the use of inflection, emphasis, and the arrangement of words, orators use word-pictures for conveying their ideas; as,

When I look around and see our prosperity in everything—agriculture, commerce, art, science, and every department of education, physical and mental, as well as moral advancement, and our colleges—I think, in the face of such an exhibition, if we can, without the loss of power, or any essential right or interest, remain in the Union, it is our duty to ourselves and to posterity to—let us not too readily yield to this temptation—do so. Our first parents, the great progenitors of the human race, were not without a like temptation when in the garden of Eden. They were led to believe that their condition would be bettered, that their eyes would be opened, and that they would become as gods. They, in an evil hour, yielded. Instead of becoming gods, they only saw their nakedness.

—ALEXANDER H. STEPHENS

The illustration commences with "Our first parents" and continues to the end. It is more effective in pointing out the danger besetting the South in listening to the temptation to sever the Union than is all the rest of the paragraph. The prophecy as to the effect of listening to the voice of the tempter is forcefully summed up in the sentence: "Instead of becoming gods, they only saw their nakedness." By means of directing the thought to the dire consequences attending the fall of Adam and Eve through listening to temptation, the orator magnifies the effects that would follow a dissolution of the union of the states. The object in employing word-pictures is to convey an idea by means of suggestion, and, when so used, they become powerful weapons in the hands of a speaker. Here is another excellent illustration:

8

Books are for the scholar's idle times. When he can read God directly the hour is too precious to be wasted in other men's transcripts of their readings. But when the intervals of darkness come, as come they must—when the sun is hid and the stars withdraw their shining—we repair to the lamps which were kindled by their ray, to guide our steps to the East again, where the dawn is. We hear, that we may speak. The Arabian proverb says, "A fig tree, looking on a fig tree, becomes fruitful."

—RALPH WALDO EMERSON

Pictures are powerful means of conveying thoughts, and often more can be expressed by deftly painting a word-picture than could be imparted by a lengthy narration. Here is a good example:

Let me picture to you the footsore Confederate soldier, as, buttoning up in his faded jacket the parole which was to bear testimony to his children of his fidelity and faith, he turned his face southward from Appomattox, in April, 1865. Think of him as ragged, half-starved, heavy-hearted, enfeebled by want and wounds, having fought to exhaustion; he surrenders his gun, wrings the hands of his comrades in silence, and lifting his tear-stained and pallid face for the last time to the graves that dot the old Virginia hills, pulls his gray cap over his brow and begins the slow and painful journey.

—*HENRY W. GRADY*

This certainly brings the whole scene before us in a moment. We see the hills of Virginia, dotted over with the graves of the dead soldiers; groups of grizzled veterans, the remnant of that wonderful fighting machine that had followed the ill-starred flag of the Confederacy under its beloved leader; the typical southern soldier wringing the hands of his comrades, and sorrowfully, but manfully, turning his face towards home. The picture, as presented by Henry W. Grady, is more eloquent than the narration of the story would have been.

Henry Watterson, a lover of oratory, and himself an orator of no mean ability, speaking at the unveiling of Lincoln's statue at Frankfort, Kentucky, on November 8, 1911, spoke thus of the great American:

Reviled as the Man of Galilee, slain even as the Man of Galilee, yet as gentle and unoffending, a man who died for men! Roll the stone from the grave and what shall we see? Just an American. The Declaration of Independence his Confession of Faith. The Constitution of the United States his Ark and Covenant of Liberty. The Union his redoubt, the flag his shibboleth.

Here is presented a striking picture by means of the simile. With the charm and skill of a true orator, Colonel Watterson employs the lowly Nazarene to symbolize the portraiture of one who, like Himself, "went about doing good," and he does it so delicately as in no manner

9

to jar or hurt the religious sensibilities of the most devout follower of the Man of Galilee. All the orator's references are biblical, and eminently fitting. The mention of the Man of Galilee, the manner of His death, the rolling of the stone away, the Ark and the Covenant, and the shibboleth,—all these keep the mind of the reader or the listener on the picture as presented by the orator, and cause the great Emancipator to stand forth clothed in the splendor of his glorious attributes, which are colored and magnified through being likened reverently to the character of Jesus.

Daniel Webster delighted in the use of pictures. Here is one from his address delivered at the laying of the corner-stone of the Bunker Hill Monument, at Charlestown, Mass., June 17, 1825:

We do not read even of the discovery of this continent, without feeling something of a personal interest in the event; without being reminded how much it has affected our own fortunes and our own existence. It is more impossible for us, therefore, than for others, to contemplate with unaffected minds that interesting, I may say that most touching and pathetic scene, when the great discoverer of America stood on the deck of his shattered bark, the shades of night falling on the sea, yet no man sleeping; tossed on the billows of an unknown ocean, yet the stronger billows of alternate hope and despair tossing his own troubled thoughts: extending forward his harassed frame, straining westward his anxious and eager eyes, till Heaven at last granted him a moment of rapture and ecstasy, in blessing his vision with the sight of the unknown world.

Here is another example taken from his speech in what is known as the White Murder Case:

An aged man, without an enemy in the world, in his own house, and in his own bed, is made the victim of a butcherly murder, for mere pay. The deed was executed with a degree of self-possession and steadiness equal to the wickedness with which it was planned. The circumstances, now clearly in evidence, spread out the whole scene before us. Deep sleep had fallen on the destined victim, and on all beneath his roof. A healthful old man, to whom sleep was sweet, the first sound slumbers held him in their soft but strong embrace. The assassin enters through the window, already prepared, into an unoccupied apartment. With noiseless foot he paces the lonely hall, half-lighted by the moon—he winds up in the ascent of stairs, and reaches the door of the chamber. Of this he moves the lock, by soft and continued pressure, till it turns on its hinges without noise; and he enters, and beholds his victim before him.

This is certainly vividly drawn, and it shows the effectiveness of stating important things by means of pictures. Writers of good prose, as well as poets, use the figure of speech for creating mental images by means of the written word, and the speaker who employs the spoken word for producing like results will surely meet with like success.

Emerson, in writing on this subject, produces a striking picture. In his essay on "Poetry and Imagination," he says:

The poet gives us the eminent experiences only—a god stepping from peak to peak, nor planting his foot but on a mountain.

Shakespeare creates a marvellous picture thus:

> Look here, upon this picture, and on this,
> The counterfeit presentment of two brothers.
> See what a grace was seated on this brow;
> Hyperion's curls, the front of Jove himself,
> An eye like Mars, to threaten and command;
> A station like the herald Mercury
> New-lighted on a heaven-kissing hill;
> A combination and a form indeed,
> Where every god did seem to set his seal
> To give the world assurance of a man.[1]

Note the ascending force of this extract from Hamlet. The drawing of the picture, delineating the brow, hair, eyes, etc., the description of the bearing, and the final summing up,

> A combination and a form indeed,
> Where every god did seem to set his seal
> To give the world assurance of a man.

It would seem to be impossible for mortal man to make a picture more vivid than is the one here presented in words by the magic art of Shakespeare.

THE USE OF WORD-PICTURES

What benefit is to be derived from the use of word-pictures?

An illustration, or picture, is quickly comprehended, and will abide with the hearer when plain facts and colorless words are forgotten. Christ did the most of His teaching by means of similitudes: "The sower and the seed," "The laborers in the vineyard," "The ten virgins," are but instances of His employment of this means of conveying an insight into difficult problems. In fact, in the Gospel according to St. Matthew, xiii:34, it is stated:

All these things spake Jesus unto the multitude in parables: and without a parable spoke he not unto them.

Henry Ward Beecher, in his sermon, "Poverty and the Gospel," used this figure of speech:

On the Niagara River logs come floating down and strike an island, and there they lodge and accumulate for a little while, and won't

---

[1] Hamlet, Act III, Scene IV.

11

go over. But the rains come, the snow melts, the river rises, and the logs are lifted up and down, and they go swinging over the falls. There is a certain river of political life, and everything has to go into it first or last; and if, in the days to come, a man separates himself from his fellows without sympathy, if his wealth and power make poverty feel itself more poor and men's misery more miserable, and set against him the whole stream of popular feeling, that man is in danger.

From what source is the speaker to take his illustrations?

From all sources: history, books, his own experience, and, best of all, nature. Emerson states the matter in this comprehensive manner:

I had rather have a good symbol of my thought, or a good analogy, than the suffrage of Kant or Plato. If you agree with me, or if Locke or Montesquieu agree, I may yet be wrong; but if the elm-tree thinks the same thing, if running water, if burning coal, if crystals, if alkalies, in their several fashions, say what I say, it must be true.

How is the speaker to make the picture so vivid that it will be immediately seen and comprehended by the listener?

By seeing it himself. The speaker must see with his mind's eye the complete picture before he utters the first word descriptive of it. He must first see the picture in its entirety and be sure of his application of it before starting on the word-picturing, and as he develops the picture step by step, or phrase by phrase, he must keep in mind not only that portion of the picture he is then describing but must retain the picture in its entirety. This will cause his mentality to go into his voice, help him to hold on to his thought, and stamp the picture upon the minds and hearts of his listeners.

THE USE OF STORIES

Stories introduced into speeches, if really introduced and not dragged in, serve many useful purposes. They attract the attention of the audience and secure for the speaker an opportunity entertainingly to commence his remarks instead of abruptly jumping into them, like a speaker bounding upon the platform instead of walking gracefully upon it; they often express in a few words what otherwise would require a long explanation; and they also permit a speaker to retire in an effective manner from an awkward or embarrassing situation. This last point is illustrated in the following story told by Rev. Joseph Parker and used by him as a wedge to get out of a meeting without offending the feelings of the other members. It created a good-natured laugh, and this made the opening that permitted the reverend gentleman gracefully to retire.

"Now, my dear children," said the good priest, "where shall we put St. Patrick? Shall we put him where the sapphire river rolls around the throne of the Almighty? No; we will not put him there. Shall we put him where the golden light plays around the golden city? No; we will not put him there. Shall we put him in a boat sailing over the golden lake when the angels are calling? No; we will not put him there." For a fourth time he demanded in a loud voice: "Where shall we put St. Patrick?" Then at that moment a peasant called out: "Well then, shure, you can put him here, for I'm going."

Robert Browning, in a most entertaining letter addressed to Elizabeth Barrett, under date of April 8, 1846, discoursed on several subjects, among them being the proposition that repentance must precede forgiveness, and to illustrate his idea he narrated the following story, which might be used effectively in a speech:

Some soldiers were talking over a watch fire abroad. One said that once he was travelling in Scotland and knocked at a cottage-door. An old woman with one child let him in, gave him a supper and a bed. Next morning he asked her how they lived, and she said, the cow, the milk of which he was drinking, and the kale in the garden, such as he was eating—were all her "marlien" or sustenance—whereon, rising to go, he for the fun, "killed the cow and destroyed the kale"—"the old witch crying out she should certainly be starved"—then he went his way. "And she was starved, of course," said a young man; "do you rue it?"—The other laughed, "Rue aught like that!"—The young man said, "I was the boy, and that was my mother—now then!"—(pierces him with his sword). "If you had rued it"—the youth said—"You should have answered it only to God!"

John P. Curran, at the trial of the Drogheda Defenders, April 23, 1794, told this story, in order to make clear his views regarding the strength that exists in unity:

Upon this principle acted the dying man whose family had been disturbed by domestic contentions. Upon his death-bed he calls his children around him; he orders a bundle of twigs to be brought; he has them untied; he gives to each of them a single twig; he orders them to be broken—and it is done with facility. He next orders the twigs to be united in a bundle, and orders each of them to try their strength upon it. They shrink from the task as impossible. Thus my children, continued the old man, it is union alone that can render you secure against the attempts of your enemies, and preserve you in that state of happiness which I wish you to enjoy.

In the celebrated case of People vs. Durant, tried in San Francisco, Cal., in the year 1895, the district attorney, William S. Barnes, as demonstrating the fallacy of direct evidence where the witness endeavors to "back up" that evidence with circumstances which existed only in the fancy of the witness, or were "manufactured out of whole cloth," used this effective illustration:

There is a time-honored story which is commonly used as an illustration in the trial of cases. It is of a will case, that contest being over its probate. Counsel asked the proponent who sealed the will and she said the testator did. She had provided the material for the sealing, but the deceased had placed the wax in the candle and had pressed the seal in her presence. Counsel then turned to the Court and said: "Your worship, it is a wafer." This is the wafer in the case.

SUMMARY

Do not the citations given in this chapter show conclusively that modern and ancient modes of constructing orations are identical, and that it would be well for all who would attain distinction as speakers to study the means employed by those who have gone before? The author replies in the affirmative, and he reiterates his advice to all students of oratory to study faithfully the productions of the great orators of all times. In doing this, the student should be careful not to be a mere copyist; he must not make an echo of himself, repeating the forms of others, but he should study the principles underlying the arts of construction and delivery as employed by the masters who preceded him, and then apply the principles in his own individual manner. A student who is taught parrot fashion—that is, by imitation—will never equal his teacher, because he will lack the one great thing of value in every art—individuality; but one who is taught by principle, as well as by example, may far excel his preceptor. Issues and problems change, orators pass into the realm of shade; but the principles of oratory continue practically the same through all climes and ages.

CHAPTER II

HOW TO CONSTRUCT AND DELIVER ORATIONS

THE APPLICATION OF THE MEANS

The previous chapter was used to show what means orators employed in constructing their oratory, and this chapter will be devoted to showing students how to adopt and use those means. It would be of little use to tell students of oratory how others made their effects unless they are shown how they can produce equal results; therefore this chapter will be a chapter of hows. It will consider the proper arrangement of all the forms of creating and delivering the oratorical message, and deal at length with the conveying of the thought by means of the putting together of words and interpreting it through an understanding and an application of inflection and emphasis. It has been shown that oratory, through all its existence, has been created by means of the effective use of negative and positive words, phrases, and sentences; correct application of apposition and opposition; proper grouping of words and phrases in the form of series; the driving home and clinching of points; and many other ways of conveying thought by means of speech, and that these means have been passed from Gorgias to Isaeus, from Isaeus to Demosthenes, from Demosthenes to Cicero, and from these masters of old transmitted to Webster, Clay, Lincoln, Roosevelt, Bryan, Watterson, and the other able and careful public speakers of our day. Not only will the arrangement of words be thoroughly considered, but their utterance will receive much attention, the aim of the author being to show how, by the inflection, emphasis, and tone of the living voice, thought can be interpreted, and an impression made by the speaker on the minds and actions of others by means of the spoken word. Attention will also be given to getting the mentality into the voice, making the soul of the speaker shine through the medium that is to make the thought apparent to the listener.

INFLECTION

What is inflection? Inflection is a bending of the voice.
How many inflections are there? Two. The rising and the falling.
What does the rising inflection signify? The rising inflection, in

the main, signifies uncertainty. Whatever is uncertain, negative, qualified, conditional, incomplete, or continuous, requires the rising inflection; as,

Uncertainty. A government having at its command the armies, the fleets, and the revenues of Great Britain, might possibly hold Ireland by the sword. . . . But, to govern Great Britain by the sword—so wild a thought has never, I will venture to say, occurred to any public man of any party.

—Macaulay

In this example the first sentence is uncertain because Ireland might possibly be held by the sword, but it is not certain that it could be. The second sentence is assertive, and requires the falling inflection.

Negative. He have arbitrary power! My Lords, the East India Company have not arbitrary power to give him; the King has no arbitrary power to give him; your Lordships have not; nor the Commons; nor the whole legislature. We have no arbitrary power to give, because arbitrary power is a thing which neither any man can hold nor any man can give.

—Burke

Here is a splendid string of negatives, not demonstratively spoken, but given in the form of clear argumentation, and for that reason every member requires the rising inflection. The opening exclamation, "He have arbitrary power," should be given the falling inflection because it is a positive denial of his right to possess it. Were this extract spoken vehemently instead of argumentatively, it would take the falling inflection on all its members; but it is clearly intended to be negatively spoken, because the orator immediately follows it with positive statements, thus denoting a contrast. Therefore the exclamation alone is given the falling inflection.

Exception. It should be remembered that only while the thought is negative should the words be given the rising inflection, and that whenever emphasis is placed on the negative word it removes the negative quality and makes the thought positive, thus necessitating the use of the falling inflection. Consequently, whenever a negative is used in the sense of a contradiction it should be given the falling inflection, because it is just as positive to deny the assertion of a speaker as it is for the speaker to make the assertion; as,

I am charged with being an emissary of France. An emissary of France! and for what end? It is alleged that I wish to sell the independence of my country! and for what end? Was this the object of my ambition; and is this the mode by which a tribunal of justice reconciles contradictions? No! I am no emissary.

—Robert Emmet

The positive statement is, "I am charged with being an emissary of France"; and the contradiction, "No! I am no emissary." Emphasis being placed on the negative word "no" necessitates the falling inflection being used in order to make the contradiction positive.

Qualified Negative. A negative is qualified when it is restricted in any manner by the use of such words as "only," "alone," "merely," etc., such words receiving the inflection and being negatived; as,

In reading great orations one not only learns something of the methods and style of the orator, but obtains an epitome of the history of the times.

—William Jennings Bryan

Mr. Bryan here states that by means of reading one learns something of the methods and style of the orator, and also gains an epitome of the history of the times; and that he does not only learn the former, but that he also gains the latter. In this sentence everything is positive except the negatived word "only," this being the only word in the sentence that is acted upon by the negative word "not," because the reader learns something of the methods and style of the orator, but not only this, because he obtains an epitome of the history of the times as well. "Only," being the negatived word (the word upon which the negative acts), it should be given the rising inflection, while the balance of the sentence, being positive, should be given the falling inflection.

Qualified. I believe in the doctrine of peace; but, Mr. President, men must have liberty before there can come abiding peace.

—John M. Thurston

The phrase, "I believe in the doctrine of peace," is qualified by the concluding statement, "men must have liberty before there can come abiding peace"; and any expression that is qualified should be given the rising inflection. In this example Senator Thurston states that he believes in peace, provided peace can be had with liberty; but that if the loss of liberty is the price exacted for peace, then he prefers war. In order to convey the meaning of this example, the first phrase should be given the rising inflection and the last phrase the falling; the qualified taking the rising, and the concluding the falling inflection.

Conditional. If ye love wealth better than liberty, the tranquility of servitude than the animating contest of freedom, go from us in peace.

—Samuel Adams

Here we have two conditional phrases and one concluding phrase. All expressions that are conditional in character require the rising inflection, and the clause that concludes the sentence takes the inflection that interprets the thought. Therefore, if the concluding clause is positive, as in this example, it should be given the falling inflection; but if negative, it should be given the rising inflection. There is no exception to the conditional clause taking the rising inflection, because it is always uncertain in character, and whatever is uncertain should always be given the rising inflection, but the concluding clause, whenever it is negative, is given the rising inflection; as,

So, on the other hand, if I take the life of another, without being aware of any intended violence on his part, it will constitute no excuse for me to prove that he intended an attack upon me.

—Sargent S. Prentiss

Continuity. Whenever the thought is continuous the rising inflection should be employed until a conclusion is reached; as,

In speaking to you, men of the greatest city of the West, men of the state which gave to the country Lincoln and Grant, men who preëminently and distinctly embody all that is most American in the American character, I wish to preach, not the doctrine of ignoble ease, but the doctrine of the strenuous life, the life of toil and effort, of labor and strife.

—Roosevelt

The thought here is continuous and incomplete until we come to the phrase "the doctrine of the strenuous life," and in order to obtain an unbroken flow of speech the rising inflection should be used until the close of the negative phrase "not the doctrine of ignoble ease," but from there to the end of the sentence the falling inflection should be used because of its positive character and the fact that the thought is practically complete with the utterance of the phrase "but the doctrine of the strenuous life," all that follows being merely an amplification.

QUESTIONS

How many kinds of questions are there? Two.
What are they called? They are called direct and indirect.
What difference is there between these two kinds of questions? The direct question may be answered by either yes or no; the indirect question is answered by a statement or explanation. Usually there is uncertainty as to the answer to the direct question, and therefore the question should generally be given the rising inflection, but as soon as uncertainty ceases to exist as to the answer to a question, it should be given the falling inflection. Therefore, if the speaker knows that the answer is sure to be yes, or if he knows that the answer is sure to be no, the question should take the falling inflection, for then there would be no uncertainty as to the reply to the question. On the other hand, if, for any reason, the quality of uncertainty exists in the indirect question, it

18

should be given the rising inflection. The general supposition regarding questions is that they usually require the rising inflection, but the reverse of this is the fact. A question should only be given the rising inflection when the speaker is not sure as to whether the answer will be yes or no, or when an indirect question is expressive of the uncertainty of the speaker; as, What did you say? Direct questions, whenever the answer is anticipated, or the question repeated with marked emphasis, or spoken with earnestness in the shape of an appeal, should be given the falling inflection; as,

Immortal spirits of Hampden, Locke, and Sidney, will it not add to your benevolent joys to behold your posterity rising to the dignity of men, and evincing to the world the reality and expediency of your systems, and in the actual enjoyment of that equal liberty, which you were happy, when on earth, in delineating and recommending to mankind?

—SAMUEL ADAMS

The falling inflection should be given this direct question because the anticipated answer is yes.

The falling inflection should be given a direct question such as,

Has the gentlemen done? has he completely done?

The reason the falling inflection is here used is that the question is repeated with marked emphasis, and whenever a question is so repeated it should be given the falling inflection on the repetition.

The falling inflection should also be given all direct questions that are earnest appeals; as,

Will you please forgive me?

Direct Question. Undoubtedly the world is better; but would it have been better if everybody had then insisted that it was the best of all possible worlds, and that we must despond if sometimes a cloud gathers in the sky, or a Benedict Arnold appeared in the patriot army, or even a Judas Iscariot among the chosen twelve?

—GEORGE W. CURTIS

Indirect Question. When, O Catiline, do you mean to cease abusing our patience? How long is that madness of yours still to mock us? When is there to be an end of that unbridled audacity of yours, swaggering about as it does now?

—Cicero

A direct question is sometimes used in the form of a statement; as,

The constitutional question is: Has Congress the power, under our Constitution, to hold in subjection unwilling vassal states?

—George F. Hoar

This is a direct question, but because it is a statement put forth to be argued it should be given the falling inflection. If a request is made of a presiding officer for information regarding what question is then before the body, and the officer replies with a direct question, he should give it the falling inflection, because he does not speak it as a question but as a statement in reply to the member's question as to what is then before the meeting.

What does the falling inflection signify?

The falling inflection, in the main, signifies certainty. The arrival at a result, commands (whether negatively or positively constructed), and all positive words, phrases, and sentences, require, as a rule, the falling inflection.

The Arrival at a Result. We are all born in subjection, all born equally, high and low, governors and governed, in subjection to one great, immutable pre-existent law, prior to all our devices, and prior to all our contrivances, paramount to all our ideas, and all our sensations, antecedent to our very existence, by which we are knit and connected to the eternal frame of the universe, out of which we cannot stir.

—BURKE

The result here is not reached until we come to the final phrase "out of which we cannot stir," and although this is a negative phrase, so far as the construction goes, it requires the falling inflection because it closes the thought and is positive in its nature.

Commands. These things I command you, that ye love one another.

—ST. JOHN, XV., 17

This is a commandment given by Jesus to His disciples, and both phrases require the falling inflection. It makes no difference whether the command is to do or not to do a certain thing, all commandments, of whatever nature, require falling inflection; as,

Thou shalt not make unto thee any graven image, or any likeness of any thing that is in heaven above, or that is in the earth beneath, or that is in the water under the earth.

—EXODUS, XX., 4

Also, Honor thy father and thy mother: that thy days may be long upon the land which the Lord thy God giveth thee.

—EXODUS, XX., 12

Positive. To the cant about the pharisaism of reform there is one short and final answer. The man who tells the truth is a holier man than the liar. The man who does not steal is a better man than the thief.

—GEORGE W. CURTIS

All positive words, phrases, and sentences require, as a rule, the falling inflection, the only exception being when the words or phrases are arranged in the form of a series. This point is fully brought out and developed in the treatment of series in another part of this chapter.

Qualified Positives. The words "only," "alone," "merely," etc., when not qualified by the negative word "not," generally qualify some other word or phrase; as,

Every thing around was wrapped in darkness, and hushed in silence, broken only by what seemed, at that hour, the unearthly clank and rush of the train.

—EDWARD EVERETT

Here "only" qualifies what the silence was broken by. The meaning being that it was broken by but one thing, and that was "the unearthly clank and rush of the train." "Only," in this example, requires the falling inflection because it is positive.

Apposition. By means of the addition of words or phrases of like natures, we illustrate and explain; as,

The hardest chemist, the severest analyzer, scornful of all but the driest fact, is forced to keep the poetic curve of nature, and his result is like a myth of Theocritus.[2]

—EMERSON

"The severest analyzer" is employed to explain what "the hardest chemist" is, therefore the two phrases are in apposition. This form of construction is often used in explaining who persons are; as,

I, Henry V, King of England, etc.

All these terms are in apposition and should receive the same inflection, because identity of inflection conveys similarity of thought. Here is another good example of apposition:

Identity of law, perfect order in physics, perfect parallelism between the laws of nature and the laws of thought exist.

—EMERSON

EMPHASIS

What is emphasis? Any impressive utterance that arrests the attention of the listener.

Is it placed merely on single words? No. It may be placed on individual words, phrases, or sentences.

Does it consist of force alone? No. Emphasis consists of time, pitch, force, quality, and location.

Time. By time is meant the rapidity of utterance; as,

---

[2] A Grecian pastoral poet who lived in the third century.

With noiseless foot he paces the lonely hall, half lighted by the moon—he winds up the ascent of stairs, and reaches the door of the chamber.

—Daniel Webster

The idea is here brought out by means of the slow, measured manner in which the murderer is described noiselessly passing through the lonely hall and winding up the stairway. If this passage were quickly and violently spoken, a mis-interpretation would be given it. Time, in this instance, gives emphasis to the thought.

The light of the newly kindled sun, indeed, was glorious. It struck upon all the planets, and waked into existence their myriad capacities of life and joy. As it rebounded from them, and showed their vast orbs all wheeling, circle beyond circle in their stupendous course, the sons of God shouted for joy.

—HORACE MANN

This passage is also made emphatic by the time employed. It requires rapidity of utterance in order to express the ideas of the awakening of life and the joy of man.

Pitch. By pitch is meant the tone of voice employed—its height or depth; as,

With simple resignation, he [Garfield] bowed to the divine decree.

—James G. Blaine

The words "With simple resignation" require simplicity of voice, but the phrase "he bowed to the divine decree" should be spoken in a low, impressive tone, the better to express the feeling of reverence. The idea is here conveyed as much by the pitch of the voice as by the words themselves.

People of Hungary! will you die under the exterminating sword of the savage Russians? If not, defend yourselves! Will you look on while the Cossacks of the far North tread under foot the bodies of your fathers, mothers, wives, and children? If not, defend yourselves! Will you see a part of your fellow citizens sent to the wilds of Siberia, made to serve in the wars of tyrants, or bleed under the murderous knout? If not, defend yourselves! Will you behold your villages in flames, and your harvests destroyed? Will you die of hunger on the land which your sweat has made fertile? If not, defend yourselves!

—LOUIS KOSSUTH

This example must be spoken in an inspiring tone; the oft-repeated phrase, "If not, defend yourselves," should be given a gradual rise in pitch on each repetition until the final one is spoken almost in a shout. It is this gradual change in pitch that increases the emphasis on this important phrase each time it is spoken.

Force. By force is meant the loudness of voice; as,

For my part, whatever anguish of spirit it may cost, I am willing to know the whole truth; to know the worst, and to provide for it.

—PATRICK HENRY

By means of the force placed upon the words "whole," "worst," and "provide," the thought is driven home with earnestness, and as the words grow in importance the force of the voice should increase. It is mainly by means of this gradual increase in the force of the voice that an ascending series is marked; as,

Our petitions have been slighted; our remonstrances have produced additional violence and insult, our supplications have been disregarded; and we have been spurned, with contempt, from the foot of the throne!

—PATRICK HENRY

The earnestness and force of the speaker's delivery should grow with each succeeding phrase, until it bursts out with its greatest power and expression on the final one. Care should be exercised to go from one phrase to another by a gradual increase of force, culminating on the concluding phrase.

All important or significant words require emphasis by means of force; as,

It must be confessed, it will be confessed; there is no refuge from confession but suicide, and suicide is confession.

—DANIEL WEBSTER

Quality. By quality is meant the kind of voice—whether it is smooth or rough, rich or poor, large or small, expressive or non-expressive of the many emotions which the human voice is capable of producing. A tone may be raucous, because it is held in the throat; it may be nasal, through being held in the head; it may be breathy, through a waste of breath; or, on the other hand, it may possess those qualities of clearness, smoothness, and richness that come only from a properly developed and correctly used vocal mechanism. The quality of the voice may be pure, aspirated, or whispered; as,

Pure Quality. This uncounted multitude before me and around me proves the feeling which the occasion has excited. These thousands of human faces, glowing with sympathy and joy, and from the impulses of a common gratitude turned reverently to heaven in this spacious temple of the firmament, proclaim that the day, the place, and the purpose of our assembling here made a deep impression on our hearts.

—DANIEL WEBSTER

This example should be spoken in a clear, ringing, buoyant voice; and, if so spoken, the quality would be pure.

Aspirated Quality. Gracious God! In the nineteenth century to talk of constructive treason!

—*WILLIAM PINKNEY*

The words, "Gracious God!" are expressive of repressed indignation and should be uttered in a tone that is only partly vocalized; and, when so spoken, the quality is aspirated. An aspirated tone is one that is surrounded with breath, only a portion of which is vocalized.

Whispered Quality. The whisper is seldom used by the orator, but is often employed by the actor. Whispered speech is speech that is produced by the articulation of breath without that breath being converted into voice. For instance, when Hamlet sees the ghost of his father he articulates, but does not vocalize, the following:

Angels and ministers of grace defend us!

—*SHAKESPEARE*

Hamlet is so awed by the presence of the spirit of his father as to be deprived of the use of his voice, although he retains the ability to speak, and when one produces speech without voice he is using the whispered quality. The whisper is articulated breath, but not vocalized breath. It is speech, but not voice.

Location. By location is meant the position that the word or phrase holds in the sentence. If the emphasis is properly built up, the speaker will move from the weaker to the stronger, from the lesser to the greater; as,

Here, then, are the three liberties: liberty of the producer, liberty of the distributer, liberty of the consumer. The first two need no discussion—they have been long, thoroughly, and brilliantly illustrated by the political economists of Great Britain, and by her eminent statesmen; but it seems to me that enough attention has not been directed to the third, and, with your patience, I will dwell on that for a moment before proceeding to other topics.

—Henry Ward Beecher

Mr. Beecher states that his intention is to speak on the liberty of the consumer; therefore, in enumerating the three liberties, he places the one he intends to discuss in the vantage position—the last.

When a word, phrase, or sentence is set against another word, phrase, or sentence, both members of the opposition require emphasis; as,

Law and arbitrary power are in eternal enmity.

—*EDMUND BURKE*

The placing of "law" against "arbitrary power" requires that the opposing words should be made emphatic by means of emphasis as well as by inflection. All words or thoughts that are contrasted (single, double, or triple opposition) should be emphasized by the application of force, and the contrast brought out through the proper placing of the inflection. It is by means of inflection and emphasis that all contrasts in delivery are marked.

The repetition of a word or phrase requires that the repetition should be made more emphatic than the first utterance by means of greater force; as,

They have answered then, that although two hundred thousand of their countrymen have offered up their lives, there yet remain lives to offer; and that it is the determination of all, yes, of all, to persevere until they shall have established their liberty, or until the power of their oppressors should have relieved them from the burden of existence.

—Daniel Webster

A series of emphatic words requires that there should be a general increase in force on all the members of the series; as,

The universal cry is—let us move against Philip—let us fight for our liberties—LET US CONQUER OR DIE.

—R. B. SHERIDAN

Where a word is used to qualify another, the qualifying word should be emphasized; as,

They planned no sluggard people, passive while the world's work calls them. They established no reactionary nation. They unfurled no retreating flag.

—ALBERT J. BEVERIDGE

The fathers planted a people, established a nation, and unfurled a flag; but they did not plant a sluggard people, establish a reactionary nation, nor unfurl a retreating flag. It is by means of placing the emphasis on the qualifying words in this example that the meaning is instantly interpreted.

Some years ago a critic,[3] in commenting on E. H. Sothern's reading of the line from The Love Chase, "The cause of causes, lady," justly criticised him for emphasizing the unimportant word of, but the critic himself fell into as great an error as the actor when he cited the following as correct placing of emphasis: My heart of hearts, the man of men, great among the greatest, mightiest in the mightiest, and cause of causes. The meaning in each instance is best brought out by placing the principal emphasis on heart, man, great, mightiest, and cause, and secondary emphasis on hearts, men, greatest, mightiest, and causes. The ideas being that it is in the very center of the heart, that he towers

---

3 Alfred Ayres in "Acting and Actors," page 128.

above all others, that it is stronger than all others, and that it is the creator of creatures. Therefore the phrases should read: My heart of hearts, the man of men, great among the greatest, mightiest in the mightiest,, the cause of causes.

The same critic, a little further on in the same book,[4] takes Julie Marlowe to task for reading the following lines from Romeo and Juliet thus:

Deny thy father and refuse thy name.

He states it should be read:

Deny thy father and refuse thy name.

In the opinion of the author, both the actress and the critic are half right and half wrong, the scene requiring that emphasis should be placed on the four words; thus,

Deny thy father and refuse thy name.

This reading clearly denotes what Juliet desires shall be done with both the father and the name; the other readings do not.

Daniel Webster, in his reply to Senator Hayne, used this striking arrangement of words to express his idea of the unity of liberty and union:

Liberty and union, now and forever, one and inseparable.

In most readers the passage is marked, liberty and union, thus making the important connective and, which has practically nothing to do with conveying the thought, all-important, and sinking into insignificance the thought words of the orator. Webster distinctly says that "liberty" and "union" are "one and inseparable," whereas by putting the emphasis on the word and the speaker distinctly states that they are two. Webster undoubtedly intended "liberty" and "union" to be synonymous—"liberty" meaning the same as "union," and "union" the same as "liberty"—what constituted the one being exactly the same as what constituted the other. Therefore, like emphasis should be placed on both words.

Every sentence contains at least one thought; and in every group of words conveying a thought some particular word carries that thought to the mind. Such words are the thought words. This can be best illustrated by examples. In her plea for mercy Portia says:

The quality of mercy is not strain'd;[5]

In this line, strain'd is the word that conveys the idea. It is not quality nor mercy that Portia desires to impress on the mind of Shylock, but the fact that mercy is not strain'd. Antonio had confessed the bond, Portia had stated that nothing but the mercy of the Jew could save him from paying the penalty, and in making this statement she had used the word must. Shylock replied by saying: "On what

---

[4] Page 157.
[5] The Merchant of Venice, Act. IV, Scene I.

26

compulsion must I?" In other words, how are you going to compel me? And it is this thought of the Jew's to which she replied.

In the same speech Portia says:

> ... we do pray for mercy,
> And that same prayer doth teach us all to render
> The deeds of mercy.

The thought words, as the author sees them, are here italicized, but his reading of the lines differs from any he has heard from the stage or seen marked by critics. The great tendency is to come down hard on the word deeds, whereas it is one of the least important words in the entire sentence; it might be omitted without injury to the thought or the sense. Mr. Alfred Ayres, from whose work, Acting and Actors, the author has before quoted, advises the laying of the stress on the word all; but there is no better reason for emphasizing that word than there is for placing the stress upon deeds. The passage in the prayer to which Portia refers is: "Forgive us our debts, as we forgive our debtors," this being a clear statement of the supplicant's understanding of the necessity of his forgiving his debtors if he is to entertain the hope of having his debts forgiven by the heavenly Father. The verse following the Lord's prayer more clearly brings out this idea: "For if ye forgive men their trespasses, your heavenly Father will also forgive you."[6] The words "pray" and "render" are, therefore, the thought words—by means of their contrast they bring out the idea—and for this reason they require the emphasis. A paraphrase will demonstrate the correctness of this statement: We ask for mercy, and that prayer tells us to give mercy. The receiving of mercy being contingent on the granting of it.

COMBINED USE OF INFLECTION AND EMPHASIS

Inflection and emphasis, as before stated, are two of the principal means at the disposal of a speaker for the interpretation of thought. By these two means of expression, and the use of the proper color-tone in the voice, the thought can be clearly conveyed. By inflection and emphasis, words, phrases, and sentences are contrasted, and by means of contrast the mind of the listener is directed to the point that the speaker wishes him to see; as,

I propose, then, in what follows to make some remarks on communion with God, or prayer in a large sense of the word; not as regards its external consequences, but as it may be considered to affect our own minds and hearts.

—CARDINAL NEWMAN

---

[6] St. Matthew, vi:14.

The speaker states that he does not intend to discuss prayer so far as its external consequences are concerned; and if he stopped there, we should know what he intended not to discuss; but when he adds the positive, "but as it may be considered to affect our own minds and hearts," we know exactly what he intends to avoid and what he intends to take up, and this double knowledge is imparted to us by means of the contrast that the Cardinal uses. It is very well to tell a person not to do a certain thing, but it is much stronger and more comprehensive if he is also told what to do. It is all well and good to be told what will not justify action on one's part, but it is far better to be told what will; as,

It is the apprehension of impending harm, and not its actual existence, which constitutes the justification for defensive action.

—SARGENT S. PRENTISS

Here we are told that both the existence and apprehension of bodily harm will justify defensive action, and the point is, therefore, placed beyond misunderstanding by means of contrast.

How many forms of contrast are there? There are three: the single, the double, and the triple.

What is the single contrast? The single contrast is where one word, phrase, or sentence is contrasted with another; as,

Helen was not a sinner, but a sufferer, and our feeling for her should not be one of hatred, but of compassion.

—GORGIAS

The sentence gives two examples of the single contrast, "sinner" being opposed to "sufferer" and "hatred" opposed to "compassion."

What is the double contrast? The double contrast is where two words or phrases are contrasted with a like number of words or phrases; as,

In fact it is a universal law, not that the stronger should yield to the weaker, but the weaker to the stronger; that the stronger should lead, and the weaker follow.

—GORGIAS

In this example, "stronger," the first time it is used, is contrasted with "weaker" the second time it is used, and the first "weaker" with the second "stronger." In the second phrase, "stronger" is contrasted with "weaker," and "lead" with "follow."

The double contrast requires, as a rule, that the first member should be given the falling inflection, the second the rising, the third the rising, and the fourth the falling, thus bringing the first and the third, the second and the fourth, in contrast; as,

For it is equally wrong and stupid to censure what is commendable, and to commend what is censurable.

—GORGIAS

This is a good illustration of the double contrast. "Censure" is contrasted with "commend," and "commendable" with "censurable." When the double contrast is contained in two phrases, the first phrase being positive and the other phrase negative, the first member should be given the rising inflection, the second the falling, the third the falling, and the fourth the rising. In this way the contrast will be clearly shown and the negative and positive qualities retained; as,

Lay not up for yourselves treasures upon earth, where moth and rust doth corrupt, and where thieves break through and steal; but lay up for yourselves treasures in heaven, where neither moth nor rust doth corrupt, and where thieves do not break through nor steal.[7]
—The Bible

In this example, "Lay not up for yourselves treasures upon earth" is contrasted with "but lay up for yourselves treasures in heaven," and as the former is negative, it requires the rising inflection, while the latter requires the falling inflection, because it is positive; "where moth and rust doth corrupt, and where thieves break through and steal" is contrasted with "where neither moth nor rust doth corrupt, and where thieves do not break through nor steal"; therefore the former, being positive, should be given the falling inflection, while the latter, being negative, should be given the rising inflection.

In the triple oppositions the inflections alternate, the first member receiving the rising inflection, the second the falling, the third the rising, the fourth the falling, the fifth the rising, and the sixth the falling; as,

> She loved me for the dangers I had passed,
> And I loved her that she did pity them.
>
> —*SHAKESPEARE*

"She" is contrasted with the second "I," "me" with "her," and "dangers" with "pity."

What is the triple contrast? The triple contrast is where three words or phrases are contrasted with three other words or phrases; as,

Both parties deprecated war; but one of them would make war rather than let the nation survive, and the other would accept war rather than let it perish.

> —*LINCOLN*

The triple contrast is between "one" and "other," "make" and "accept," "survive" and "perish." This is a splendidly constructed sentence, and contains more information than many paragraphs made up of numerous sentences. It is because of the masterly arrangement of contrasts that so much is stated in so small a space.

---

[7] Matthew, vi:19–20.

How are the contrasts to be brought out? By means of inflection and emphasis. The single contrast requires that when both members are positive the first should be given the rising inflection and the second the falling; as,

The human mind is the brightest display of the power and skill of the Infinite mind with which we are acquainted.

—JOHN TODD

The contrast is between the words "human" and "Infinite," and as both of them are positive, "human" is given the rising inflection and "Infinite" the falling, thus marking, by means of the different inflections, the difference between the words. All words that are contrasted are given emphasis as well as inflection.

Whenever the words or phrases that are contrasted consist of negatives and positives, the former should be given the rising inflection and the latter the falling inflection, irrespective of their location; as,

They fell and were buried; but they never can die.

—GEORGE W. CURTIS

In this example the positive statement that the heroes "fell and were buried" requires the falling inflection, while the negative one that "they never can die" should be given the rising inflection in order to mark the contrast.

PARENTHESIS

What is a parenthesis? A parenthesis is a secondary idea that is interjected into a main idea in order to amplify or explain it; as,

He who has a memory that can seize with an iron grasp and retain what he reads—the ideas, simply, without the language, and judgment to compare and balance—will scarcely fail of being distinguished.

—JOHN TODD

The main idea is, "He who has a memory that can seize with an iron grasp and retain what he reads, will scarcely fail of being distinguished"; the secondary, or parenthetical, idea being, "the ideas, simply, without the language, and judgment to compare and balance." This is a long and important parenthesis. It contains two thoughts, "the ideas, simply, without the language," "and judgment to compare and balance," which materially amplify the main thought and at the same time qualify it.

What is the use of the parenthesis? It is of great use to the extempore speaker in that it permits him, after he has started his

30

sentence, to explain or amplify his thought before coming to a conclusion; as,

A whole family, just, gentle and pure, were thus, in their own house, in the night time, without any provocation, without one moment's warning, sent by the murderer to join the assembly of the just.

—WILLIAM H. SEWARD

Seward starts with the idea of stating that a whole family were foully murdered, but after commencing to express his thought, he desires to qualify it, so he halts it to interject the fact that this whole family were "just, gentle, and pure." Were it not for the use of the parenthesis, he would have been compelled to use another sentence. Care should be exercised in using parentheses, as they tend to confuse the listener unless properly spoken.

How should a parenthesis be spoken? In order to show that the speaker has left the main idea and taken up a secondary one, he should change the pitch of the voice on leaving the main idea, or while speaking the parenthesis, and immediately resume the original pitch on resuming the main idea.

The following is a striking example of the use of parenthesis. It is a long, loose sentence, but full of information that may be better expressed in this manner than by a number of short sentences:

This great nation, filling all profitable latitudes, cradled between two oceans, with inexhaustible resources, with riches increasing in an unparalleled ratio, by agriculture, by manufactures, by commerce, with schools and churches, with books and newspaper thick as leaves in our forests, with institutions sprung from the people, and peculiarly adapted to their genius; a nation not sluggish, but active, used to excitement, practiced in political wisdom, and accustomed to self-government, and all its vast outlying parts held together by a federal government, mild in temper, gentle in administration, and beneficent in results, seemed to have been formed for peace.

—HENRY WARD BEECHER

The main thought consists of the short sentence, "This great nation seemed to have been formed for peace," and all that explains its situation, its resources, and its government is parenthetical. This illustration is not cited as a good example for speakers to follow, but it is merely given to show one of the means employed by Mr. Beecher, an eloquent speaker, in expressing his ideas. The subject of the construction of sentences is dealt with at length in the chapter on Composition.

PAUSE

Pauses should be regulated by the sense and not by grammatical punctuation. A pause is sometimes required where no mark of punctuation is placed and at times a mark of punctuation should be passed over quickly in order to not retard the conveyance of the speaker's thought. The pauses used by the speaker, but note employed by the grammarian, are called rhetorical pauses and are used for emphasis; as,

Go, forget that you have a wife and children, to ruin, and remember only—that you have France to save.[8]

THE SERIES

What is a series? A series is a group of three or more important positive words or phrases, of different meanings, yet so closely related as to be capable of being welded into one thought; as,

Let old issues, old questions, old differences, and old feuds be regarded as fossils of another epoch.

—ALEXANDER H. STEPHENS

The group that constitutes the series is composed of "old issues," "old questions," "old differences," "old feuds," which, united should all "be regarded as fossils of another epoch."

What use is the series? The series allows a speaker to gather many forces, amalgamate them, thus uniting the feeble powers of the number into the powerful strength of the one, and to direct the united force to one point; as,

We are among the sepulchres of our fathers. We are on ground distinguished by their valor, their constancy, and the shedding of their blood.

—DANIEL WEBSTER

The orator tells the assembly that they are on ground distinguished by the valor of their fathers, but he does more: he tells them that the ground was also distinguished by their constancy and the shedding of their blood. The series enables the speaker to weld together "valor," "constancy," and "blood," thus combining the three virtues shown by the fathers, and this arrangement, the blending of the three reasons, gives the one strong reason, the patriotism of our fathers, for honoring the ground upon which the people were gathered. Cicero thus clearly defines a series and tells what it accomplishes: "For there is

---

[8] Spoken to D'Aguesseau by his wife when he went to confront his enraged King. Quoted by Wendell Phillips in his address on "Idols."

such an admirable continuation and series of things that each seems connected with the other, and all appear linked together and unified." This is exactly what a series is: Words or phrases that are closely connected with one another and are all linked together; as,

We welcome you to the immeasurable blessings of rational existence, the immortal hope of Christianity, and the light of everlasting truth!

—*DANIEL WEBSTER*

How many kinds of series are there? Two, the commencing and the concluding.

What is a commencing series? A commencing series is always an incomplete one, so far as the sense is concerned, as it requires something more than the series to complete the sense. It generally commences a sentence; as,

It is only when public opinion, or the strong power of government, the formidable array of influence, the force of a nation, or the fury of a multitude is directed against you, that the advocate is of any use.

—*JAMES. T. BRADY*

The series ends with "or the fury of a multitude," and the sense is made complete by "is directed against you, that the advocate is of any use."

A series is often composed of qualifying words; as,

What though it breaks like lightning from the cloud? The electric fire had been collecting in the firmament through many a silent, calm, and clear day.

—*ORVILLE DEWEY*

The words "silent, calm, and clear" qualify the word day and constitute a commencing series, because they require the word day to complete the thought.

What is a concluding series? A series is considered a concluding one when the series is complete with the close of the series. It generally concludes the sentence; as,

The remarkable people of this world are useful in their way; but the common people, after all, represent the nation, the age, and the civilization.

—*HENRY WARD BEECHER*

The series consists of "the nation," "the age," "the civilization"; a group of three important things which the common people represent.

Here is a good example of a concluding series of phrases:

With such consecrated service, what could we not accomplish; what riches we should gather for her; what glory and prosperity we

33

should render to the union; what blessings we should gather into the universal harvest of humanity.

—HENRY W. GRADY

A series constitutes sometimes a parenthesis; as,

For no cause, in the very frenzy of wantonness, by the red hand of murder, he was thus thrust from the full tide of this world's interests, from its hopes, its aspirations, its victories, into the visible presence of death—and he did not quail.

—JAMES. G. BLAINE

This example opens with a commencing series which ends with "by the red hand of murder," the sense of which is completed by "he was thrust from the full tide of this world's interest into the visible presence of death," but the thought is interrupted by the orator to interject the parenthetical clause "from its hopes, its aspirations, its victories," and as what completes the sense, "the full tide of this world's interest," precedes the series, it is a concluding series.

Is there any difference as to how the two series should be spoken? Yes. The commencing series requires the falling infection on every member except the last, which should be given the rising inflection; as,

From the very beginning I chose an honest and straightforward course in politics, to support the honor, the power, the glory of my fatherland.

—DEMOSTHENES

The series is embraced in the words "the honor, the power, the glory," and as the sense is incomplete with the close of the series, requiring "of my fatherland" to complete the sense, it is a commencing series. The proper delivery of this series requires that "honor" should be given the falling inflection, "power" the falling, and "glory" the rising.

The concluding series requires the falling inflection on every member except the next to the last, which should be given the rising inflection; as,

He thinks the whole world sees it in his face, reads it in his eyes, and almost hears its workings in the very silence of his thoughts.

—DANIEL WEBSTER

This is an excellent example of a concluding series of phrases. The first phrase, ending with "face," requires the falling inflection; the second, ending with "eyes," requires the rising inflection; the third, ending with "thoughts," requires the falling inflection.

34

SERIES OF CONTRASTS

What is a series of contrasts? A series of contrasts is where there are at least three contrasts arranged in the form of the series; as,

Ask, and it shall be given you; seek, and ye shall find; knock, and it shall be opened unto you.[9]

—THE BIBLE

The series consists of three phrases, and the series must be brought out by giving the first phrase the falling inflection, the second phrase the rising inflection, and the third phrase the falling inflection; and as there are three contrasts, "ask" being contrasted with "given," "seek" with "find," and "knock" with "opened," we must, in order to retain the concluding series, give "ask" the rising inflection, "given" the falling, "seek" the falling, "find" the rising, "knock" the rising, and "opened" the falling.

If the contrasts form a commencing series, the inflections should be applied according to the rules regarding the series; as,

Sink or swim, live or die, survive or perish, I give my hand and heart to this vote.

—DANIEL WEBSTER

"Sink" should be given the rising inflection, "swim" the falling, "live" the rising, "die" the falling, "survive" the falling, and "perish" the rising, for by so doing the contrasts will be marked and the series retained. The series consists of "sink or swim, live or die, survive or perish," and as it requires "I give my hand and heart to this vote" to complete the sense, it is a commencing series.

MODULATION

What is modulation? Modulation, in a broad sense, is coloring the voice so as to make it explain by its tones the meaning of the spoken words. It consists principally of inflection and pitch, but the elements of emphasis also enter into it. By means of modulation action is given to the voice—it rises, it falls, it glides, it leaps, it bounds; all sounds are described—the moaning of the winds, the rush of waters, the tramp of marching armies; all emotions are expressed—the shout of joy, the cry of pain, the huzzah of victory. The inflection of the voice interprets its meaning—whether it is negative, positive, conditional, etc., the pitch of the voice expresses the emotion—whether it is joyous, sad, indifferent, etc. The speaking voice is divided into three registers, the medium, the upper and the lower. The tones of the middle register

---

[9] St. Matthew, vii:7.

are the customary tones of the voice, and they are used for giving expression to anything that is ordinary. They are expressive of unemotional thoughts; as,

Some persons, for example, tell us that the acquisition of knowledge is all very well, but that it must be useful knowledge—meaning thereby that it must enable a man to get on in a profession, pass an examination, shine in conversation, or obtain a reputation for learning.

—*ARTHUR JAMES BALFOUR*

This is a plain, simple statement, spoken without emotion of any kind, and therefore should be pitched in an ordinary key. The matter need not necessarily be unimportant to be spoken in the medium register, but it must be simple in its character and unimpassioned in its nature, and for these reasons it is spoken in the ordinary tones of the voice.

The lower register is expressive of solemnity, sorrow, and all deep-seated emotions; as,

If the spirits of the illustrious dead participate in the concerns and cares of those who were dear to them in this transitory life, Oh, ever dear and venerated shade of my departed father, look down with scrutiny upon the conduct of your suffering son, and see if I have, even for a moment, deviated from those principles of morality and patriotism which it was your care to instil into my youthful mind, and for which I am now to offer up my life!

—*ROBERT EMMET*

The upper register is used for expressing the emotions of a light and joyous nature; as,

Advance, then ye future generations! We would hail you, as you rise in your long succession, to fill the places which we now fill, and to take the blessings of existence where we are passing, and soon shall have passed, our own human duration. We bid you welcome to this pleasant land of the fathers. We bid you welcome to the healthful skies and the verdant fields of New England. We greet your accession to the great inheritance which we have enjoyed. We welcome you to the blessings of good government and religious liberty. We welcome you to the treasures of science and the delights of learning. We welcome you to the transcendent sweets of domestic life, to the happiness of kindred and parents, and children. We welcome you to the immeasurable blessings of rational existence, the immortal hope of Christianity, and the light of everlasting truth!

—*DANIEL WEBSTER*

Some of the stronger emotions, such as anger, defiance, and grief, when not deeply felt, are expressed on the upper register; as,

36

We do not come as aggressors. Our war is not a war of conquest; we are fighting in the defense of our homes, our families and posterity. We have petitioned, and our petitions have been scorned; we have entreated, and our entreaties have been disregarded; we have begged, and they have mocked when our calamity came. We beg no longer; we entreat no more; we petition no more. We defy them.

—*WILLIAM JENNINGS BRYAN*

The following vivid description of the delivery of the Blind Preacher, by the orator William Wirt, is a splendid example of modulation in a comprehensive sense, because it depends on the distinctive colors that are placed in the voice, as well as on inflection and emphasis, for its effective presentation.

It was some time before the tumult had subsided, so far as to permit him to proceed. Indeed, judging by the usual, but fallacious, standard of my own weakness, I began to be very uneasy for the situation of the preacher. For I could not conceive how he would be able to let his audience down from the height to which he had wound them, without impairing the solemnity and dignity of the subject, or perhaps shocking them by the abruptness of the fall. But, no! the descent was as beautiful and sublime as the elevation had been rapid and enthusiastic.

The first sentence, with which he broke the awful silence, was a quotation from Rousseau: "Socrates died like a philosopher, but Jesus Christ, like a God."

I despair of giving you any idea of the effect produced by this short sentence, unless you could perfectly conceive the whole manner of the man, as well as the peculiar crisis in the discourse. Never before did I completely understand what Demosthenes meant by laying such stress on delivery. You are to bring before you the venerable figure of the preacher; his blindness, constantly recalling to your recollection old Homer, Ossian, and Milton, and associating with his performance the melancholy grandeur of their geniuses; you are to imagine that you hear his slow, solemn, well-accented enunciation, and his voice of affecting, trembling melody; you are to remember the pitch of passion and enthusiasm to which the congregation were raised; and then the few minutes of portentous, death-like silence which reigned throughout the house; the preacher removing his white handkerchief from his aged face (even yet wet from the recent torrent of his tears), and, slowly stretching forth the palsied hand which holds it, begins the sentence, "Socrates died like a philosopher," then, pausing, raising his other hand, pressing them both clasped together with warmth and energy to his breast, lifting his "sightless balls" to heaven, and pouring his whole soul into his trembling voice—"but Jesus Christ, like a God!" If he had been indeed and in truth an angel of light, the effect could scarcely have been more divine.

In this chapter and the one preceding are given some of the mechanical means of constructing speeches and delivering them, and in thus telling the student of oratory the specific way of accomplishing results, this book differs from the many that treat, or profess to treat, of oratory. Demosthenes says: "To censure is easy for any man; to show what measures the cause requires is the part of a counsellor." This is a nugget of wisdom, and in adopting it the author has used the injunction do instead of issuing a number of don'ts, as is the custom of many teachers. He tells primarily what to do and how to do it, and only in a secondary manner does he use the negative way of instruction. In this chapter, students are shown what means were employed by those who succeeded in mastering the art of vocal expression and how they may adopt them in aiming to accomplish the same results; and the author has no hesitancy in stating that if the student will properly qualify himself to become an orator by a diligent study of the method therein contained, he will rise to eminence in a field of labor that repays with honors and renown all who toil in it. This chapter treats of the mechanical means of producing oratory and making orators, but the psychological, or mental, means, which must be used in conjunction with the mechanical in order that there may be life in the production, will receive due attention in later chapters. Unless the mentality enters into the work of the orator, it will be devoid of action, and consequently not oratory; for, in the words of Demosthenes: "All speech without action appears vain and idle."

CHAPTER III

CONSTRUCTION

Spoken matter is a speech only when it possesses three divisions: an opening, a body, and a conclusion. Without possessing these three divisions it may be a talk, but it is not a speech. This can be best explained by the author quoting from one of his previous works:[10]

"Every speech, no matter what its length or what its subject, should possess three parts: an opening or statement, a body or argument, a conclusion or appeal. The opening should contain a statement of the facts to be presented, or the points upon which the argument is to be made; the body should be given over to a presentation of the facts, a narration of the story, a description of the scene, or an argument of the cause; and the conclusion should be devoted to summing up of the facts, an application of the story or the scene, or a deduction from the argument on the points.

"The opening may contain as many statements as the speaker desires, but he must make sure to argue upon and drive home in the body of the speech all that he mentions in the opening. Every statement in the opening must be like a plank in a platform, and all such planks, or statements, must be fastened together properly in the argument, otherwise there will be gaps in the platform, or statement, through which the speaker's argument is liable to fall to failure."

A rambling story is not a speech; a talk that has not a clear opening, a convincing argument, or a logical conclusion, is not a speech; a statement without a body is not a speech. All these things may be talks, but only a well-defined, clearly-mapped-out discourse can be dignified with the name of speech. In order that one may be a speech-maker and not a babbler, he must work in accordance with a well-defined plan. He should carefully gather the material that is to be used, arrange the parts of the speech in their proper places, and deliver the speech in the best possible manner. No matter how excellent the material may be, it will prove of little value to the speaker unless it is arranged consecutively; built, as it were, point on point, or fact on fact, and developed according to his prearranged plan. It should be so knitted together as to cohere and form a structure that, resting on a firm foundation, will be compact and complete. Desultory talking is not speech making. The speaker should possess a definite object, and keep to that object until it has been clearly presented and convincingly

---

[10] "Speech-Making," page 1. By Edwin Gordon Lawrence (The A. S. Barnes Company).

demonstrated. Order should reign everywhere—in the arrangement of the words, the presentation of the ideas, and the delivery of the matter. Lack of attention to these details is the cause of many failing as public speakers who, had they given proper attention to the perfection of the means to be employed, might have become clear thinkers and masterly presenters of well-ordered thoughts. Length has nothing whatever to do with the question as to whether spoken matter is a speech or not. One might speak for an hour and not deliver a speech; and, on the other hand, a perfectly constructed speech might be produced in a minute or less. Here is a matter that occupies less than two lines, or, to be exact, twenty-two words, and yet it possesses all the requirements of a speech:

The light of the body is the eye: if therefore thine eye be single, thy whole body shall be full of light.[11]

We have the proposition that "The light of the body is the eye"; the argument, "if therefore thine eye be single"; and the conclusion, "thy whole body shall be full of light."

Specimen divisions of speeches of Demosthenes are here employed to emphasize these points, and students are advised to study closely the means adopted by this master of oratory and rhetoric in arranging his speeches. Two examples of each of the three divisions of a speech, and one example of a complete speech, are here presented in order that students may gain a practical and comprehensive idea regarding the construction of speeches.

DIVISIONS OF A SPEECH

OPENING

Against the Law of Leptines (355 b. c.). It was chiefly, men of the jury, because I deemed it good for Athens that the law should be repealed, but partly on account of the son of Chabrias, that I engaged to support these men to the utmost of my ability. It is plain enough, men of Athens, that Leptines, or whoever else defends the law, will have nothing to say for it on the merits, but will allege that certain unworthy persons obtaining immunity have evaded the public services, and will lay the greatest stress upon this point. I will pass by the injustice of such proceeding—for a complaint against some to take the honour from all—for it has in a manner been explained, and is doubtless acknowledged by you; but this I would gladly ask him: Granting most fully that not some but all were unworthy, why did he consider that you and they were to be dealt with alike? By enacting that none should be exempted, he took the exemption from those that enjoyed it; by adding

---

[11] St. Matthew, vi:22.

that it should be unlawful to grant it thereafter, he deprived you of the power of granting. He can not surely say that, as he deprived the holders of their privilege because he deemed them unworthy of it, in the same manner he thought the people unworthy to have the power of giving their own to whom they pleased. But possibly he may reply that he framed the law so because the people are easily misled. Then what prevents your being deprived of everything, yea, of the government itself, according to such argument? For there is not a single department of your affairs in which this has not happened to you. Many decrees have you at various times been entrapped into passing. You have been persuaded ere now to choose the worse allies instead of the better. In short, amid the variety of your measures there must, I conceive, happen something of this kind occasionally. Shall we therefore make a law prohibiting the council and the people hereafter from passing bills and decrees? I scarcely think so. We ought not to be deprived of a right, in the exercise of which we have been deceived; rather should we be instructed how to avoid such error, and pass a law, not taking away our power, but giving the means of punishing those who deceive us.

On the Navy Boards (354 b. c.). It appears to me, O Athenians, that the men who praise your ancestors adopt a flattering language, not a course beneficial to the people whom they eulogize. For attempting to speak on subjects which no man can fully reach by words they carry away the reputation of clever speakers themselves, but cause the glory of those ancients to fall below its estimation in the minds of the hearers. For my part, I consider the highest praise of our ancestors to be the length of time which has elapsed during which no other men have been able to excel the pattern of their deeds. I will myself endeavour to show in what way, according to my judgment, your preparations may most conveniently be made. For thus it is. Though all of us who intend to speak should prove ourselves capital orators, your affairs, I am certain, would prosper none the more; but if any person whomsoever came forward, and could show and convince you what kind and what amount of force will be serviceable to the state, and from what resources it should be provided, all our present apprehensions would be removed. This will I endeavour to do, as far as I am able, first briefly informing you what my opinion is concerning our relations with the king.

BODY

The first Philippic (351 b. c.). First, I say, you must not despond, Athenians, under your present circumstances, wretched as they are; for that which is worst in them as regards the past is best for the future. What do I mean? That your affairs are amiss, men of Athens, because you do nothing which is needful; if, notwithstanding you performed your duties, it were the same, there would be no hope of amendment.

Consider, next, what you know by report, and men of experience remember, how vast a power the Lacedaemonians had not long ago, yet how nobly and becomingly you consulted the dignity of Athens, and undertook the war against them for the rights of Greece. Why do I mention this? To show and convince you, Athenians, that nothing, if you take precaution, is to be feared; nothing, if you are negligent goes as you desire. Take for examples the strength of the Lacedaemonians then, which you overcame by attention to your duties, and the insolence of this man now, by which through neglect of our interest we are confounded. But if any among you, Athenians, deem Philip hard to be conquered, looking at the magnitude of his existing power, and the loss by us of all our strongholds, they reason rightly, but should reflect, that once we held Pydna and Potidaea and Methone and all the region round about as our own, and many of the nations now leagued with him were independent and free, and preferred our friendship to his. Had Philip then taken it into his head that it was difficult to contend with Athens, when she had so many fortresses to infest his country, and he was destitute of allies, nothing that he has accomplished would he have undertaken, and never would he have acquired so large a dominion. But he saw well, Athenians, that all these places are the open prizes of war, that the possessions of the absent naturally belong to the present, those of the remiss to them that will venture and toil. Acting on such principle, he has won everything and keeps it, either by way of conquest or by friendly attachment and alliance; for all men will side with and respect those whom they see prepared and willing to make proper exertion. If you, Athenians, will adopt this principle now, though you did not before, and every man, where he can and ought to give his service to the state, be ready to give it without excuse, the wealthy to contribute, the able-bodied to enlist; in a word, plainly, if you will become your own masters, and cease each expecting to do nothing himself while his neighbour does everything for him, you shall then with Heaven's permission recover your own, and get back what has been frittered away, and chastise Philip. Do not imagine that his empire is everlastingly secured to him as a god. There are who hate and envy him, Athenians, even among those that seem most friendly; and all feelings that are in other men belong, we may assume, to his confederates. But now they are all cowed, having no refuge through your tardiness and indolence, which I say you must abandon forthwith. For you see, Athenians, the case, to what pitch of arrogance the man has advanced who leaves you not even the choice of action or inaction, but threatens and uses (they say) outrageous language; and, unable to rest in possession of his conquests, continually widens their circle and, while we dally and delay, throws his net all around us. What, then, Athenians, when will you act as becomes you? In what event? In that of

42

necessity, I suppose. And how should we regard the events happening now? Methinks to freemen the strongest necessity is the disgrace of their condition. Or tell me, do you like walking about and asking one other, Is there any news? Why, could there be greater news than a man of Macedonia subduing Athenians, and directing the affairs of Greece? Is Philip dead? No, but he is sick. And what matters it to you? Should anything befall this man you will soon create another Philip if you attend to business thus. For even he has been exalted not so much by his own strength but by our negligence. And, again, should anything happen to him; should fortune, which still takes better care of us than we of ourselves, be good enough to accomplish this, observe that, being on the spot, you would step in while things were in confusion and manage them as you pleased; but as you are, though occasion offered Amphipolis, you would not be in a position to accept it, with neither forces nor counsels at hand.

However, as to the importance of a general zeal in the discharge of duty, believing you are convinced and satisfied, I say no more.

On the Liberty of the Rhodians (351 b. c.) One of the events for which I consider you should be thankful to the gods is that a people, who to gratify their own insolence went to war with you not long ago, now place their hopes of safety in you alone. Well may we be rejoiced at the present crisis, for if your measures thereupon be wisely taken the result will be that the calumnies of those who traduce our country you will practically and with credit and honour refute. The Chians, Byzantines, and Rhodians accused us of a design to oppress them, and therefore combined to make the last war against us. It will turn out that Mausolus, who contrived and instigated these proceedings, pretending to be a friend of the Rhodians, has deprived them of their liberty; the Chians and Byzantines, who called them allies, have not aided them in misfortune, while you, whom they dreaded, are the only people who have wrought their deliverance. And this being seen by all the world, you will cause the people in every state to regard your friendship as the token of their security; nor can there be a greater blessing for you than thus to obtain from all men a voluntary attachment and confidence.

I marvel to see the same persons advising you to oppose the king on behalf of the Egyptians, and afraid of him in the matter of the Rhodian people. All men know that the latter are Greeks, the former a portion of his subjects. And I think some of you remember that when you were debating about the king's business I first came forward and advised—nay, I was the only one, or one of two, that gave such counsel—that your prudent course in my opinion was not to allege your quarrel with the king as the excuse for your arming, but to arm against your existing enemies, and defend yourselves against him also if he attempted to injure you. Nor did I offer this advice without obtaining your approval, for you agreed with me. Well, then, my reasoning of today is consistent with the argument on that occasion; for, would the king take me to his counsels, I should advise him as I advise you, in defense of his own possessions to make war upon any Greeks that opposed him, but not to think of claiming dominions to which he had no manner of title. If now it be your general determination, Athenians, to surrender to the king all places that he gets possession of, whether by surprise or by deluding certain of the inhabitants, you have determined, in my judgment, unwisely; but if in the cause of justice you esteem it your duty either to make war, if needful, or to suffer any extremity, in the first place, there will be the less necessity for such trials, in proportion as you are resolved to meet them; and, secondly, you will manifest a spirit that becomes you.

That I suggest nothing new in urging you to liberate the Rhodians, that you will do nothing new in following my counsel, will appear if I remind you of certain measures that succeeded. Once, O Athenians, you sent Timotheus out to assist Ariobarzanes, annexing to the decree "that he was not to infringe your treaty with the king." Timotheus, seeing Ariobarzanes had openly revolted from the king, and that Samos was garrisoned by Cyprothemis, under the appointment of Tigranes, the king's deputy, renounced the intention of assisting Ariobarzanes, but invested the island with his forces and delivered it. And to this day there has been no war against you on that account. Man will not fight for aggressive purposes so readily as for defensive. To resist spoliation they strive with all their might. Not so to gratify ambition; this they will attempt if there be none to hinder them; but if prevented, they regard not their opponents as having done them an injury.

My belief is that Artemisia would not even oppose this enterprise now if our state were embarked in the measure. Attend a moment and see whether my calculations be right or wrong. I consider, were my king succeeding in all his designs in Egypt, Artemisia would make a strenuous effort to get Rhodes into his power, not from affection to the king, but from a desire, while he tarried in her neighborhood, to confer an important obligation upon him, so that he might give her the most friendly reception; but since he fares as they report, having miscarried in his attempts, she judges that this island—and so the fact is—would be of no further use to the king at present, but only a fortress to overawe her kingdom and prevent disturbances. Therefore it seems to me she would rather you had the island, without her appearing to have surrendered it, than that he should obtain possession. I think, indeed, she will send no succours at all, but if she do they will be scanty and feeble. As to the king, what he will do I can not pretend to know; but this I will maintain, that it is expedient for Athens to have it immediately understood whether he means to claim the Rhodian city or not; for, if he should, you will have to deliberate not on the concerns of Rhodes only, but on those of Athens and all Greece.

Even if the Rhodians who are now in the government had held it by themselves I would not have advised you to espouse their cause; nor though they promised to do everything for you. But I see that in the beginning, in order to put down the democracy, they gained over a certain number of citizens, and afterward banished those very men when they had accomplished their purpose. I think, therefore, that people who have been false to two parties would be no steadier allies to you. And never would I have proffered this counsel had I thought it would benefit the Rhodian people only; for I am not their state friend, nor is any of them connected with me by ties of private hospitality. And even if both these causes had existed I would not have spoken unless I had considered it for your advantage. Indeed, as far as the Rhodians are concerned, if the advocate for their deliverance may be allowed to say so, I am rejoiced at what has happened—that, after grudging to you the recovery of your rights, they have lost their own liberty; and, when they might have had an alliance on equal terms with Greeks and their betters, they are under subjection to barbarians and slaves, whom they have admitted into their fortresses. I would almost say that, if you determine to assist them, these events have turned out for their good. For, during prosperity, I doubt whether they would have learned discretion, being Rhodians; but since they are taught by experience that folly is mightily injurious to men, they may possibly perhaps become wiser for the future; and this I think would be no small advantage to them. I say, therefore, you should endeavour to rescue these people, and not harbour resentment, considering that you too have often been deceived by miscreants, but for no such deceit would you allow that you merited punishment yourselves.

Observe also, men of Athens, that you have waged many wars both against democracies and against oligarchies—this, indeed, you know without my telling—but for what cause you have been at war with either perhaps not one of you considers. What are the causes? Against democratical states your wars have been either for private grievances, when you could not make public satisfaction, or for territory, or boundaries, or a point of honour, or the leadership; against oligarchies for none of these matters, but for your constitution and freedom. Therefore I would not hesitate to say I think it better that all the Greeks should be your enemies with a popular government than your friends under oligarchal. For with freemen I consider you would have no difficulty in making peace when you chose, but with people under an oligarchy even friendship I hold to be insecure. It is impossible that the few can be attached to the many, the seekers of power to the lovers of constitutional equality.

CONCLUSION

Against the Law of Leptines (355 b. c.). One might pursue the argument and show that in no single respect is the law proper or expedient for you; but, that you may comprehend the whole question at once, and that I may have done speaking, do what I now advise. Make your comparison; consider what will happen to you if you condemn the law, and what if you do not; then keep in mind what you think will be the consequence in either event, that you may choose the better course. If now you condemn the law, as we advise, the deserving will have their rights from you; and if there be any undeserving party, as I grant there may be, such a one, besides being deprived of his honour, will suffer what penalty you think proper according to the amended statute, while the commonwealth will appear faithful, just, true to all men. Should you decide in its favour, which I trust you will not, the good will be wronged on account of the bad, the undeserving will be the cause of misfortune to others, and suffer no punishment themselves, while the commonwealth (contrary to what I said just now) will be universally esteemed faithless, envious, base. It is not meet, O Athenians, that for so foul a reproach you should reject fair and honourable advantages. Remember, each of you individually will share in the reputation of your common judgment. It is plain to the bystanders and to all men that in the court Leptines is contending with us, but in the mind of each of you jurymen generosity is arrayed against envy, justice against iniquity, all that is virtuous against all that is base. If you follow the wiser counsels, and give judgment in my favour, you will yourselves have the credit of a proper decision, and will have voted what is best for the commonwealth; and should occasion ever arise, you will not lack men willing at their own risk to defend you.

You must give your earnest attention to these things, and be careful that you are not forced into error. Many a time, O Athenians, instead of it being proved to you that measures were just, they have been extorted from you by the clamour and violence and impudence of the speakers. Let not this happen now; it would not be well. What you have determined to be just, keep in mind and remember until you vote, that you may give your votes conscientiously against evil counsellors. I marvel when you punish with death those who debase the coin, if you will give ear to persons who render the whole commonwealth false and treacherous. You will not surely! O Jupiter and the gods!

I have nothing more to add, as you seem fully to understand what has been said.

On the Navy Boards (354 b. c.). Not to trouble you, men of Athens, with over-many words, I will give you a summary of my advice and retire. I bid you prepare yourselves against existing enemies, and I declare that with this same force you should resist the king and all other people, if they attempt to injure you; but never inflict an injustice either in word or deed. Let us look that our actions, and not our speeches on the platform, be worthy of our ancestors. If you pursue this course you will do service not only to yourselves but also to them who give the opposite counsel, since you will not be angry with them afterward for your errors committed now.

A COMPLETE SPEECH

The First Olynthiac (349 b. c.). I believe, men of Athens, you would give much to know what is the true policy to be adopted in the present matter of inquiry. This being the case, you should be willing to hear with attention those who offer you their counsel. Besides, that you will have the benefit of all preconsidered advice, I esteem it part of your good fortune that many fit suggestions will occur to some speakers at the moment, so that from them all you may easily choose what is profitable.

The present juncture, Athenians, all but proclaims aloud that you must yourselves take these affairs in hand if you care for their success. I know not how we seem disposed in the matter. My own opinion is, vote succour immediately, and make the speediest preparations for sending it off from Athens, that you may not incur the same mishap as before; send also ambassadors to announce this, and watch the proceedings. For the danger is that this man, being unscrupulous and clever at turning events to account, making concessions when it suits him, threatening at other times (his threats may well be believed), slandering us and urging our absence against us, may convert and wrest to his use some of our main resources. Though, strange to say, Athenians, the very cause of Philip's strength is a circumstance favorable to you. His having it in his sole power to publish or conceal his designs, his being at the same time general, sovereign, paymaster, and everywhere accompanying his army, is a great advantage for quick and timely operations in war; but for a peace with the Olynthians, which he would gladly make, it has a contrary effect. For it is plain to the Olynthians that now they are fighting not for glory or for a slice of territory, but to save their country from destruction and servitude. They know how he treated those Amphipolitans who surrendered to him their city, and those Pydneans who gave him admittance. And generally, I believe, a despotic power is mistrusted by free states, especially if their dominions are adjoining. All this being known to you, Athenians, all else of importance considered, I say you must take heart and spirit, and apply yourselves more than ever to the war, contributing promptly, serving personally, leaving nothing undone. No plea or pretence is left you for declining your duty. What you were all so clamorous about, that the Olynthians should be pressed into a war with Philip, has of itself come to pass, and in a way most advantageous to you. For, had they undertaken the war at your instance, they might have been slippery allies, with minds but half resolved, perhaps; but since they hate him on a quarrel of their own, their enmity is like to

47

endure on account of their fears and their wrongs. You must not then, Athenians, forego this lucky opportunity, nor commit the error which you have often done heretofore. For example, when we returned from succouring the Euboeans, and Hierax and Stratocles of Amphipolis came to this platform, urging us to sail and receive possession of their city, if we had shown the same zeal for ourselves as for the safety of Euboea you would have held Amphipolis then and been rid of all the troubles that ensued. Again, when news came that Pydna, Potidaea, Methone, Pagasae, and the other places (not to waste time in enumerating them) were besieged, had we to any one of these in the first instance carried prompt and reasonable succour, we should have found Philip far more tractable and humble now. But, by always neglecting the present and imagining the future would shift for itself, we, O men of Athens, have exalted Philip, and made him greater than any King of Macedon ever was. Here, then, is come a crisis, that of Olynthus, self-offered to the state, inferior to none of the former. And methinks, men of Athens, any man fairly estimating what the gods have done for us, notwithstanding many untoward circumstances, might with reason be grateful to them. Our numerous losses in way may justly be charged to our own negligence; but that they happened not long ago, and that an alliance to counterbalance them is open to our acceptance, I must regard as manifestations of divine favour. It is much the same as in money matters. If a man keep what he gets he is thankful to fortune; if he lose it by imprudence, he loses withal his memory of the obligations. So in political affairs, they who misuse their opportunities forget even the good which the gods send them, for every prior event is judged commonly by the last result. Wherefore, Athenians, we must be exceedingly careful of our future measures, that by amendment therein we may efface the shame of the past. Should we abandon these men too, and Philip reduce Olynthus, let any one tell me what is to prevent him marching where he pleases? Does any of you, Athenians, compute or consider the means by which Philip, originally weak, has become great? Having first taken Amphipolis, then Pydna, Potidaea next, Methone afterward, he invaded Thessaly. Having ordered matters at Pherae, Pagasae, Magnesia, everywhere exactly as he pleased, he departed for Thrace, where, after displacing some kings and establishing others, he fell sick; again recovering, he lapsed not into indolence, but instantly attacked the Olynthians. I omit his expeditions to Illyria and Paeonia, that against Arymbas, and some others.

Why, it may be said, do you mention all this now? That you, Athenians, may feel and understand both the folly of continually abandoning one thing after another, and the activity which forms part of Philip's habit and existence, which makes it impossible for him to rest content with his achievements. If it be his principle ever to do more than he has done, and yours to apply yourselves vigorously to nothing, see what the end promises to be. Heavens! which of you is so

48

simple as not to know that the war yonder will soon be here if we are careless? And should this happen, I fear, O Athenians, that as men who thoughtlessly borrow on large interest, after a brief accommodation, lose their estate, so will it be with us; found to have paid dear for our idleness and self-indulgence, we shall be reduced to many hard and unpleasant shifts, and struggle for the salvation of our country.

To censure, I may be told, is easy for any man; to show what measures the case requires is the part of a counsellor. I am not ignorant, Athenians, that frequently when any disappointment happens you are angry, not with the parties in fault, but with the last speakers on the subject; yet never, with a view to self-protection, would I suppress what I deem for your interest. I say, then, you must give a twofold assistance here: first, save the Olynthians their towns, and send our troops for that purpose; secondly, annoy the enemy's country with ships and other troops; omit either of these courses, and I doubt the expedition will be fruitful. For, should he, suffering your incursion, reduce Olynthus, he will easily march to the defense of his kingdom; or, should you only throw succour into Olynthus, and he, seeing things out of danger at home, keep up a close and vigilant blockade, he must in time prevail over the besieged. Your assistance, therefore, must be effective and twofold.

Such are the operations I advise. As to a supply of money: you have money, Athenians; you have a larger military fund than any people, and you receive it just as you please. If you will assign this to your troops you need no further supply; otherwise you need a further, or rather you have none at all. How then? some man may exclaim; do you move that this be a military fund? Verily, not I. My opinion, indeed, is that there should be soldiers raised, and a military fund, and one and the same regulation for receiving and performing what is due; only you just without trouble take your allowance for the festivals. It remains, then, I imagine, that all just contribute; if much be wanted, much; if little, little. Money must be had; without it nothing proper can be done. Other persons propose other ways and means. Choose which you think expedient, and put hands to work while it is yet time.

It may be well to consider and calculate how Philip's affairs now stand. They are not, as they appear, or as an inattentive observer might pronounce, in very good trim, or in the most favourable position. He would never have begun this war had he imagined he must fight. He expected to carry everything on the first advance, and has been mistaken. This disappointment is one thing that troubles and dispirits him; another is the state of Thessaly. That people were always, you know, treacherous to all men, and just as they ever have been they are to Philip. They have resolved to demand the restitution of Pagasae, and have prevented his fortifying Magnesia; and I was told they would no longer allow him to take the revenue of their harbours and markets, which they say should be applied to the public business of Thessaly, not received by Philip. Now, if he be deprived of this fund, his means will be much straitened for paying his mercenaries. And surely we must suppose that Paeonians and Illyrians, and all such people, would rather be free and independent than under subjection, for they are unused to obedience, and the man is a tyrant. So report says, and I can well believe it, for undeserved success leads weak-minded men into folly; and thus it appears often that to maintain prosperity is harder than to acquire it. Therefore must you, Athenians, looking on his difficulty as your opportunity, assist cheerfully in the war, sending embassies where required, taking arms yourselves, exciting all other people, for if Philip got such an opportunity against us, and there was a war on our frontier, how eagerly think you he would attack you! Then are you not ashamed that the very damage which you suffer, if he had the power, you dare not seize the moment to inflict on him?

And let not this escape you, Athenians, that you have now the choice whether you shall fight there, or he in your country. If Olynthus hold out, you will fight there and distress his dominions, enjoying your own home in peace. If Philip take that city, who shall then prevent his marching here? Thebans? I wish it be not too harsh to say they will be ready to join in the invasion. Phocians? who can not defend their own country without your assistance. Or some other ally? But, good sir, he will not desire! Strange, indeed, if, what he is thought foolhardy for prating now, this he would not accomplish if he might. As to the vast difference between a war here or there, I fancy there needs no argument. If you were obliged to be out yourselves for thirty days only, and take the necessaries for camp-service from the land (I mean without an enemy therein), your agricultural population would sustain, I believe, greater damage than what the whole expense of the late war amounted to. But if a war should come, what damage must be expected? There is the insult, too, and the disgrace of the thing, worse than any damage to right-thinking men.

On all these accounts, then, we must unite to lend our succour, and drive off the war yonder; the rich, that, spending a little from the abundance which they happily possess, they may enjoy the residue in security; the young, that, gaining military experience in Philip's territory, they may become redoubtable champions to preserve their own; the orators, that they may pass a good account of their statesmanship, for on the result of measures will depend your judgment of their conduct. May it for every cause by prosperous!

CHAPTER IV

COMPOSITION

Words make sentences, sentences form paragraphs, and paragraphs are developed into speeches. Words should be vital and instantly spring into position so that the thought may be quickly conveyed. They should be appropriate in that they may become the time, place, and circumstance in which they are used. They should not be employed for their own sake, but merely for the reason that they fit in properly with their fellows and adequately convey the speaker's meaning. Words are important on account of their expressive power, and this is greatly influenced by their location; as,

Many times the attempt was made to stretch the royal authority far enough to justify military trials; but it never had more than temporary success.

—*JEREMIAH S. BLACK*

In this sentence the word "temporary" is important for the reason that it qualifies the word "success," and the ability properly to place words in a sentence so as to make them most effective in the performance of their duty is as important to the speaker as is the advantageous marshaling of an army to its general.

A sentence should contain one complete thought, and but one, and this thought should be presented from only one point of view. By remembering this, speakers will avoid confusing their listeners, as a sentence containing one thought presented from one point is most likely to be clear. The mind of the speaker grasps instantly such sentences, sees all around them, as it were, and as quickly presents them in the mind of the listener. Students of speech-making are strongly advised to observe this rule of unity in constructing their sentences.

Other essential qualities to the formation of good sentences are force and ease. Force is best represented in short sentences, and ease in long ones, although a sentence may, at times, lack ease because it is too long. A sentence that is so involved that its meaning is not instantly clear will lack in ease as well as in clearness, and is sure to be deficient in force. When a speaker wishes to employ force he should move from a weaker word to a stronger; as, Byron, Milton, and Shakespeare are representative English poets. When he wishes a sentence that is made up of a negative and a positive to be forceful he should place the negative first; as,

A man is fed, not that he may be fed, but that he may work.

—RALPH WALDO EMERSON

When the object of the speaker is to be argumentative instead of assertive he should place the positive first; as,

Territory, like other property, can only be acquired for constitutional purposes, and cannot be acquired and governed for unconstitutional purposes.

—GEORGE F. HOAR

Sentences should be feeders, thus suggesting other sentences. They should connect one with the other at both ends like links forming a chain. The essential qualities of sentences are correctness, force, ease, unity, and clearness.

As there should be perfect ease in going from word to word in a sentence, so there should be like ease in going from sentence to sentence in a paragraph. In fact, a paragraph is much like a large sentence, the only real difference is that it is made of sentences whereas a sentence is composed of words. A paragraph, like a sentence, should be a unit, and one paragraph should grow out of another exactly as sentences should do, and thus will the many paragraphs form the speech in the same manner as do the words form the sentences and the sentences form the paragraphs.

The four forms of English composition are exposition, argumentation, narration, and description. Exposition teaches; argumentation convinces and persuades; narration tells; description shows. In oratory we have five classes: philosophic, demonstrative, forensic, deliberative, and social, and the four forms of composition may be employed in any of the five classes of oratory. Speakers, as a rule, use the narrative for the statement; exposition, argumentation, or description, for the body; and sometimes one form and sometimes another for the conclusion. A speaker might adopt the narrative form for stating his points, the argumentative for making them clear, and the descriptive for driving them home.

EXPOSITION

Exposition means the interpreting of a passage or a work, explaining and expounding its meaning, analyzing its parts, and laying bare to the reader or listener all that might be obscure. A splendid example of exposition is the following extract from The American Scholar, by Ralph Waldo Emerson:

If it were only for a vocabulary, the scholar would be covetous of action. Life is our dictionary. Years are well spent in country labors; in town—in the insight into trades and manufactures; in frank intercourse

52

with many men and women; in science; in art; to the one end of mastering in all their facts a language by which to illustrate and embody our perceptions. I learn immediately from any speaker how much he has already lived through the poverty or the splendor of his speech. Life lies behind us as the quarry from whence we get tiles and cope-stones for the masonry of today. This is the way to learn grammar. Colleges and books only copy the language which the field and the work-yard made.

But the final value of action, like that of books, and better than books, is, that it is a resource. That great principle of undulation in nature, that shows itself in the inspiring and expiring of the breath; in desire and satiety; in the ebb and flow of the sea; in day and night; in heat and cold; and as yet more deeply ingrained in every atom and every fluid, is known to us under the name of polarity—these "fits of easy transmission and reflection," as Newton called them, are the law of nature because they are the law of spirit.

The mind now thinks; now acts; and each fit reproduces the other. When the artist has exhausted his materials, when the fancy no longer paints, when thoughts are no longer apprehended, and books are a weariness—he has always the resource to live. Character is higher than intellect. Thinking is the function. Living is the functionary. The stream retreats to its source. A great soul will be strong to live, as well as strong to think. Does he lack organ or medium to impart his truths? He can still fall back on this elemental force of living them. This is a total act. Thinking is a partial act. Let the grandeur of justice shine in his affairs. Let the beauty of affection cheer his lowly roof. Those "far from fame," who dwell and act with him, will feel the force of his constitution in the doings and passages of the day better than it can be measured by any public and designed display. Time shall teach him that the scholar loses no hour which the man lives. Herein he unfolds the sacred germ of his instinct, screened from influence. What is lost in seemliness is gained in strength. Not out of those, on whom systems of education have exhausted their culture, comes the helpful giant to destroy the old or to build the new, but out of unhandseled savage nature, out of terrible Druids and Berserkirs, come at last Alfred and Shakespeare.

I hear therefore with joy whatever is beginning to be said of the dignity and necessity of labor to every citizen. There is virtue yet in the hoe and the spade, for learned as well as for unlearned hands. And labor is everywhere welcome; always we are invited to work; only be this limitation observed, that a man shall not for the sake of wider activity sacrifice any opinion to the popular judgments and modes of action.

53

ARGUMENTATION

Argumentation means the stating of points or facts, the logical presentation of them, and the drawing of conclusions from a consideration of the premises. Its objects are to convince and persuade the reader or listener. Argumentation that stops with conviction is incomplete—it must persuade as well as convince in order to be effective. A speaker accomplishes practically nothing if he convinces an audience but does not persuade it to do the thing he desires. Arguments may be direct or indirect. They are direct when aimed at a stated conclusion, and they are indirect when they are employed to disprove what is opposed to the speaker's contention. The most effective form of argument is where the two forms, direct and indirect, are employed, thus not only demolishing one contention but clearly establishing the other. It is comparable to the contrast in oratory where the statement is made that a certain thing is not only not of a certain class but specifically belongs to another one. This is "clinching" the argument, and it leaves not a loophole for the escape of the opponent.

Here is an excellent piece of argumentative oratory, taken from an address of William H. Seward in the celebrated Freeman case.

"Thou shalt not kill," is a commandment addressed, not to him alone, but to me, to you, to the Court, and to the whole community. There are no exceptions from that commandment, at least not in civil life, save those of self-defense, and capital punishment for crimes in the due and just administration of the law. There is not only a question, then, whether the prisoner has shed the blood of his fellow-man, but the question whether we shall unlawfully shed his blood. I should be guilty of murder if, in my present relation, I saw the executioner waiting for an insane man and failed to say, or failed to do in his behalf, all that my ability allowed. I think it has been proved of the prisoner at the bar, that during all this long and tedious trial, he has had no sleepless nights, and that even in the daytime, when he retires from the halls to his lonely cell, he sinks to rest like a wearied child, on the stone floor, and quietly slumbers till roused by the constable with his staff, to appear again before the jury. His counsel enjoy no such repose. Their thoughts by day and their dreams by night are filled with oppressive apprehension that, through their inability or neglect, he may be condemned.

I am arraigned before you for undue manifestations of zeal and excitement. My answer to all such charges shall be brief. When this cause shall have been committed to you, I shall be happy indeed if it shall appear that my only error has been that I have felt too much, thought too intensely, or acted too faithfully.

If my error would thus be criminal, how great would yours be if you should render an unjust verdict? Only four months have elapsed since an outraged people, distrustful of judicial redress, doomed the prisoner to immediate death. Some of you have confessed that you approved that lawless sentence. All men now rejoice that the prisoner was saved for this solemn trial. But this trial would be as criminal as that precipitate sentence, if, through any wilful fault or prejudice of yours, it should prove but a mockery of justice. If any prejudice of witnesses, or the imagination of counsel, or any ill-timed jest, shall, at any time, have diverted your attention; or if any prejudgment which you have brought into the jury box, or any cowardly fear of popular opinion shall have operated to cause you to deny to the prisoner that dispassionate consideration of his case which the laws of God and man exact of you, and if, owing to such an error, this wretched man fall from among the living, what will be your crime? You have violated the commandment, "Thou shalt not kill." It is not the form or letter of the trial by jury that authorizes you to send your fellow-man to his dread account, but it is the spirit that sanctifies that glorious institution; and if, through pride, passion, timidity, weakness, or any cause, you deny the prisoner one iota of all the defense to which he is entitled by the law of the land, you yourselves, whatever his guilt may be, will have broken the commandment, "Thou shalt do no murder."

NARRATION

Narration is recounting the particulars of events, or enumerating facts; telling of occurrences or things in regular order. Specifically, it is that part of explanation that allows the subject in its relations to the movement of time. In simple words, it is a continuous telling.

The narrative form of composition is beautifully employed by Daniel Webster in his first Bunker Hill Monument address, the following being an extract from that admirable speech:

The society whose organ I am was formed for the purpose of rearing some honorable and durable monument to the memory of the early friends of American independence. They have thought that for this object no time could be more propitious than the present prosperous and peaceful period; that no place could claim preference over this memorable spot; and that no day could be more auspicious to the undertaking than the anniversary of the battle which was here fought. The foundation of that monument we have now laid. With solemnities suited to the occasion, with prayer to Almighty God for His blessing, and in the midst of this cloud of witnesses, we have begun the work. We trust it will be prosecuted, and that, springing from a broad foundation, rising high in massive solidity and unadorned grandeur, it may remain as long as Heaven permits the works of man to last, a fit emblem, both of the events in memory of which it is raised, and of the gratitude of those who have reared it.

DESCRIPTION

Description is showing of things by means of language-pictures; telling the attributes that make up the whole. Word-pictures are created by means of explaining the individual parts of a theme or view as they affect the entire thing.

As a piece of word-picturing the following description of the breaking of day, by Edward Everett, is certainly magnificent:

Much as we are indebted to our observatories for elevating our conceptions of the heavenly bodies, they present, even to the unaided sight, scenes of glory which words are too feeble to describe. I had occasion, a few weeks since, to take the early train from Providence to Boston, and, for this purpose, rose at two o'clock in the morning. Every thing around was wrapped in darkness, and hushed in silence, broken only by what seemed, at that hour, the unearthly clank and rush of the train. It was a mild, serene, mid-summer's night; the sky was without a cloud; the winds were hushed. The moon, then in the last quarter, had just risen; and the stars shown with a spectral lustre but little affected by her presence. Jupiter, two hours high, was the herald of the day: the Pleiades, just above the horizon, shed their sweet influence in the east: Lyra sparkled near the zenith: Andromeda veiled her newly discovered glories from the naked eye, in the south: the steady Pointers, far beneath the pole, looked meekly up from the depths of the north to their sovereign.

Such was the glorious spectacle as I entered the train. As we proceeded, the timid approach of twilight became more perceptible. The intense blue of the sky began to soften; the smaller stars, like little children, went first to rest; the sister beams of the Pleiades soon melted together; but the bright constellations of the west and north remained unchanged. Steadily the wondrous transfiguration went on. Hands of angels, hidden from mortal eyes, shifted the scenery of the heavens; the glories of night dissolved into the glories of the dawn. The blue sky now turned more softly gray; the great watch-stars shut up their holy eyes; the east began to kindle. Faint streaks of purple soon blushed along the sky; the whole celestial concave was filled with the inflowing tides of the morning light, which came pouring down from above in one great ocean of radiance; till at length, as we reached the blue hills, a flash of purple fire blazed out from above the horizon, and turned the dewy tear-drops of flower and leaf into rubies and diamonds. In a few seconds the everlasting gates of the morning were thrown wide open, and the Lord of Day, arrayed in glories too severe for gaze of man, began his course.

56

EXPOSITION

The Conspiracy to Murder. A conspiracy to kill and murder does not owe its criminality to the length of time it may occupy in its progress, from its first conception to its ultimate adoption—a conspiracy may be formed the very instant before the step is taken to put it into effect. If a number of people meet accidentally in the street, and conspire together to kill and murder at the moment, it is as essentially the crime of conspiracy as if it had been intended for a year before, and hatched from that year to the moment of its accomplishment.

—*JOHN P. CURRAN, Trial of John Costly for conspiracy to murder, Dublin, Feb. 23, 1804*

Circumstantial Evidence of Guilt. I need not pause to remind you how much caution, how much candor, and how much intelligence are requisite in appreciating circumstantial evidence in any case. That kind of evidence may clearly prove guilt. That many times, however, it has also shed innocent blood, and many times it has stained a fair name, I need not pause for a moment to illustrate or remind you. Instead of doing that, I think I shall be better occupied, under the direction of his honor, in reminding you of the two great rules by which circumstantial evidence is to be weighed, appreciated, and applied by the jury. Those rules, gentlemen, are these:

In the first place, that the jury shall be satisfied that they conduct, as a necessary result and conclusion, to the inference of guilt. It is a rule that may be called a golden rule in the examination and application of this kind of evidence which we call circumstantial, that should it so turn out that every fact and circumstance alleged and proved to exist is consistent, on the one hand with the hypothesis of guilt and on the other hand consistent, reasonably and fairly, with the hypothesis of innocence, then those circumstances prove nothing at all. Unless they go so far as to establish as a necessary conclusion this guilt which they are offered with a view to establish, they are utterly worthless and ineffectual for the investigation of truth. I had the honor to read to the court this morning, and possibly in your hearing, an authority in which that familiar and elementary doctrine was laid down, a doctrine every day applied, everywhere recognized as primary in the appreciation of this kind of evidence. It is not enough that the circumstances relied upon are plainly and certainly proved. It is not enough to show that they are consistent with the hypothesis of guilt. They must also render the hypothesis of innocence inadmissible and impossible, unreasonable and absurd, or they have proved nothing at all.

—*RUFUS CHOATE, in the Dalton divorce case*

Stare Decisis. The people, in forming the organic law of the government of this state, very wisely foresaw that, in its action and progress, questions of interpretation of the settlement of legal principles, and of their application, would frequently arise; and thence the necessity of constituting some tribunal with general appellate and supervisory powers, whose decisions should be final and conclusively settle and declare the law. This was supposed to have been accomplished in the organization of this court. Heretofore this court, under the Constitution, has been looked to by the people as the tribunal of the last resort in the state; and it has hitherto been supposed that when this court has decided a case upon its merits such decision not only determined the right of the parties litigant in that particular case, but that it also settled the principles involved in it as permanent rules of law, universally applicable in all future cases embracing similar facts, and involving the same or analogous principles. These decisions thus became at once public law, measures of private right, and landmarks of property. They determined the right of persons and of things. Parties entered into contracts with each other with reference to them, as to the declared and established law; law equally binding upon the courts and the people. But the doctrine recently put forth would at once overturn this whole body of law founded upon the adjudications of this court, built up as it has been by the long continued and arduous labors, grown venerable with years, and interwoven as it has become with the interests, and habits, and the opinions of the people. Under this new doctrine all would again be unsettled—nothing established. Like the ever returning but never ending labors of the fabled Sisyphus, this court, in disregard to the maxim of "stare decisis," would, in each recurring case, have to enter upon its examination and decision as if all were new, without any aid from the experience of the past, or the benefit of any established principle or settled law. Each case with decision being thus limited as law to itself alone would in turn pass away and be forgotten, leaving behind it no record of principle established, or light to guide, or rule to govern the future.

—*LUTHER BRADISH. Opinion given as Presiding Judge
of Court of Errors, in Hanford v. Archer,
Dec., 1842, at Albany, N. Y.*

ARGUMENTATION

The Obligation of Contract. We contend that the obligation of a contract—that is, the duty of performing it—is not created by the law of the particular place where it is made, and dependent on that law for its existence; but that it may subsist, and does subsist, without the law, and independent of it. The obligation is in the contract itself, in the assent of the parties, and in the sanction of universal law. This is the doctrine of Grotius, Vattel, Burlamaqui, Pothier, and Rutherford. The contract, doubtless, is necessarily to be enforced by the municipal law of the place where performance is demanded. The municipal law acts on the contract after it is made, to compel its execution, or give damages for its violation. But this is a very different thing from the same law being the original or fountain of the contract.

Let us illustrate this matter by an example. Two persons contract together in New York for the delivery, by one to the other, of a domestic animal, a utensil of husbandry, or a weapon of war. This is a lawful contract, and, while the parties remain in New York it is to be enforced by the laws of that state. But, if they remove with the article to Pennsylvania or Maryland, there a new law comes to act upon the contract, and to apply other remedies if it be broken. Thus far the remedies are furnished by the laws of society. But suppose the same parties to go together to a savage wilderness, or a desert island beyond the reach of the laws of any society. The obligation of the contract still subsists, and is as perfect as ever, and is now to be enforced by another law, that is the law of nature; and the party to whom the promise was made has a right to take by force the animal, the utensil, or the weapon that was promised him. The right is as perfect here as it was in Pennsylvania, or even in New York.

—DANIEL WEBSTER, in Ogden v. Saunders

Parent and Child. The next greatest tie is that of parent and child. If in God's providence a man has not only watched over the cradle of his child, but over the grave of his offspring, and has witnessed earth committed to earth, ashes to ashes, and dust to dust, he knows that the love of a parent for his child is stronger than death. The bitter lamentation, "Would to God I had died for thee," has been wrung from many a parent's heart. But when the adulterer's shadow comes between the parent and child, it casts over both a gloom darker than the grave. What agony is equal to his who knows not whether the children gathered around his board are his own offspring or an adulterous brood, hatched in his bed. To the child it is still more disastrous. Nature designs that children shall have the care of both parents; the mother's care is the chief blessing to her child—a mother's honor its priceless inheritance. But when the adulterer enters a family, the child is deprived of the care of one parent, perhaps of both. When death, in God's providence, strikes a mother from the family, the deepest grief that preys upon a husband's heart is the loss of her nurture and example to his orphan child; and the sweetest conversation between parent and child is when they talk of the beloved mother who is gone. But how can a daughter hear that mother's name without a blush? Death is merciful to the pitiless cruelty of him whose lust has stained the fair brow of innocent childhood by corrupting the heart of the mother, whose example must stain the daughter's life.

—EDWIN M. STANTON, in Sickles' trial

Distrust of Witnesses. Are they witnesses to be trusted with report of evidence by words? Are they witnesses to remember words where everything may depend upon the exact expression, upon the order of the language, upon dropping an epithet here and inserting an epithet there, by which the guilt of adultery is confessed? Is this a body of witnesses that are to be trusted to report words, that are the issues of life, with certainty and accuracy? I submit that, on the outside of it, the whole case of confession to be listened to by this jury is a conclusive and rational distrust which would leave my client in no fear at all of the result. Here is a man that cannot be trusted to carry ten bushels of yellow, flat corn across the city for fear that he would steal half of it; who cannot be trusted to take a hat full of uncounted bills to New York. A man who has not honesty enough, or fairness enough, to weight the hind quarter of an ox—shall he be trusted to weigh out gold dust and dimes, and count the pulses of life? A man not honest enough, a combination not honest enough, to carry a letter without mutilating it into a falsehood, to prove words in which honesty, intelligence, and fairness may be entirely omitted. We come, then, to this examination of confession exactly in this state of the case: It is probability, amounting almost to a miracle, that a confession should be made under any circumstances at all. Confessions themselves are never to be acted upon by the jury unless they know, upon their oaths, that they have the very words spoken in the sense in which they came. They never can have that assurance if they have not a clear and undoubting confidence in the speaker that reports them. And their case opens, I say, with this: that a moral miracle is to be established on the testimony of confessions, by the evidence of witnesses, as a body, manifestly and apparently undeserving a moment's confidence.

—RUFUS CHOATE, in Dalton divorce case

NARRATION

The History of Trial by Jury. I might begin with Tacitus, and show how the contest arose in the forest of Germany more than two thousand years ago; how the rough virtues and sound common sense of that people established the right of trial by jury, and thus started on a career which has made their posterity the foremost race that ever lived in all the tide of time. The Saxons carried it to England, and were ever ready to defend it with their blood. It was crushed out by the Danish invasion; and all that they suffered of tyranny and oppression during the period of their subjugation resulted from the want of trial by jury. If that had been conceded to them the reaction would not have taken place which drove back the Danes to their frozen homes in the north. But those ruffian sea-kings could not understand that, and the reaction came. Alfred, the greatest of revolutionary heroes and the wisest monarch that ever sat on a throne, made the first use of his power, after the Saxons restored it, to reëstablish their ancient laws. He had promised them that he would, and he was true to them because they had been true to him. But it was not easily done; the courts were opposed to it, for it limited their power—a kind of power that everybody covets—the power to punish without regard to law. He was obliged to hang forty-four judges in one year for refusing to give his subjects a trial by jury. When the historian says he hung them, it is not meant that he put them to death without a trial. He had them impeached before the grand council of the nation, the Witenagemot, the parliament of that time. During the subsequent period of Saxon domination no man on English soil was powerful enough to refuse a legal trial to the meanest peasant. If any minister or any king, in war or in peace, had dared to punish a freeman by tribunal of his own appointment, he would have roused the wrath of the whole population; all orders of society would have resisted it; lord and vassal, knight and squire, priest and penitent, bocman and socman, master and thrall, copyholder and villein, would have risen in one mass and burnt the offender to death in his castle, or followed him in his flight and torn him to atoms. It was again trampled down by the Norman conquerors; but the evils resulting from the want of it united all classes in the effort which compelled King John to restore it by the Great Charter. Everybody is familiar with the struggles which the English people, during many generations, made for their rights with the Plantagenets, the Tudors, and the Stuarts, and which ended finally in the revolution of 1688, when the liberties of England were placed upon an impregnable basis by the Bill of Rights. Many times the attempt was made to stretch the royal authority far enough to justify military trials; but it never had more than temporary success.

—JUDGE JEREMIAH S. BLACK, in the Milligan
case, U. S. Supreme Court,
Washington, D. C., Dec., 1866

Testimony. I will go through the case fairly and discuss it fully. I will nothing extenuate, nor aught set down in malice. I will base my argument upon the testimony, not as I would have it, but as it is. I will speak not to the world, but to you, who can correct and hold me in judgment, if I fail to redeem the promises of fairness and candor which

I make. Heaven can witness for me that I desire no fame at the expense of these unfortunate men. I will use no bitter words, I will affect no bitter loathing; I will assail neither man, woman, nor child, except under the urgent pressure of duty and necessity. I wish I could be spared the painful task of doing so at all.

—*J. A. VAN DYKE, in conspiracy case,*
Detroit, Mich., Sept., 1851

DESCRIPTION

Conscience. Lady Macbeth must needs walk by night in her sleep and rub her hands as if to wash them, and cry out: "Out, damned spot, out I say!" But all Neptune's ocean will not wash the stain away; all the perfumes of Arabia will not sweeten the murderer's hand. Conscience, the greatest gift of God, the child itself of God, working and acting obedient to the same law by which your system and mine, by their nature, will attempt to throw off disease, that which is imperfect and that which is poison, I say by that same law conscience seeks to throw off its load of guilt.

—*STATE'S ATTORNEY FRANK M. NYE, in People v.*
Hayward, Minneapolis, Minn., Dec., 1895

Consent Under Protest. Sir, the consent of Maine to part with her soil and her sovereignty was given with a bleeding heart; it was like the consent of him who bares his own right arm to the surgeon's knife when advised that his life can only be preserved by its amputation; she consented as one consents to commit to kindred dust the children of his body; she consented as the red man consents to be driven from his happy hunting grounds, the graves of his fathers and the banks of the streams where he sported in childhood; she consented, as was said by another, as "the victim consents to execution because he walks and is not dragged to the scaffold which has been erected to receive him."

—*DANIEL S. DICKINSON, Speech in reply to*
Webster on the Northwestern Boundary
question, U. S. Senate, April 9, 1846

Duties of Juries. Gentlemen of the jury, I have about concluded my duties in this case. Yours will follow. I ask from you nothing in the world but the intelligent judgment of twelve intelligent men on the evidence before you. I have only one little picture more to offer. It is Burns's picture of the Scottish farmer in the seclusion of his family. His day's work done, he draws his little family about him. He has laid aside his cap and has taken the old family Bible from its shelf. He calls Jane and James and the old mother and reads to them from God's promises. Then all bow their heads in prayer. "In scenes like these old Scotia's grandeur lies." Some of you here are wont to keep that sacred tryst. Into that tryst you would never admit this paper.

—*GENERAL BLACK, in People v. Dunlap,*
New York, Feb. 4, 1896

CHAPTER V

PARAPHRASING

Paraphrasing is the reproduction of the sense of a passage, a composition or a speech, in other than the terms used by the original writer or speaker. It is the holding on to the original structure and thought, but a clothing of them in entirely new language. It is an amplification of an idea, a redressing of it; the use of new terms or different language for the presentation of an old thought; as,

What would have been the consequences, sir, if we had been conquered? Were we not fighting against that majesty? Would the justice of our opposition have been considered? The most horrid forfeitures, confiscations, and attainders would have been pronounced against us.

In paraphrasing this extract from a speech by Patrick Henry we should keep in mind his thought only and pay no attention to the language he used in expressing the thought. We should borrow his idea, but we should clothe it in language of our own; as,

Let me ask you, sir, what would have resulted from our having been conquered by Great Britain? It was the exercise of power by that nation that we combated. Would she, had our struggle for liberty failed, have considered that we fought for what we believed to be right? No, sir, history would have but repeated itself. Our patriots would have died on the gallows, their children would have been deprived of their inheritance, and no cruelty would have been too great for the conquering nation to have inflicted upon her rebellious colonies.

What good is to be derived from paraphrasing?

It trains the mind through the exercising of the power of mental concentration that is necessary in order to hold on to the thought; it helps to form the habit of constructing a framework; it aids in making a speaker arrange his thoughts consecutively; it improves the speaker's style, and it enlarges his vocabulary.

On a first attempt it will seem almost impossible for many to paraphrase. They are apt to think the original matter so well constructed, and the thought so perfectly expressed, as to render any other arrangement of it ridiculous and practically out of the question. They cannot bring to mind words common to themselves with which to clothe the ideas of another. In trying to remember the words of the original writer or speaker they lose the thought and are unable to proceed. To all such, the author says: continue in the work; cease to think of words at all, keep the framework in mind, lay hold of the thought, and words to convey the thought will leap forward to do the work. They may not, at first, be the best possible words, but words that will answer the purpose of carrying the thought to the mind of the listener will flow freely, and with study and practice the vocabulary will become larger and more effective.

Paraphrasing helps to develop the imaginative quality by cultivating the power of producing mental images, seeing with the mind's eye, as it were. If a speaker will hold on to his picture or his theme, he will have no trouble in drawing the one or developing the other. In presenting a picture, the speaker must keep the entire scene in his mind when describing it in detail; and when developing a theme, it must be in the speaker's mental vision in its entirety while he develops it step by step, point by point; as,

God called man in dreams into the vestibule of heaven, saying, "Come up higher, and I will show thee the glory of My house"; and to His angels who stood about His throne, He said, "take him, strip him of his robes of flesh; cleanse his affections; put a new breath into his nostrils; but touch not his human heart—the heart that fears, and hopes, and trembles." A moment, and it was done, and the man stood ready for his unknown voyage. Under the guidance of a mighty angel, with sounds of flying pinions, they sped away from the battlements of heaven. Some time, on the mighty angel's wings, they fled through Saharas of darkness, wildernesses of death. At length, from a distance not counted, save in the arithmetic of heaven, light beamed upon them—a sleepy flame, as seen through a hazy cloud. They sped on, in their terrible speed, to meet the light; the light with lesser speed came to meet them. In a moment the blazing of suns around them—a moment, the wheeling of planets; then came long eternities of twilight; then again, on the right hand and the left, appeared more constellations. At last, the man sank down, crying, "Angel, I can go no further; let me lie down in the grave, and hide myself from the infinitude of the universe, for end there is none." "End is there none?" demanded the angel. And, from the glittering stars that shown around, there came a choral shout, "End there is none!" "End is there none?" demanded the angel again, "And it is this that awes thy soul?" I answer, "End there is none to the universe of God! Lo, also, there is no beginning!"

This is a story taken from the German and used by O. M. Mitchell in his address "The Immensity of the Creation," and it made a striking illustration. It will be an easy matter to paraphrase this vivid portraiture if the student will keep in mind the idea of the angel and the man flying through space as the scene shifts. There is a continuous change in the surroundings as the angel and man continue to fly through space, but the mind of the speaker should accompany them and see all the changes that occur without losing sight of the angel and the man, as they are the picture, the surroundings being merely the accessories or details, and while these are being described the angel and the man must still be in view. The angel and the man must be seen standing at the portals of heaven, they must be seen speeding from the battlements of that glorious place. The scene now shifts to a desert of darkness, but still the angel and the man are within the mental vision of the speaker. Now a ray of light, breaking through a misty cloud, showers its brightness upon them. The scene has again changed, but the picture of the angel and the man remains. The light grows in brightness and immensity, other details enter into the picture—the suns, the planets, and the twilight—but still the angel and the man are there. Again the scenery is shifted, the man sinks down in weariness, the chorus of angel voices is heard as the multitude of stars open their portals to let out the heavenly shout, "End there is none," but still the picture is there—the picture of the angel and the man.

In developing a theme, the same principle prevails. It is for this reason that it is wise to have in a speech but one proposition to expound, one subject to discuss, one object to accomplish. By dragging in many points, instead of developing the one, the speaker is apt to ramble, the listener to become confused, and the speech to fail. By this it is meant that there must be one grand central idea or point around which all others must revolve. This principal idea, proposition, or point must be like the hub of a wheel—it may have any number of spokes, but they must all radiate from the hub. It is like the picture of the angel and the man flying through space—the scene changes, but the angel and the man are always present to the imaginative eye of the speaker—and it is for this reason he is able to describe so vividly his picture or develop his theme to make them apparent even to the mind of the unimaginative listener.

Let us consider the developing of a theme in place of the drawing of a picture. For this purpose we will take an extract from a speech of that clear reasoned and eminent theologian, William Ellery Channing:

The grand idea of humanity, of the importance of man as man, is spreading silently, but surely. Even the most abject portions of society are visited by some dreams of a better condition for which they were designed. The grand doctrine, that every human being should have the means of self-culture, of progress in knowledge and virtue, of health, comfort, and happiness, of exercising the powers and affections of a man—this is slowly taking its place as the highest social truth. That the world was made for all, and not for a few; that society is to care for all, that no human being shall perish but through his own fault; that the great end of government is to spread a shield over the rights of all—these propositions are growing into axioms, and the spirit of them is coming forth in all the departments of life.

How beautifully Dr. Channing holds on to his theme through the entire passage. He starts by telling us what the grand idea of humanity is, and then he proceeds to expound it. The first laying down of the proposition is, that "the importance of man as man" (this is the grand idea of humanity) is becoming universal. He then amplifies the idea by stating that even the lowest specimens of humanity are awakening to a realization of it. He then develops what this idea consists of—the right of all men to education, proper housing, and sufficient food, in short, the right to live as human beings—and asserts that it has become the most important of the social truths. He then enumerates what at one time were considered debatable opinions but are now recognized as undeniable facts. Notice how, while he brings in many statements, they all radiate from the one proposition that "the importance of man as man is spreading silently, but surely," and never once does he permit you to lose sight of the theme, because he continuously has it before his mental eye. No matter what he says, "the importance of man as man" is uppermost, just as was the picture of the angel and the man, and if the student in paraphrasing the passage will keep that one point in mind, he should have no serious difficulty in presenting it in a new garb clearly to the minds of others. A carrying out of this principle will enable an extempore speaker to form his matter with perfect ease, and this is one reason why paraphrasing is beneficial to the student of public speaking. It is a valuable stepping stone that should be used by all in attempting to attain proficiency in the art of expressing thought by means of the spoken word.

Any material that comes to hand may be used for the purpose of paraphrasing provided it be properly constructed and expressed in good language. These are two important points to remember in choosing selections for paraphrasing, as students are sure to be influenced by the construction and diction of the matter they employ for this purpose.

The following extracts furnish splendid matter for paraphrasing.

EDUCATION

HORACE MANN

From her earliest history, the policy of this country has been to develop the minds of all her people, and to imbue them with the principles of duty. To do this work most effectually, she has begun with the young. If she would continue to mount higher and higher toward the summit of prosperity, she must continue the means by which her present elevation has been gained. In doing this, she will not only exercise the noblest prerogative of government, but will coöperate with the Almighty in one of His sublimest works.

The Greek rhetorician, Longinus, quotes from the Mosaic account of the creation what he calls the sublimest passage ever uttered: "God said, 'Let there be light,' and there was light!" From the centre of black immensity effulgence burst forth. Above, beneath, on every side, its radiance streamed out, silent, yet making each spot in the vast concave brighter than the line which the lightning pencils upon the midnight cloud. Darkness fled as the swift beams spread onward and outward, in an unending circumfusion of splendor. Onward and outward still they move to this day, glorifying, through wider and wider regions of space, the infinite Author from whose power and beneficence they sprang. But not only in the beginning, when God created the heavens and the earth, did he say, "Let there be light!" Whenever a human soul is born into the world, its Creator stands over it, and again pronounces the same sublime words, "Let there be light."

Magnificent, indeed, was the material creation, when, suddenly blazing forth in mid-space, the new-born sun dispelled the darkness of the ancient night. But infinitely more magnificent is it when the human soul rays forth its subtler and swifter beams; when the light of the senses irradiates all outward things, revealing the beauty of their colors and the exquisite symmetry of their proportions and forms; when the light of reason penetrates to their invisible properties and laws, and displays all those hidden relations that make up all the sciences; when the light of conscience illuminates the moral world, separating truth from error, and virtue from vice. The light of the newly kindled sun, indeed, was glorious. It struck upon all the planets, and waked into existence their myriad capacities of life and joy. As it rebounded from them, and showed their vast orbs all wheeling, circle beyond circle in their stupendous courses, the sons of God shouted for joy. The light sped onward, beyond Sirius, beyond the pole-star, beyond Orion and the Pleiades, and is still spreading onward into the abysses of space. But the light of the human soul flies swifter than the light of the sun, and outshines its meridian blaze. It can embrace not only the sun of our system, but all suns and galaxies of suns; ay! the soul is capable of knowing and enjoying Him who created the suns themselves; and when these starry lusters that now glorify the firmament shall wax dim, and fade away like a wasted taper, the light of the soul shall still remain, nor time, nor cloud, nor any power but its own perversity, shall ever quench its brightness. Again I would say, that whenever a human soul is born into the world, God stands over it and pronounces the same sublime fiat, "Let there be light!" and may the time soon come, when all human governments shall coöperate with the Divine government in carrying this benediction and baptism into fulfilment!

DIGGING FOR THE THOUGHT

JOHN RUSKIN

When you come to a good book, you must ask yourself, "Am I inclined to work as an Australian miner would? Are my pickaxes and

68

shovels in good order, and am I in good trim myself—and my sleeves well up to the elbows, and my breath good, and my temper?" And, keeping the figure a little longer, even at the cost of tiresomeness, for it is a thoroughly useful one, the metal you are in search of being the author's mind or meaning, his words are as the rock which you have to crush and smelt in order to get at it. And your pickaxes are your own care, wit, and learning; your smelting-furnace is your own thoughtful soul. Do not hope to get at any good author's meaning without those tools and that fire. Often you will need sharpest, finest chiselling, and patientest fusing before you can gather one grain of the metal.

And, therefore, first of all, I tell you earnestly and authoritatively (I know I am right in this), you must get into the habit of looking intensely at words, and assuring yourself of their meaning, syllable by syllable—nay, letter by letter. For, though it is only by reason of the opposition of letters in the function of signs to sounds that the study of books is called "literature", that a man versed in it is called, by the consent of nations, a man of letters, instead of a man of books or of words, you may yet connect with that accidental nomenclature this real fact—that you might read all the books in the British Museum (if you could live long enough) and remain an utterly illiterate, uneducated person; but that if you read ten pages of a good book, letter by letter, that is to say, with real accuracy, you are forevermore in some measure an educated person. The entire difference between education and non-education (as regards the merely intellectual part of it) consists in this accuracy. A well-educated gentleman may not know many languages, may not be able to speak any but his own, may have read very few books; but whatever language he knows, he knows precisely; whatever word he pronounces, he pronounces rightly. Above all, he is learned in the peerage of words, knows the words of true descent and ancient blood, at a glance, from words of modern canaille; remembers all their ancestry, their inter-marriages, distant relationship, and the extent to which they were admitted, and offices they held among the national noblesse of words at any time and in any country. But an uneducated person may know, by memory, many languages,and talk them all, and yet truly know not a word of any—not a word even of his own. An ordinarily clever and sensible seaman will be able to make his way ashore at most ports; yet he has only to speak a sentence of any language to be known for an illiterate person. So also the accent, or turn of expression of a single sentence, will at once mark a scholar. And this is so strongly felt, so conclusively admitted, by educated persons, that a false accent or a mistaken syllable is enough, in the parliament of any civilized nation, to assign to a man a certain degree of inferior standing forever.

HISTORICAL READING

ARTHUR JAMES BALFOUR

It is no doubt true that we are surrounded by advisers who shall tell us that all study of the past is barren except in so far as it enables us to determine the laws by which the evolution of human societies is governed. How far such an investigation has been up to the present time fruitful in results I will not inquire. That it will ever enable us to trace with accuracy the course which states and nations are destined to pursue in the future, or to account in detail for their history in the past, I do not indeed believe.

We are borne along like travelers on some unexplored stream. We may know enough of the general configuration of the globe to be sure that we are making our way towards the ocean. We may know enough by experience or theory of the laws regulating the flow of liquids, to conjecture how the river will behave under the varying influences to which it may be subject. More than this we cannot know. It will depend largely upon causes which, in relation to any laws which we are ever likely to discover, may properly be called accidental, whether we are destined sluggishlyto drift among fever-stricken swamps, to hurry down perilous rapids, or to glide gently through fair scenes of peaceful cultivation.

But leaving on one side ambitious sociological speculations, and even those more modest but hitherto more successful investigations into the causes which have in particular cases been principally operative in producing great political changes, there are still two modes in which we can derive what I may call "spectacular" enjoyment from the study of history.

There is first the pleasure which arises from the contemplation of some great historic drama, or some broad and well-marked phase of social development. The story of the rise, greatness, and decay of a nation is like some vast epic which contains as subsidiary episodes the varied stories of the rise, greatness, and decay of creeds, of parties and of statesmen. The imagination is moved by the slow unrolling of this great picture of human mutability, as it is moved by the contrasted permanence of the abiding stars. The ceaseless conflicts, the strange echoes of long forgotten controversies, the confusion of purpose, the successes which lay deep the seeds of future evils, the failures that ultimately divert the otherwise inevitable danger, the heroism which struggles to the last for a cause foredoomed to defeat, the wickedness which sides with right, and the wisdom which huzzahs at the triumph of folly—fate, meanwhile, through all this turmoil and perplexity, working silently toward the predestined end—all these form together a subject the contemplation of which need surely never weary.

But there is yet another and very different species of enjoyment

70

to be derived from the records of the past, which requires a somewhat different method of study in order that it may be fully tasted. Instead of contemplating, as it were, from a distance, the larger aspects of the human drama, wemay elect to move in familiar fellowship amid the scenes and actors of special periods.

We may add to the interest we derive from the contemplation of contemporary politics a similar interest derived from a not less minute and probably more accurate knowledge of some comparatively brief passage in the political history of the past. We may extend the social circle in which we move—a circle perhaps narrowed and restricted through circumstances beyond our control—by making intimate acquaintances, perhaps even close friends, among a society long departed, but which, when we have once learnt the trick of it, it rests with us to revive.

It is this kind of historical reading which is usually branded as frivolous and useless, and persons who indulge in it often delude themselves into thinking that the real motive of their investigation into bygone scenes and ancient scandals is philosophic interest in an important historical episode, whereas in truth it is not the philosophy which glorifies the details, but the details which make tolerable the philosophy.

Consider, for example, the use of the French Revolution. The period from the taking of the Bastille to the fall of Robespierre is of about the same length as very commonly intervenes between two of our general elections. On these comparatively few months libraries have been written. The incidents of every week are matters of familiar knowledge. The character and the biography of every actor in the drama has been made the subject of minute study; and by common admission there is no more fascinating page in the history of the world.

But the interest is not what is commonly called philosophic, it is personal. Because the Revolution is the dominant fact in modern history, therefore people suppose that the doings of this or that provincial lawyer, tossed into temporaryeminence and eternal infamy by some freak of the revolutionary wave, or the atrocities committed by this or that mob, half-drunk with blood, rhetoric, and alcohol, are of transcendent importance.

In truth, their interest is great, but their importance is small. What we are concerned to know as students of the philosophy of history is, not the character of each turn and eddy in the great social cataract, but the manner in which the currents of the upper stream drew surely in toward the final plunge, and slowly collected themselves after the catastrophe, again to pursue, at a different level, their renewed and comparatively tranquil course.

Now, if so much of the interest of the French Revolution depends on our minute knowledge of each passing incident, how much more necessary is such knowledge when we are dealing with the quiet nooks and corners of history—when we are seeking an introduction, let us say, into the literary society of Johnson or the fashionable society of Walpole! Society, dead or alive, can have no charm without intimacy, and no intimacy without interest in trifles.

If we would feel at our ease in any company, if we wish to find humour in its jokes and point in its repartees, we must know something of the beliefs and prejudices of its various members—their loves and their hates, their hopes and their fears, their maladies, their marriages, and their flirtations. If these things are beneath our notice, we shall not be the less qualified to serve our queen and country, but need make no attempt to extract pleasure out of one of the most delightful departments of literature.

EULOGY OF GENERAL GRANT
DEAN FARRAR

Every true man derives his patent of nobleness direct from God. Did not God choose David from the sheepfolds to make him ruler of his people Israel? Was not the "Lord of life and all the worlds" for thirty years a carpenter at Nazareth? Do not such careers illustrate the prophecy of Solomon, "Seest thou the man diligent in his business? he shall stand before kings." When Abraham Lincoln sat, book in hand, day after day, under the tree, moving around it as the shadow moved, absorbed in mastering his task; when James Garfield rang the bell of Hiram Institute, day after day, on the very stroke of the hour, and swept the school room as faithfully as he mastered the Greek lesson; when Ulysses Grant, sent with his team to meet some men who were to load the cart with logs, and finding no men there, loaded the cart with his own boy strength—they showed in conscientious duty and thoroughness the qualities which were to raise them to rule the destinies of men.

But the youth was not destined to die in that deep valley of obscurity and toil in which it is the lot—perhaps the happy lot—of many of us to spend our little lives. The hour came: the man was needed.

In 1861 there broke out the most terrible war of modern days. Grant received a commission as colonel of volunteers, and in four years the struggling toiler had risen to the chief command of a vaster army than has ever been handled by any mortal man. Who could have imagined that four years could make that stupendous difference? But it is often so. The great men needed for some tremendous crisis have often stepped as it were through the door in the wall which no one had noticed, and, unannounced, unheralded, without prestige, have made their way silently and single-handed to the front.

And there was no luck in it. He rose, it has been said, by the upward gravitation of natural fitness. It was the work of inflexible faithfulness, of indomitable resolution, of sleepless energy, of iron purpose, of persistent tenacity. Inbattle after battle, in siege after siege, whatever Grant had to do he did it with his might. He undertook, as General Sherman said, what no one else would have adventured, till his very soldiers began to reflect some of his own indomitable determination. With a patience which nothing could tire, with a firmness which no obstacle could daunt, with a military genius which embraced the vastest plans, yet attended to the smallest minutiæ, he defeated one after another every great general of the Confederates except General Stonewall Jackson.

Grant had not only to defeat armies, but to "annihilate resources"—to leave no choice but destruction or submission. He saw that the brief ravage of the hurricane is infinitely less ruinous than the interminable malignity of the pestilence, and that in that colossal struggle victory—swift, decisive, overwhelming, at all costs—was the truest mercy. In silence, in determination, in clearness of insight, he was your Washington and our Wellington. He was like them also in this, that the word "can't" did not exist in his soldier's dictionary, and that all he achieved was accomplished without bluster and without parade.

After the surrender at Appomattox the war of the Secession was over. It was a mighty work, and Grant had done it mightily. Surely the light of God, which manifests all things in the slow history of their ripening, has shown that for the future destinies of a mighty nation it was a necessary and a blessed work. The Church hurls her most indignant anathema at unrighteous war, but she never refused to honor the faithful soldier who fights in the cause of his country and his God. The gentlest and most Christian of poets has used the tremendous words that—

> God's most dreaded instrument,
> In working out a pure intent,
> Is man—arrayed for mutual slaughter;
> Yea, carnage is his daughter.

We shudder even as we quote the words; but yet the cause for which Grant fought—the unity of a great people, the freedom of a whole race of mankind—was as great and noble as that when at Lexington the embattled farmers fired the shot which was heard round the world. The South has accepted that desperate and bloody arbitrament. Two of the Southern generals will bear General Grant's funeral pall. The rancor and the fury of the past are buried in oblivion. True friends have been made out of brave foemen, and the pure glory and virtue of Lee and of Stonewall Jackson will be part of the common national heritage with the fame of Garfield and of Grant.

CHAPTER VI

A SERIES OF PRACTICAL HOWS

HOW TO BREATHE

And the Lord God formed man of the dust of the ground, and breathed into his nostrils the breath of life; and man became a living soul.[12]

—The Bible

These words were spoken several thousand years ago by one of the wisest of men, who was inspired by the Master of Life to utter words of wisdom for the guidance of the children of men. From the moment those divine words were spoken it seems as though man has been aiming to get along with as little of the breath of God as possible. The divine breath is given as freely now as it was at the time of the creation, and it is ever present to those who are willing to receive it, as, like God's love, it is not withheld from us, but we withhold ourselves from it. No soul is ever lost save through its own determination to go to destruction, and no body suffers for the want of the life-giving breath except through sin, ignorance, or wilfulness. The great English preacher, Charles H. Spurgeon, in a lecture ɩo his students, thus expressed himself: "The next best thing to the grace of God for a preacher is oxygen." As the world cannot live without the grace of God, the body cannot exist without oxygen; and this oxygen is the life-giving property of the air which is drawn into the lungs and distributed through the body by means of the blood. Correct breathing insures physical health in that it causes the blood to circulate properly through all the veins as well as through the arteries, thus carrying off the particles that otherwise would remain in the system, decomposing and poisoning the body with their dead matter. Proper breathing brightens the eye, makes ruddy the cheek, raises the spirits, clarifies the mind, ennobles the soul, and forms the voice. Sir George Mivart, the noted English naturalist, voiced a self-evident fact when he said: "Of all the functions of the body that of respiration is the most conspicuously necessary for the maintenance of life," but while it is understood by all thinking animals that they must breathe in order that they may live, it is not so clearly evident to man that he must breathe correctly in order that pure vocal tones may be produced and expressive speech formed.

The question of breath. This is of the greatest importance to the

---

[12] St. Matthew, vi:22.

speaker, as by the action of the breathing muscles the voice is controlled in all things except modulation. Speech is breath and voice before it becomes speech, and the form it takes as it starts on its journey at the moment of its creation it must retain until it ceases to exist. Breath possesses three forms, effusive, expulsive, and explosive, and whichever of these forms it assumes at the start, it must retain during its transition into voice and speech. After the pressure of the breathing muscles against the lungs has forced the breath into the larynx and produced voice through the vibration of the vocal cords until that voice has been formed into articulated sounds by the action of the hard and soft palate, the tongue, the teeth, and the lips, it must remain, so far as its form is concerned, exactly as it started. Effusive breath can produce only effusive voice, effusive voice can be converted into only effusive speech, and in no manner can this form be altered after the breath has been expelled from the lungs. The voice is affected and modified by the resonance chambers, the organs of articulation, and the mentality of the speaker, but it must be one of the three forms, effusive, expulsive, or explosive, and it must retain this form from its birth to its death.

Respiration. Respiration is the process of taking air into the lungs and sending it out. This process of breathing is twofold, inhalation and exhalation. Inhalation is the taking in of the air, and exhalation is the sending out of the breath. Normal persons breathe about twenty times a minute; that is, they inhale twenty times and exhale twenty times during that period. When the air is received into the lungs, the oxygen is extracted from it, eaten up, as it were, and distributed through the system; and, on the exhalation, the carbonic gas and organic matter is carried out. If a person is confined within a limited space, and little air permitted to enter, he will soon consume most of the oxygen contained therein, poison the atmosphere with the carbonic gas which he throws off, and die for the want of the life-giving property—oxygen. It is estimated that almost half the deaths are caused through improper breathing and the inhalation of vitiated air. Five hundred cubic feet of air every twenty-four hours is not too much for every human being.

The lungs are the organs of respiration. They are two in number, the right and the left. The right lung possesses three distinct chambers, and the left lung is made up of two. The average adult has a lung capacity, in round numbers, of three hundred and fifty cubic inches, and uses about thirty cubic inches for an ordinary inhalation and exhalation, although it would be well if he used forty, or even fifty, cubic inches of his capacity. There are one hundred cubic inches of air always in the lungs of an adult which cannot be forced out by physical exertion and the human animal live. As soon as this reserve force of air is about to be drawn upon, nature cries out against its use, causes the being to pant, and forces him to seek other supplies.

The two lungs are joined to the trachea, or air tube, by means of the bronchial tubes, and at the upper end of the trachea is the larynx, or voice box. In the larynx are the two true vocal cords, the vibration of which produces voice; and this voice, passing into the mouth, is moulded into speech by the organs of articulation.

Control of the breath. There are muscles that act on the lungs and regulate the entrance of air and the exit of breath. The muscles are: pectoral, dorsal, costal, intercostal, abdominal, and the diaphragm. The pectoral muscles hold up the chest and thus allow the air to enter the upper lobes of the lungs. The dorsal muscles press inward from the back and assist the abdominal muscles to regulate the action of the diaphragm. The costal and intercostal muscles cause the ribs to expand and contract, thus enlarging and decreasing the capacity of the cavity that contains the lungs. The abdominal muscles act directly on the diaphragm, causing it to fall and rise. The diaphragm supports the lungs and is the only muscle that comes in contact with them.

This is all the information regarding the anatomy of the breathing muscles that is necessary to an understanding of the instructions here given for gaining a knowledge of their proper use and management in connection with the production of speech.

How is one to breathe properly? By inflating the lungs fully from their base to their apex.

How can this be accomplished? By bringing into use all the muscles that act on the lungs, particularly the abdominal muscles and the diaphragm. When inhaling there should be an expansion of the base of the lungs; and when exhaling there should be a contraction. The upper lobes of the lungs should be expanded all the time, the chest should be held upward and outward, whether the person is inhaling or exhaling; the air is first drawn into the lower lobes, then gradually rises and forces the air out of the upper lobes, and immediately takes its place, the upper lobes being filled with air all the time, whereas the lower lobes are only filled immediately following the full inhalation, as they commence to decrease in size as soon as the air starts to rise into the upper lobes. Breathing should be accomplished without an apparent effort, and air should be taken whenever the speaker feels it required; he should not continue speaking until the breath is almost exhausted, but he should replenish while he feels confident of his ability to utter several more words without taking another breath.

Breathing should not be audible, but the air should be allowed to quietly and naturally enter the lungs. This can be accomplished by expanding the abdominal muscles, thus drawing down the diaphragm, releasing the pressure from the lungs and permitting the air to enter them. It requires no effort to inhale. All that is necessary is to create a vacuum in the lungs, by taking the pressure of the diaphragm from them, and the air will flow in freely. Avoid "smelling" the air into the lungs—take bites out of the atmosphere, as it were, and permit the air to enter the mouth as well as the nose. Habitual mouth breathing is wrong, and one should always breathe through the nose when not producing voice, but when speech is required it is necessary to allow the air to enter through both passages. Unless this is done, the breathing will be forced and the speaker will always be short of breath.

It is advisable to exercise physically while practicing breathing, therefore walking, running, and climbing are great aids in building up the organs of respiration, and when the exercising must be done indoors, it is advisable to go through physical movements in conjunction with the breathing. Movements of the arms that represent swimming, bending the bow, sawing wood, chopping down trees, etc., are highly beneficial as aids in developing deep and full breathing, and if one is so situated that one can row, swim, cut down trees, etc., in reality, the exercise brought about by such means will be of incalculable benefit in building up the breathing mechanism. Most persons cease to breathe correctly because of a non-use of some of the muscles and organs of respiration, and the exercises that are here recommended will compel the employment of all the neglected adjuncts to correct breathing, and thus bring about effective respiration.

HOW TO PRODUCE AND USE THE VOICE

A man was not made to shut up his mind in itself, but to give it voice and to exchange it for other minds.[13]

In order that man may enter into commerce with other men for the exchange of mental commodities he must have a medium of communication, and the greatest and noblest of all means is the human voice. We are thus admonished by one who was entitled to speak, for he knew how to convey his thought by word of mouth as well as by pen:

Remember that talking is one of the fine arts—the noblest, the most important, and the most difficult—and that its fluent harmonies may be spoiled by the intrusion of a single harsh note.[14]

Let all who would excel as public speakers heed this wise warning and seek to obtain voices capable of producing "fluent harmonies."

What is voice? Voice is vocalized breath. It is formed in the larynx, or voice box, and is produced by the breath acting on the vocal cords and causing them to vibrate. Immediately as voice is produced it should pass from the larynx into the mouth and be converted into speech; one of the worst vocal faults, throatiness, arises from a failure to do this. Voice can be modulated; that is, its pitch can be raised and lowered, and the whole gamut of vocal tones can be played upon by

---

[13] William Ellery Channing in "Self-Culture."
[14] Oliver Wendell Holmes in "Autocrat of the Breakfast Table."

means of the change in pitch. The pitch of the voice is regulated by the tension of the vocal cords and the distinctive resonance chamber into which the vibration is placed. There are three such chambers; the chest, the throat, and the head. Voice and resonance should not be confounded. Resonance is a part of voice, it is the spirit or essence, as it were, and enters into the different chambers and thus affects the tone of the voice; but the voice itself, the body of the sound, must be placed on the lips. There are three divisions to the speaking voice, the lower, the middle, and the upper, and by moving the tone from one division to another the voice is modulated. As before stated, the tension of the vocal cords and the chamber into which the resonance enters regulate the pitch of the voice. Tones on the lower register require a lesser tension of the vocal cords than do tones on the upper register, and the low tones require that the resonance be placed in the cavity of the chest, while the high tones necessitate the resonance being placed in the head. The speaker, however, must not allow his thought to dwell on the placing of the resonance; he must think only of getting the speech into the air, because the resonance, or the spirit of the voice, will enter the proper chamber if the passage is free and the speaker thinks of where he wishes the voice to go, and pays no attention as to whence it comes. The voice instantly obeys the thought, if the mechanism works properly, consequently it is well for the speaker to think of the end he has in view and not cumber the vocal machine by worrying about the means to be employed in accomplishing that end. While cultivating and disciplining the voice it is necessary to think of the means, and to make a conscious effort to use those means, but when in the act of producing speech no conscious thought should be directed toward that act. All effort used while in the process of producing speech must be subconscious, and entirely free from physical effort.

How to obtain a good voice. Mainly by ceasing to abuse it, for most of the vocal defects are acquired by bad habits. Improper breathing is responsible for work begin placed upon the larynx which nature never intended it to perform, and this overworking, or straining, of the larynx produces throaty tones and causes an irritation of that organ which finally develops into laryngitis. A failure to form the sounds on the lips is the cause of mouthing, and a lack of moulding the voice into correct sound deprives the sound of its carrying power, because of its exit being impeded. For instance, round sounds like o require a round mould to pass through, and if, instead of such a mould, a flat one is formed, the sound is barely able to squeeze through after having lost half of its vitality in the effort. Speak the word soul with the lips rounded while uttering the vowel o and then attempt to speak the same word with the lips flattened when producing that sound, and the necessity of moulding will be instantly apparent. Shakespeare says: "Speak the speech, I pray you, as I pronounced it to you trippingly on the tongue," and if speakers would follow this splendid advice which

Hamlet gives to the players, throaty tones would be abolished. But how are speakers to do this? By thoroughly developing the breathing muscles by proper exercise, so as to enable them to perform their functions correctly, thereby taking away the strain from the larynx and permitting the opening of the throat, bringing the voice forward and moulding it on the lips. These are the only means that will enable anyone to speak "trippingly on the tongue," and the importance of so doing is forcefully expressed by Cardinal Newman, that master of English composition, in the following:

Our intercourse with our fellow men goes on, not by sight but by sound, not by eyes but by ears. Hearing is the social sense and language is the social bond.

HOW TO PRODUCE SPEECH EFFECTS

The first duty of man is to speak, that is his chief business in this world, and talk, which is the harmonious speech of two or more, is by far the most accessible of pleasures. It costs nothing; it is all profit; it completes our education; it founds and fosters our friendships; and it is by talk alone that we learn our period and ourselves.[15]

Speech is the one great outward evidence that separates the human from the brute, and the more this faculty is cultivated the higher man rises in the scale of civilization. Speech permits man to clothe the immortal thought in palpable shape and present it to other minds exactly as it is perceived by the original thinker. It makes manifest that which otherwise would remain in the realm of the unseen, and permits of that communion of mind with mind which strengthens and uplifts mankind. It is the humanizing medium, the glorifying agent, and the magnifying reflector of the soul.

How is speech produced? Speech is produced by the organs of articulation acting on the voice, cutting it up, joining, blending, and moulding the separate sounds, until symbols are produced that represent thoughts.

The Greek rhetorician and orator, Gorgias, speaking more than two thousand four hundred years ago, said:

The power of speech is mighty. Insignificant in themselves, words accomplish the most remarkable ends. They have power to remove fear and assuage pain. Moreover then can produce joy and increase pity.

Words really possess the magic power ascribed to them by this master of words, this great writer and speaker of Greece at the time when she flourished in the magnificent days of Pericles, the days when Athens was adorned by buildings, pictures, and statuary, and her

---

[15] Robert Louis Stevenson.

citizens listened to oratory that has never been surpassed. Printed words are mighty when read by the intelligent reader, but spoken words are mightier when voiced by the imaginative speaker. Then they become living things, impregnated by the voice of the speaker, and they go forth to the mind of the listener carrying their interpreted message with them. This power of expression is what Gorgias meant in his reference to words, and it is this life of words that we are to consider, this explaining by tone, pitch, force, time, and color of the voice the meaning of the spoken words.

It is the tone of voice in which a thought is uttered that gives the thought its power for good or evil, for pleasure or for pain, for success or failure. Words spoken in one manner will be devoid of meaning; spoken in another, they will be illumined with the light of reason. Words that are spoken as words will remain nothing but words, but those that are spoken as thoughts will disappear as words, and the ideas will step forward and be seen in the expressive countenance and heard in the tones of the voice.

There is a soul to the voice just as there is a soul to the body, and unless this soul rays forth its light in the form of vocal color, it will be as devoid of spirituality, as bereft of all magnetic influence, as is the lifeless clay after the soul has winged its flight from the earthly habitation. It is for this reason that words struck offat white heat often sound much better than they read; they have leaped into existence willingly to perform their errand and, being full of the mentality of the being who created them, they go on their mission in a manner to carry conviction and bring about persuasion.

To speak effectively. In the first place, by having good working tools for the making of speech. This means that one must use the muscles and organs of breath, sound, and speech in such manner as to produce the voice with ease and utter the words distinctly and with the desired force. Secondly, one should so master inflection, emphasis, pitch, and color as to be able to present the thought precisely as he conceives it. The whole vocal mechanism, in both its physical and mental parts, must be under perfect control, and this control can only be gained by patient practice. Attention to technique is necessary if one desires to become an artist in any department of life, and unless the seeker after oratorical honors pays particular attention to controlling those different parts of the mental and physical being that are employed in the labor of producing speech, he will never become a master of that art. Nature may have endowed him with exceptional powers, but unless those powers are developed and practiced, they will be taken away. Students of oratory are strongly advised to master deep breathing, articulation, modulation, emphasis, and delivery, for unless they do so they will never possess the power of conveying thought by means of the spoken word, no matter how many or what manner of beautifulthoughts they may have. A means of conveying the message is as necessary to the speaker as is the possession of the message. No matter what glorious messages speakers may have within their minds, they will do no one but themselves any good unless they can convey those messages to others, and a speaker without a well-trained and expressive voice is as badly off as is a farmer with an abundant crop and no means of getting his produce to market.

A special set of exercises for the strengthening, coloring, and general building up of the speaking voice is here appended, and students are urged to practice the exercises faithfully.

VOCAL EXERCISES

Breath. Remember that breath is the foundation of voice, and that correct breathing is necessary to the production of correct speech. Breathe by means of the abdominal muscles and diaphragm, thus using the lungs from bottom to top and retaining control over the voice; at the same time, freeing the larynx from all pressure and permitting the vocal tone to come smoothly into the mouth, where it is articulated into speech.

All animals, brute and human, male and female, possess organs of respiration that are similar in their nature and that work in precisely the same manner. It is a mistake to think that women breathe naturally in a different manner from men. Many do so habitually, but it is only on account of their mode of dress or failure to takeproper exercise, for all animals sustain life by means of similar action of like organs of respiration.

First Exercise: Close the mouth, draw a full breath into the lungs through the nose, being careful not to "smell" the air in but to take it in noiselessly; then, open the mouth and allow the breath to come into the air, as to blowing upon a pane of glass to form a coating of moisture. The chest must neither rise nor fall when inhaling or exhaling, it should be held up and out all the time, the expansion and contraction taking place at the base of the lungs. In order to obtain this full expansion and complete contraction of the lower lobes of the lungs during respiration, it is necessary to draw the abdominal muscles outward on the inhalation and inward on the exhalation. The outward action of the abdominal muscles will cause the diaphragm to flatten, thus removing the pressure of that muscle from the base of the lungs and permitting the air to enter all the lobes. The inward action of the abdominal muscles will cause the diaphragm to arch, thus pressing on the base of the lungs and forcing out the breath. The main expansion and contraction should take place below and around the diaphragm, that portion of the body from the navel up to the floating ribs and extending all around the body, bringing into play the lower costal and dorsal muscles as well as the abdominal muscles and the diaphragm.

Second Exercise: Inhale as in the first exercise, then exhale through the mouth in the form of a sigh, using a quicker and stronger action of the abdominal musclesin forcing out the breath than was used in the first exercise.

Third Exercise: Inhale as in the previous exercise, then exhale through the mouth in the form of an aspirated cough, being careful, however, not to allow the whispered sound to strike upon the rim of the larynx or to remain back in the pharynx, but bring it forward so as to have it explode in the air and not in the throat or mouth.

Deep breathing should be practiced until it becomes automatic, because the speaker who makes a conscious effort to control the breathing mechanism will be stilted and artificial in his utterance. Breathing must be absolutely subconscious, and these exercises should be practiced until it becomes so. While practicing, a conscious effort must be made to use the breathing muscles properly; but as soon as this has been accomplished, the thought must be taken from the means and the disciplined muscles will then work automatically.

VOICE

Voice is produced in the larynx, the voice box, but it must be immediately brought into the mouth, converted into speech, and sent on its way to perform its mission. The breath acting on the vocal cords causes them to vibrate, and this vibration is called voice. In producing voice no more breath should be used than is necessary to produce the desired sound. If too much breath is used, and it escapes through the larynx without beingconverted into voice, it will drown the voice and breathy tones will be formed. Breath must always be kept back of the voice, it must never be permitted to escape at the sides or around the tone; if it does so escape, the tone cannot be pure, breath will be wasted, the larynx will soon tire, and the speech will be muffled and lack power.

First Exercise: Form the sound of m. This is done by closing the mouth and sending the voice sound into the cavity of the head and then through the nose into the air. Bear in mind that you are to produce the sound of m and not speak the letter m. Prolong the sound on the one pitch for ten seconds, take a full breath, and repeat the sound, practicing in this manner for five minutes at a time.

Second Exercise: Use the voice sound of m as in the previous exercise, but instead of sustaining the one tone, vary it by producing medium, high, and low tones. Hum a tune, keeping the mouth closed, using the one sound of m, and sending the voice through the head passages into the air. This exercise will prove wonderfully beneficial if it is patiently practiced. Any tune may be used for this purpose, but be sure that the voice is brought well forward and comes into the air through the nasal passages.

Third Exercise: Hum the sound of m, then open the mouth and produce the vowel sound of a, gliding from the humming sound into the full open sound of a; as, ma. Exercise on the other four vowels, e, i, o, u, in like manner: as, me, mi, mo, mu.

Fourth Exercise: On the same pitch that you would use in asking an ordinary question, such as "Are you going out today?" repeat the vowels a, e, i, o, u, using a full breath for each sound and sustaining it on the same pitch, and as long as you can conveniently. Then lower the voice to the deepest tone you can produce with ease and repeat the exercise. Then raise the voice as high as you can without straining and repeat the exercise. Practice in such a way as to bring into play all the tones of the voice and gradually to increase its compass. Avoid force in increasing the vocal range. Produce tones only that come with ease.

Fifth Exercise: Use the ordinary speaking pitch of the voice and repeat the vowels a, e, i, o, u, with the explosive force; pushing the sounds out as though they did not wish to leave and you were compelled to keep up the pressure in order to prevent them coming back. Be particular to press with the diaphragm only. Practice on low and high tones also.

Sixth Exercise: Repeat the exercise on the same register but use the explosive force, shooting the sounds into the air like the report of a pistol. Practice on low and high tones also.

It is a good plan to practice with speech the same as with voice. That is, produce speech in the three forms, effusive, expulsive, and explosive, and on the three registers, medium, lower, and upper. Any matter can be used for this purpose, special material not being necessary.

In order to bring speech forward and carry it into theair, set before you an imaginary target and direct the voice toward it, raising and lowering the target as you desire to raise and lower the tone. Remember to think the voice out, as you can get it out no other way.

HOW TO STRENGTHEN THE MEMORY

If any one ask me what is the only and great art of memory, I shall say it is exercise and labor. To learn much by heart, to meditate much, and, if possible, daily, are the most efficacious of all methods. Nothing is so much strengthened by practice or weakened by neglect as memory.

—Quintilian

These words, uttered by the scholarly rhetorician of Rome during the first century of the Christian era, are as true today as when they were first spoken. Application, concentration, association, opposition, and use are the principal means for the effectual training and strengthening of the memory. Many systems have been devised for memory training, but none of them is of more than superficial use, the majority making it more difficult to remember the means whereby the thought is to be recalled than to remember the thought itself. They are cumbersome, burdensome, and unworkable. Loisette, in his much exploited system, Assimilative Memory, advises paying particular attention to the location of figures in order to remember them, and he cites the following example:

"Pike's Peak, the most famous in the chain known as the Rocky Mountains in America, is fourteen thousand onehundred and forty-seven feet high. . . . There are two fourteens in these figures, and the last figure is half of fourteen."

This is all very well in this particular instance of Pike's Peak, but what are we to do with mountains that are ten thousand and eighty-five feet, seven thousand and forty-nine feet, or five thousand six hundred and fifty-one feet in height? The specific case works out nicely, but the general case cannot be worked out at all.

It is the object of this work to show how to do things and not to controvert the advice given by other authors, its mission being constructive and not destructive, therefore nothing further will be said regarding the Loisette or any other system of memory training; but specific advice will be given regarding the best way of laying hold of and retaining what enters the mind.

Application is one means of strengthening the memory. Whatever you desire to retain, be sure you apply your mind to it until you have it firmly impressed thereon. Do not merely see or hear a fact and then permit it to pass into forgetfulness; but, if you wish to retain it, apply your thought to it, think deeply and strongly on it, on all the circumstances pertaining to it, and then pass it into the chamber of memory, there to repose until you desire to awaken it. Study it carefully before putting it away.

Concentration is another valuable adjunct in memory training. Focus all your mental power upon the thing, person, or theme you wish to remember. Bear all your mental heat upon the one spot, and you will be able to burn through whatever keeps your object from you, and after having once been perceived in this manner by the mental eye that object will never be forgotten.

A lawyer may be examining a witness and ask that witness if he remembers seeing John Smith on a certain occasion. The witness may say he has no recollection of having done so. The lawyer may say, "Do you not remember that on the twenty-first day of June you attended a meeting of the directors of the Second National Bank which was called to elect a new president?" and this part of the happenings of that day may then bring all the other occurrences to the mind of the witness, and he may then say, "Oh yes! John Smith gave me his check for $500 on that date. I now remember that fact quite well." This would be re-collecting.

Association of words, events, or ideas, helps wonderfully in strengthening the memory, in that it enables one to group together quickly scattered parts and thus recall things in their entirety. This is what the lawyer did for the witness when he mentioned the meeting of the board of directors of the bank, and by means of the association of events enabled the witness to recall that the meeting of the directors took place on the day that Smith paid him the five hundred, in this manner re-collecting the scattered parts of the events of the twenty-first day of June and bringing Smith clearly into the picture. In trying to remember any occurrence, endeavor to bring to mind some incident in connection with it, and if successful in so doing, the whole train of events pertaining to that occurrence will soon move regularly along in the channels of the mind.

Opposition. A knowledge and use of the rule of opposition will greatly assist the memory. Suppose an advocate should say, "The thoughtless members of the community may censure me for entering upon the prosecution of this case," and should desire to make the thought more comprehensive, he could do so by placing a phrase against the one quoted and say, "but the sober-minded men and women will surely commend me for performing my duty as I understand it." Double and triple oppositions may be used as aids to the memory; as: The Biblical account of the flood states that God was angry with His children of earth because of their many sins, and He determined to destroy all animal life except that of the chosen few who were to accompany Noah into the ark. After the rains had ceased and the waters had subsided, Noah feared to return to the land, but God dispelled that fear by placing a bow in the heavens as a covenant between Him and man that never again would He permit a deluge of water to visit the earth. After four years of civil war, after the land of America had been deluged with blood, we set our Nation's flag against the cloud as a covenant between North and South that never again, in this dear country of ours, shall brother's hand be raised in enmity against his brother.

The whole idea of this passage can be kept clearly in mind by setting "deluge" against "civil war," "bow" against "flag." Keep the idea, or the picture, before you,and there will be no difficulty in remembering what you desire to say, nor will there be any trouble experienced in finding words to express the idea.

When reading, do not bother about words, but dig down deep for the thought, lay hold of it, impress it on the memory, and the substance of what you read (the really valuable part of it) will remain with you forever. In this letter to Mrs. Bixby, dated Nov. 21, 1864, President Lincoln says:

85

I have been shown in the files of the War Department a statement of the Adjutant General of Massachusetts, that you are the mother of five sons who have died gloriously on the field of battle.

The points to remember are that five brothers died gloriously on the field of battle, and that a mother gave those treasures to her country. The pictures to place upon memory's wall are the raging battle, and the lonely mother at home. Those two pictures tell the whole story, and by gazing on them the complete narrative can be given.

Use. Use is another of the great aids in memory training. Employ the mind. Keep it busy. Make it alert through exercise. Train it to move quickly from point to point, picture to picture. Work it hard while you work it, but give it frequent periods of rest. Do not cumber the brain with a mass of words. Learn words by all means, learn their meaning, relationship, and power, but do not try to remember them merely as words. Think of them, rather, in their relationship with one another—their power of conveying an idea or explaining a thought, their ability to paint a picture or make clear a point—think of them collectively and not individually, and they can be marshalled easily in phrases and sentences where the speaker would stumble over them in attempting to bring them forward one by one.

Sound Education. A sound general education forms a splendid foundation for a good memory, and if you have not had the benefit of schooling in early life, you should take up a course of instructive reading at the earliest possible moment. Study history, the sciences, the arts. Read the lives of men—the pivotal men of all periods—and select one, two, or three master works and thoroughly saturate yourself with their style as well as their substance. The author has many times recommended the Bible and Shakespeare for this purpose, and subsequent years of experience have only strengthened his belief in the efficiency of these immortal works.

Reflection. This is a great help in memory training. Continuously hover over your subject, brood over it, keep it before the mental camera until a perfect negative is taken, from which a positive may be formed at any time. Accustom yourself to see your subject on every side; use your spiritual eye so that you may see not only through but all around your theme, and then you will be able to present it in an intelligent and convincing manner because of your being complete master of it. You will know it.

The old saying that "one nail drives out another" does not apply to the mind. If a fact or picture is placed within the storehouse of the brain, it will be at the disposal of the possessor as long as "memory holds a seat" within the human globe. A fact cannot be clearly grasped until it is thoroughly understood, a picture cannot be seen unless all its details are collectively grasped by the eye, and it is only when the fact is understood and the picture clearly seen that they can be placed within the chambers of the mind to be brought forth by memory at will. Some of the parts of the fact, or the details of the picture, may be lost, they may all be scattered, and then it is the duty of the memory to re-collect them and join them together so as to bring to mind the image of the original fact or picture.

A good memory is of the greatest importance to the orator; in fact, no one who does not possess this attribute can be an orator in the true sense of the word. Without it, the speaker must rely on written matter; but with it, he can take those flights of fancy which memory alone makes secure because of the assurance he possesses of his ability to hold his facts securely in mind and return to them at any time. He thus gains confidence.

The object of education is to train the mind, to discipline it, and to bring it into subjection to the will. If the student accomplishes this purpose, he will then be able to concentrate his thought, to rivet it upon any subject, train the whole force of his intellect upon it, and overcome what would otherwise be insurmountable. It is for this reason that memory is so valuable to the orator. If he possesses a good memory, he may reasonably look for thegreatest success; but if it is poor, his failure is equally certain. If, therefore, your memory fails to answer your purpose, set to work to strengthen it. This can be done by careful and systematic training along the lines here set forth. Be patient, diligent, and persevering; make use of your own thoughts—that is, think for yourself and do not merely utter the thoughts of others—and it will not be long before you will receive the help of that matchless confidence which knowledge and memory alone are able to give.

Memory, like walking, breathing, thinking, and all other actions of the body and the spirit, must be subconscious in order to be right and serviceable to man, and any conscious thought concerning the means to be employed in order to remember will surely bring about a defeat of the purpose. Practice in remembering, as in all things, makes perfect.

HOW TO ACQUIRE CONFIDENCE, AND TO CONTROL AN AUDIENCE

Preparedness. Instructions as to how a speaker can acquire confidence may be summed up in one word—preparedness. He must be sure of his audience, his subject, and himself. The way to make sure of his audience is to study it, find out its prejudices (all audiences possess prejudices), and endeavor to lead it without letting it know that it is being led. There must be a master when speaker and audience come into contact, and it is the duty of the speaker to see that the mastery is not inthe hands of the audience. The speaker should be similar in his relationship with the audience as is the director with the orchestra, and he should always aim to keep the audience subject to his will. If it breaks away from him, there will be nothing but discord, and the speech, if delivered at all, will be a failure. If, however, the audience is hostile to the speaker and at first refuses to listen to him, and he is capable of resisting its onslaught, he may achieve as signal a triumph as did Henry Ward Beecher at Liverpool, England, October 16, 1863, when, after struggling for three hours against the turbulent mob of southern sympathizers gathered for the avowed purpose of preventing the delivery of his speech in behalf of the Union, he finally mastered the disturbers, presented his cause, and won a marvellous victory. To show the forces that Beecher had to contend with, and over which he triumphed, the opening of the speech he then delivered is here given, with the interruptions noted in brackets:

For more than twenty-five years I have been made perfectly familiar with popular assemblies in all parts of my country except the extreme South. There has not for the whole of that time been a single day of my life when it would have been safe for me to go South of Mason's and Dixon's line in my own country, and for one reason: my solemn, earnest, persistent testimony against that which I consider to be the most atrocious thing under the sun—the system of American slavery in a great free republic. [Cheers.] I have passed through that early period when right of free speech was denied to me. Again and again I have attempted to address audiences that, for no other crime than that of free speech, visited me with all manner of contumelious epithets; and now since I have been in England, although I have met with greater kindness and courtesy on the part of most than I deserved, yet, on the other hand, I perceive that the southern influence prevails to some extent in England. [Applause and uproar.] It is my old acquaintance: I understand it perfectly—[laughter]—and I have always held it to be an unfailing truth that where a man had a cause that would bear examination he was perfectly willing to have it spoken about. [Applause.] And when in Manchester I saw those huge placards: "Who is Henry Ward Beecher?" [laughter, cries of "Quite right" and applause] and when in Liverpool I was told that there were those blood-red placards, purporting to say what Henry Ward Beecher had said, and calling upon Englishmen to suppress free speech—I tell you what I thought. I thought simply this: "I am glad of it." [Laughter.] Why? Because if they had felt perfectly secure that you are the minions of the South and the slaves of slavery, they would have been perfectly still. [Applause and uproar.] And, therefore, when I saw so much nervous apprehension that if I were permitted to speak [hisses and applause]—when I found they were afraid to have me speak [hisses, laughter, and "No, no!"], when I found they considered my speaking damaging to their cause [applause], when I found that they appealed from facts and reasoning to mob law [applause and uproar] I said, no man need tell me what the heart and secret counsel of these men are. They tremble

88

and are afraid. [Applause, laughter, hisses, "No, no!" and a voice, "New York mob."] Now, personally, it is a matter of very little consequence to me whether I speak here tonight or not. [Laughter and cheers.] but one thing is very certain, if you do permit me to speak here tonight you will hear very plain talking. [Applause andhisses.] You will not find a man [interruption], you will not find me to be a man that dared to speak about Great Britain three thousand miles off, and then is afraid to speak to Great Britain when he stands on her shores. [Immense applauses and hisses.] And if I do not mistake the tone and temper of Englishmen, they had rather have a man who opposes them in a manly way [applause from all parts of the hall] than a sneak who agrees with them in an unmanly way. [Applause and "Bravo."] Now if I can carry you with me by sound convictions, I shall be immensely glad [applause]; but if I cannot carry you with me by facts and sound arguments, I do not wish you to go with me at all; and all that I ask is simply fair play. [Applause, and a voice, "You shall have it, too."]

Public speakers should see that their subject fits the occasion, and particularly should they make it appear as though it intimately concerned the audience to which it is addressed. Mr. Beecher was extremely wise in selecting the themes upon which he spoke in his memorable tour through Great Britain in 1863, when he presented the cause of the Federal Government of the people of England and Scotland. When he spoke in Manchester his theme was the effect slavery had on the manufacturing interests; in Glasgow, where were located the shipyards where blockade-runners were being built for the Confederate States, and the laboring classes were thus personally concerned in the struggle between the States, he pointed out the degraded effect slavery had upon labor; in the cultured city of Edinburgh, he discussed the philosophy and the history of slavery; thus presenting his subject, on each occasion that he spoke, in a manner to interest his audiences.This showed great tact on Mr. Beecher's part and accounts, in a large measure, for his success in winning the masses of the people of Great Britain to the cause of the Union.

Julius M. Mayer, ex-Attorney General of the State of New York, at a political meeting held at Cooper Union, on November 4, 1911, after speaking on general political topics for a considerable time, said: "I want to discuss just one thing." A voice in the audience then cried out: "Go ahead, then, and do it." The rebuke was deserved. The speaker, the last on the list, had been announced to speak specifically on one question, but instead of immediately taking up his theme, which was the Levy Election Law, he started to discuss matters foreign to his subject; consequently the audience, which had listened to two long speeches by abler campaigners than Mr. Mayer, were tired out and restless before he really took up his subject, the result being that half the audience left before the speaker had touched on the topic he was designated to discuss, and the other half were not disposed to listen to him patiently. They had listened while they were being amused by the witty speech of Job E. Hedges, enthused by the impassioned, eloquent address of William A. Prendergast, and would have given attention to the remarks of Mr. Mayer had he immediately taken up his subject; but they were unwilling to listen to an indifferent speaker discuss matters with which the majority of them were thoroughly familiar. Let this experience of Mr. Mayer's be a lesson to speakers, and may it admonish them not to try the patience of an audience.

Francis P. Bent, who, at the time, was Vice-Chairman of the Board of Aldermen of the City of New York, and who is a clever campaign speaker, on a recent occasion quoted, in an address before a social club, the following passage from Shakespeare's Henry V:

> In peace there's nothing so becomes a man
> As modest stillness and humility:
> But when the blast of war blows in our ears,
> Then imitate the action of the tiger.

This last word was scarcely out of his mouth when some one cried out: "The Tammany Tiger?" A shout then arose from the assembly. Alderman Bent was not one particle disconcerted, but simply replied: "My friend, I do not suppose that Shakespeare, in writing those lines, intended to prophesy the coming of the Tammany Tiger, nor did I specifically have that specimen of the animal in view when I used the quotation, but I have no hesitation in saying that of all the fighting machines of which I have read, or with which I have come in contact, I know of none that excelled the Tammany Tiger in its ability to put up a good fight." He then went on with his speech, amid the hearty applause of his audience. In this instance, Alderman Bent typified the ready speaker.

Another occasion on which a speaker cleverly turned an interruption recently came to the personal attention of the author. John F. Hylan, a City Magistrate of the Borough of Brooklyn, New York City, was the last speaker on the programme at the opening of a Democratic Club in that section, previous to the election of 1911. His Honor had a few pet truths in the form of facts stowed away in his brain which he desired to impart to his Democratic brethren. Judges, as we are informed by Shakespeare, are "full of wise saws and modern instances," and Magistrate Hylan, whom the author has known for many years, is no exception to the rule; consequently, he proceeded to do his little "preaching." After enumerating many of the points he wished to drive home, particularly some pertaining to Jeffersonian principles, he finally said: "I know these are dry facts." A Democratic brother here spoke up: "You bet they are; and I'm dry, too." Of course the audience roared with laughter, and it looked as though the dryness alluded to by the thirsty one had put an end to the speech; but Magistrate Hylan, not one whit abashed, replied: "Your thirst will be attended to by the steward of the club in a few moments, and I will endeavor to moisten my remarks for you by stating that they shall soon come to a close."

If a speaker will not antagonize his audience through lack of tact, will keep to his subject, will be earnest in manner and language, not overtax the patience of his listeners by needlessly prolonging his discourse, and will put his mentality into his voice, he will surely be rewarded with the attention of his audience, and he will be able to sway it to his will and compel it, unknowingly, to do his bidding.

The speaker can only be sure of his subject after having considered it on all sides. He must look through it, beneath it, above it, on all sides of it, consider it carefullyfrom every possible standpoint, after which he may safely feel that he knows his subject and is prepared to speak upon it.

In order that he may be sure of himself, the speaker must be equipped physically, vocally, and mentally to carry out the task he has assumed. He must have a body capable of resisting the fatigue of standing, a voice that will serve as a vehicle for conveying the message, and a mind of sufficient power to originate, develop, and present the thought. All these parts may be made equal to the task of properly performing these important duties, and the speaker who is thus equipped will possess that perfect confidence which the consciousness of being prepared for the work he undertakes alone can give. If he possesses a justified confidence in his subject, in the art of expression, and in himself, he will be the master of all three, and by their means he will control his audience.

Self-consciousness is the cause of many speakers failing who otherwise are fitted for their task. The speaker must learn to avoid thinking of himself even indirectly. He should never permit himself to wonder what his auditors are thinking of him or his effort—should permit no thought to wander to them in quest of finding out their thoughts concerning him—but he should concentrate all his mental power upon his subject in order that he may send it out to his audience, drive it home, and command attention to his thought. If he does this, his will be the dominant mind, his attention will all be directed where it belongs—on his subject—and he will have no time norinclination to think of himself. Let him remember to think outward and not inward; to concern himself with his subject and not his audience; and, most of all, not himself; to keep his mentality ever active, ever seeking his picture or his theme; self-consciousness will then disappear, taking with it all uncertainty and nervousness, and leaving him master of the situation because of his being master of himself. This self-mastering is of the utmost importance to the public speaker; therefore he should do all in his power to cultivate and strengthen it. Without it, he is like a ship without a rudder; but with it, he possesses not only the means of controlling his course, but also the knowledge of directing it and the certainty of reaching his destination. He is then the purposeful speaker, conscious only of his ability to perform his task, and not creating imaginary difficulties which, once created, would surely overwhelm him.

HOW TO ACQUIRE FLUENCY OF SPEECH

A good working vocabulary is obtained best by studying words, learning their meaning, their origin, and their connections; finding out how many words express practically the same idea; what words are directly opposed to other words; and, in fact, becoming perfectly familiar with them in every way. A comparatively small number of words, if thoroughly mastered, will be of more service to a speaker than will a much larger number with which he is only indifferently acquainted. It is not so much the number of tools that a workman possesses that insures thesuccessful performance of his work, but the skill with which he manipulates those that he has at his disposal. So it is with the speaker. Let him thoroughly master a small vocabulary, because the effort he puts forth to become fully acquainted with his limited stock of words will, in itself, increase them and give him confidence in their use, and he will be better off than the less informed speaker with the greater vocabulary.

An easy flow of language is secured only by practice in speaking. No matter how many words one may have at one's disposal, they will be valueless unless the possessor has also the courage to use them. All who desire fluency of speech should practice continually to convey thought by word of mouth. Enter into conversation at every favorable opportunity with persons of education and refinement, doing as much of the talking as the proprieties will permit, bearing in mind that only by using a faculty is it developed and strengthened. Speak before public gatherings as often as possible, commencing in a modest manner by speaking for a few moments, and gradually gather confidence and power by demonstrating to yourself that you have the ability to acquire the art of speech. After satisfying yourself on that point, all that remains for you to do is to go ahead and acquire it.

HOW TO ACQUIRE PROFICIENCY IN GESTURE

Gesticulation, even more than speech, should be characteristic of the speaker, and entirely free from parade or pretense. Any gesticulation that calls attention to itself,and not to the thought it is intended to express, is wrong and should not be made. The aim of gesture should be to amplify, illustrate, or strengthen the spoken word, and it should only be employed in the furtherance of these objects.

Nothing tends more to give the speaker an appearance of affectation than does a superabundance of gesture, and nothing makes a speaker more awkward than does the making of ungainly gestures. The best speakers of today use very few gestures, these being mainly expressive of emphasis; and most strong gestures, both descriptive and active, have been abolished by English and American orators. The speakers of ancient days, and those of the eighteenth and the nineteenth centuries, were profuse in the use of gesture, but the declamatory style of delivery has given way to the colloquial form, which does not permit of making of many gestures, particularly those of the arms and hands, and depends more on the vocal expression than it does on the physical. While speakers are advised to be sparing in their use of gesture, there is a certain class that may be employed effectively, the movements of this class not being considered by audiences, as a rule, as gestures. These are the movements and expressions of the face, and consist of the distinctive light of the eye—whether languid, animated, sorrowful, gay, loving or threatening; the play of the lips—indicating scorn, strength, or weakness; and the state of the brow—whether smooth or contracted. All these gestures, however, after they have been thought out and clearly understood, may be left to be governed bythe same force that controls the coloring of the voice, and if the mentality of the speaker so acts as to cause the voice to properly express the thought, it will also move the body to work in harmony with it and to correspondingly convey the idea by means of physical expression.

The question of gesticulation may easily be discussed at such length as to make a book, but the author does not deem it wise to put forth any new system of gesture, nor advise the use of any of the many old ones, but will content himself with stating a few serious errors to be avoided by all speakers, and by giving some general principles that should be adopted: Do not put your hands in your pockets, nor appear not to know what to do with them. Refrain from playing with your watch chain, or running your fingers through your hair. Let your arms hang easily at your side, and appear unconscious of the fact that you possess hands. Do not always point upward when talking of heaven or the sky, nor put your hand on your breast when speaking of love or conscience. Do not attempt to describe the action of every thing—such as the flowing of rivers, rolling of clouds, or leaping of cataracts. Avoid using too many active gestures—that is, gestures expressive of the action of your own mind, such as anger, fear, and joy. Do not tear your hair, stamp your feet, nor give any other such outward manifestation of your feelings. Keep away from reading desks, tables, and all articles of furniture. Stand on your feet, in clear view of the audience; look outward and upward, and let the assembly see that you are not afraidto show yourself. Use gestures sparingly until you find the ones that feel easy to you; and all gestures that come without effort it is safe to consider natural, for if they feel easy to you, they are likely to look natural and to be effective. Finally, follow Hamlet's advice to the players:

Do not saw the air too much with your hand, thus; but use all gently: for in the very torrent, tempest, and, as I may say, whirlwind of your passion, you must acquire and beget a temperance that may give it smoothness. . . . Be not too tame neither, but let your own discretion be your tutor; suit the action to the word, the word to the action; with this special observance, that you o'erstep not the modesty of nature.[16]

_____

[16] Hamlet, Act III, Scene II.

CHAPTER VII

THE GRECIAN ORATORS

WHAT CONSTITUTED THEIR ART

When you shall say, "As others do, so will I: I renounce, I am sorry for it, my early visions; I must eat the good of the land and let learning and romantic expectation go, until a more convenient season"; then dies the man in you; then once more perish the buds of art, and poetry, and science, as they have died already in a thousand thousand men. The hour of that choice is the crisis of your history, and see that you hold yourself fast by the intellect.

—RALPH WALDO EMERSON: Dartmouth Address

If a man would become a truly great orator, he must put aside all mere selfish desires and heed only the call of the best that is in him. He must have visions, and realize them; he must act according to his own understanding, and not become the pliant tool of another, be that other a political boss, a political machine, or an unholy ambition; he must be himself, and refuse to echo the thoughts of others; and, as a foundation upon which all these virtues are to be built, must be the one great virtue of industry.

Through all climes and in all ages men have achieved eminence as orators by persevering efforts only, and while, at times, an orator, full-fledged and ready for the fray,has burst into the list and played his part upon the stage of action, such occurrences have been so rare as to make them but examples of the exception that proves the rule. Therefore, let him who would become proficient in the art of speech make up his mind to labor in order to attain that proficiency.

At the same time, we should remember that this labor need not necessarily be hard, need not be what is termed laborious, because the main requisite is that we should not interfere with nature in her work. It is perfectly natural for man to breathe properly, and yet how few do so; it is natural for man to speak, and yet how few speak properly! If we aim to remove the defects or errors that interfere with Nature doing properly her assigned task, we need not worry but that she will perform it. Take up the work of becoming a public speaker because you love the art of oratory, labor at it because you desire to accomplish it, and it will submit to you because all arts love to be mastered.

The history of oratory is a history of the world, just as the history of a great central character is an epitome of the history of his time, and as it is best to study the lives of the makers of history in order to understand the events of history, so it is best to examine the orators in order that we may learn of oratory.

In ancient times oratory was considered the art of arts because it embraced all other arts and was therefore the most difficult of achievements. Positions of honor and renown were bestowed upon those who were capable of giving fitting expression to their thoughts in public. Poets sang the praises of orators and made them the heroes of their songs. The psalmists and prophets are but types of the orator, and the actor of today is the outcome of the player of old who was more a speaker than he was an actor.

Every citizen, at one time, was his own lawyer, spoke in his own defense, and advocated his own cause. Then came the era of the speech writers, who prepared the matter for the citizen to deliver; and finally, the professional advocate of today who appears in behalf of his client and acts and speaks for him.

Let us consider the productions of the orators of that marvellous period in the world's history which dates from 500 to 300 years previous to the coming of Christ; and in doing so, let us not forget that they are all translations into a foreign tongue, and that in their transition from one language into another they have lost much of their force and beauty. Another thing to bear in mind is that an oration does not read as it sounds. It lacks the magnetism of the living speaker, the presence of the assembled multitude, the concern in the subject, and the gravity of the interest at stake, to lend a completeness to the words and to impregnate them with the expression that life alone possesses, turning the dead words into living thoughts. Here, in these orations, we possess the mere bodies—mummies, they might well be termed—the spirit having departed ages ago; but by the influence of the imaginative mind of the reader they may be compelled to assume some semblance of their former greatness.

The best way of judging of the power of orators, and the influence of oratory, is to study the effect they had on the subjects with which they dealt, the audiences they addressed, and on posterity, which looks with an unprejudiced eye. All great orations have not accomplished the purposes for which they were uttered, but they have all had a decided influence on shaping the thoughts of man and directing his actions many years after the orators who uttered the words have passed back in to the elements whence they came. Demosthenes did not succeed in saving his loved Athens from the clutches of Philip, but his burning words in behalf of liberty have stirred the hearts of men in other lands and other ages and caused them to battle in behalf of the principles for which the ancient Grecian spoke; Edmund Burke and the Earl of Chatham did not succeed in turning Lord North from his determination to subdue the colonies of North America by force of arms, but their noble speeches inspired their brother Whigs in America to rush to arms and sacrifice their all in the struggle for independence; Abraham Lincoln, in his debate with Stephen A. Douglas, did not prevail on the electorate of the State of Illinois to return legislators who would elect him to the United States Senate, but his clear reasoning and masterful presentation of facts in that famous debate drew the attention of the nation to him and contributed much toward making him President of the United States. Oratory cannot fail in ultimately accomplishing its object, although it may not accomplish the specific object that the speaker had in mindat the time of uttering the oration, because truth must always ultimately triumph, and real oratory is always truth.

Oratory requires a large theme. Men cannot grow eloquent over a ship subsidy; they may rhetorically wave the flag of their country and claim the land will go to ruin unless the subsidy is granted, but there can be no genuine enthusiasm, no eloquence, over such a cause. When Henry Clay declared that the American flag should be honored wherever it floated, that its folds should protect its citizens on sea as well as on land, he had a theme of such magnitude that was able to move his country to take up arms in defense of the doctrine he espoused. When Lincoln started on his mission to preserve the Union, he held a tremendous question in hand—the question whether government by the people should pass from the earth—and this question brought as a response the immortal Gettysburg Address. William H. Grady, when speaking to the North on the subject of the New South, had a theme of vast importance—the theme of a reunited country. Theodore Roosevelt, in adopting "Conservation of Natural Wealth" as his subject, brought to the minds of his countrymen a truth to which they had blindly closed their eyes since the settlement of the Western Hemisphere. These are subjects upon which, if the man is prepared, he can grow eloquent; and as soon as the people seriously consider questions of moment to themselves and their posterity, men will come forward who are able to discuss such questions with eloquence that willequal that of the past. Oratory is not dead, nor is it sleeping; it is merely awaiting the sound of the voice it knows to cause it to come forth. It is no use calling to it in a foreign tongue—it must be spoken to in the voice of truth. Right, liberty, justice, the rights of man to enjoy the blessings of life—these are themes that will cause eloquence to become once more the art of arts.

EXAMPLES OF GRECIAN ORATORY[17]

For the benefit of the student of oratory, specimen orations are

---

[17] It may be doubted whether any compositions which have ever been produced in the world are equally perfect in their kind with the great Athenian orations.— Macaulay's Essay, Athenian Orators

here given of ten of the most famous Grecian orators. Short biographical and other notes accompany each selection, as guides to the student regarding the careers of the orators and the circumstances under which the orations were delivered.

ANTIPHON

Antiphon, the oldest of the ten Attic orators, and founder of Grecian political oratory, was the first to systematize the rules and principles for the guidance of public speakers. He was born at Rhamnus, Attica, about 480 b. c., and, because of his activity in establishing the oligarchy of the Four Hundred, was executed at Athens in 411 b. c., after a change had taken place in the government. He was noted for his readiness in debate, and gained great renown by composing orations by which many accused of capital offenses defended themselves.

The following oration was composed by Antiphon for a man by the name of Helus, who was accused of having murdered Herodes, who, while on a journey with Helus, mysteriously disappeared.

On The Murder of Herodes. (Helus, a Mitylenean, having been accused of the murder of Herodes, who had mysteriously disappeared from the boat in which the two had embarked in company, defended himself in the following speech, composed for him by Antiphon):

I could have wished, gentlemen, that I possessed the gift of eloquence and legal experience proportionate to my adversity. Adversity I have experienced in an unusual degree, but in eloquence and legal experience I am sadly deficient. The result is that, in circumstances where I was compelled to suffer personal ill-usage on a false charge, legal experience did not come to my rescue; and here, when my salvation depends on a true statement of the facts, I feel embarrassed by my incapacity for speaking. Many an innocent man has been condemned because of his inability to present clearly the truth and justice of his cause. Many a guilty man, on the other hand, has escaped punishment through skilful pleading. It follows, then, that if the accused lacks experience on these matters, his fate depends rather on the representation of his prosecutors than on the actual facts and true version of the case.

I shall not ask you, gentlemen, to give me an impartial hearing. And yet I am aware that such is the practice of most men on trial, who have no faith in their own cause or confidence in your justice. No, I make no such request, because I know full well that, like all good men and true, you will grant me the same hearing that you grant the prosecution. I do ask you, however, to be indulgent if I commit any indiscretion of speech, and to attribute it ratherto my inexperience

98

than to the injustice of my cause. But if my argument has any weight I pray you will ascribe it rather to the force of truth than rhetorical art.

I have always felt that it is not just either that one who has done wrong should be saved through eloquence, or that one who has done no wrong should be condemned through lack of eloquence. Unskilful speaking is but a sin of the tongue; but wrongful acts are sins of the soul. Now it is only natural that a man whose life is in danger should commit some indiscretion of speech; for he must be intent not only on what he says but on the outcome of the trial, since all that is still uncertain is controlled rather by chance than by providence. This fact inspires great fear in a man whose life is at stake. In fact, I have often observed that the most experienced orators speak with embarrassment when their lives are in danger. But whenever they seek to accomplish some purpose without danger they are more successful. My request for indulgence, then gentlemen, is both natural and lawful; and it is no less your duty to grant it than my right to make it.

I shall now consider the case for the prosecution in detail. And first I shall show you that I have been brought to trial here in violation of law and justice, not on the chance of eluding your judgment—for I would commit my life to your decision, even if you were bound by no oath to pronounce judgment according to law, since I am conscious that I have done no wrong and feel assured that you will do me justice: no, my purpose in showing you this is rather that the lawlessness and violence of my accusers may bear witness to you of their better feeling towards me.

First, then, though they imprisoned me as a malefactor, they have indicted me for homicide—an outrage that no one has ever suffered in this land. For I am not a malefactor, or amenable to the law of malefactors, which has to do only with thieves and highwaymen. So far, then, as they have dealt with me by summary process, they have made it possible for you to make my acquittal lawful and righteous.

But they argue that homicide is a species of malefaction. I admit that it is a great crime, as great as sacrilege or treason. But these crimes are dealt with each according to its own particular laws. Moreover, they compel me to undergo trial in this place of public assemblage, where all men charged with murder are usually forbidden to appear; and furthermore they would commute to a fine in my case the sentence of death imposed by law on all murderers, not for my benefit, but for their own private gain, thereby defrauding the dead of lawful satisfaction. Their reason for so doing you will perceive as my argument advances.

In the second place, you all know that the courts decide murder cases in the open air, for no reason than that the judges may not assemble in the same place with those whose hands have been defiled with blood, and that the prosecutor may not be sheltered beneath the same roof with the murderer. This custom my accusers have utterly disregarded. Nay, they have even failed to take the customary solemn oath that, whatever other crimes I may have committed, they will prosecute me for murder alone, and will allow no meritorious act of mine to stand in the way of my condemnation. Thus do they prosecute me unsworn; and even their witnesses testify against me without having taken the oath. And then they expect you, gentlemen, to believe these unsworn witnesses and condemn me to death, when they have made it impossible for you to accept such testimony by their violation and contempt of the law.

But they contend if I had been set free I would have fled. What motive could I have had? For, if I did not mind exile, I might have refused to come home when summoned,and have incurred judgment by default, or, having come, might have left voluntarily after my first trial. For such a course is open to all. And yet my accusers in their lawlessness seek to deprive me alone of the common right of all Greeks.

This leads me, gentlemen, to say a word about the laws that govern my case. And I think you will admit that they are good and righteous, since, though very ancient, they still remain unchanged—an unmistakable proof of excellence in laws. For time and experience teach men what is good and what is not good. You ought not, therefore, judge by the arguments of my accusers whether the laws are good or bad, but rather judge by the laws whether their claims are just or unjust. So perfect, indeed, are the laws that relate to homicide, that no one has ever dared to disturb them. But these men have dared to constitute themselves lawmakers in order to effect their wicked purposes, and disregarding these ordinances they seek unjustly to compass my ruin.

Their lawlessness, however, will not help them, for they well know that they have no sworn witness to testify against me. Moreover, they did not make a single decisive trial of the matter, as they would have done if they had confidence in their cause. No, they left room for controversy and argument, as if, in fact, they meant to dispute the previous verdict. The result is that I gain nothing by an acquittal, since it will be open to them to say that I was acquitted as a malefactor, not as a murderer, and catching me again they will ask to have me sentenced to death on a charge of homicide. Wicked schemers! Would ye have the judges set aside a verdict obtained by fair means, and put me a second time in jeopardy of my life for the same offense? But this is not all. They would not even allow me to offer bail according to law, and thus escape imprisonment, though theyhave never before denied this privilege even to an alien. And yet the officers in charge of malefactors conform to the same custom. I, alone, then, have failed to derive advantage from this common right conferred by law. This wrong they have done me for two reasons: First, that they might render me helpless to prepare for my defense; and, second, that they might influence my friends, through anxiety for my safety, to bear false witness against me. Thus, would they bring disgrace upon me and mine for life.

In this trial, then, I am at a disadvantage in respect to many points of your law and of justice. Nevertheless, I shall try to prove my innocence. And yet I realize that it will be difficult immediately to dissipate the false impression which these men have long conspired to create. For it is impossible for any man to guard against the unexpected.

Now, the facts in the case, gentlemen, are briefly these: I sailed from Mitylene in the same boat with Herodes, whom I am accused of having murdered. Our destination was the same—Aenus, but our objectives were different. I went to visit my father, who happened to be at Aenus at that time; Herodes went to sell some slaves to certain Thracian merchants. Both the slaves and the merchants sailed with us.

To confirm these statements I shall now offer the testimony of competent witnesses.

To continue, then, we were compelled by a violent storm to put in at a port on the Methymnian coast, and there we found the boat on which they allege I killed Herodes.

Now I would have you bear in mind that this whole affair took place not through design on my part, but through chance. For it was by chance that Herodes undertook the voyage with me. It was by chance that we encountered the storm, which compelled us to put in at the Methymnian port. And it was by chance that we found the cabined boat in which we sought shelter against the violence of the storm.

After we had boarded the other boat and had taken some wine, Herodes left us, never to return. But I did not leave the boat at all that night. On the day after Herodes disappeared, however, I sought him as diligently as any of our company, and felt his loss as keenly. It was I who proposed sending a messenger to Mitylene, and when no one else was willing to go I offered to send my own attendant. Of course, I would not have done this if I had murdered Herodes, for I would be sending an informant against myself. Finally, it was only after I was satisfied by diligent search that Herodes was nowhere to be found, that I sailed away with the first favorable wind. Such are the facts.

What inference can you draw from these facts other than that I am an innocent man? Even these men did not accuse me on the spot, while I was still in the country, although they knew of the affair. No, the truth was too apparent at that time. Only after I had departed, and they had had an opportunity to conspire against me, did they bring this indictment.

Now the prosecution have two theories of the death of Herodes. One is that he was killed on shore, the other that he was cast into the sea. First, then, they say that I killed Herodes on shore, by striking him on the head with a stone. This is impossible, since, as I have proved, I did not leave the boat that night. Strange that they should pretend to have accurate knowledge of the manner of his death, and yet not be able satisfactorily to account for the disappearance of his body. Evidently this must have happened near the shore, for, since it was night, and Herodes was drunk, his murderer could have had no reason to take him far from the shore. However that may be, two days' search failed to produce any trace of him. This drives them to their second hypothesis—that I drowned Herodes. If that were so, there would be some sign in the boat that the man was murdered and cast into the sea. No such sign, however, appears. But they say they have found signs in the boat in which he drank the wine. And yet they admit he was not killed in that boat. The utter absurdity of this second view is shown by the fact that they cannot find the boat they say I used for the purpose of drowning Herodes, or any trace of it.

It was not till after I sailed away to Aenus, and the boat in which Herodes and I made the voyage had returned to Mitylene, that these men made the examination that led to the discovery of blood. At once they concluded that I killed Herodes on that very boat. But when they found that this theory was inadmissible, since the blood was proved to be that of sheep, they changed their course and sought to obtain information by torturing the crew. The poor wretch whom they first subjected to torture said nothing compromising about me. But the other, whom they did not torture till several days later, keeping him near them in the meantime, is the one who has borne false witness against me.

All that is possible for you to learn, gentlemen, from the testimony of human witnesses, you have now heard. It remains to consider the testimony of the gods, expressed by signs. For by reliance on these heaven-sent signs you will best secure the safety of the state both in adversity and in prosperity. In private matters, too, you ought to attach great weight to these signs. You all know, of course, that, when a wicked man embarks in the same boat with a righteous man, the gods not infrequently cause the shipwreck and destruction of both because of the sinfulness of one alone. Again, the righteous, by association with the wicked, have been brought, if not to destruction, at least into the greatest dangers that divine wrath can send. Finally, the presence of guilty men at a sacrifice has often caused the omens to be unfavorable. Thus do the gods testify to the guilt and wickedness of man.

In the light of divine testimony, then, my innocence is established. For no mariner with whom I have sailed has ever suffered shipwreck. Nor has my presence at a sacrifice ever caused the omens to be unfavorable.

Now, I feel sure, gentlemen, that if the prosecution could find evidence that my presence on shipboard or at a sacrifice had ever caused any mishap, they would insist upon this as the clearest proof of my guilt. Since, however, this divine testimony is adverse to their claims, they ask you to reject it, and to have faith in their representation. Thus do they run counter to the practice of reasonable men. For, instead of testing words by facts, they seek to overthrow facts by words.

Having now concluded my defense, gentlemen, against all that I can recall of the charge against me, I look to you for acquittal. On that depends my salvation and the fulfilment of your oath. For you have sworn to pronounce judgment according to law. Now, I am not liable to the laws under which I was arrested, while as to the facts with which I am charged I can still be brought to trial in the legal form. And if two trials have been made out of one, the fault is not mine, but that of my accusers. When, however, my worst enemies give me the chance of a second trial, surely you, the impartial awarders of justice, will never pronounce on the present issue a premature verdict of murder. Be not so unjust; rather leave something for that other witness, Time, who aids the zealous seekers of eternal truth. I should certainly desire that in cases of homicide the sentence be in accordance with law, but that the investigation, in every possible instance, be regulated by justice. In this way the interests of truth and right would best be secured. For in homicide cases an unjust sentence banishes truth and justice beyond recall. If, then, you condemn me, you are bound to abide by the sentence, however guiltless I may be. No one would dare, through confidence in his innocence, to contravene the sentence passed upon him, nor, if conscious of guilt, would he rebel against the law. We must yield not only to the truth, but to a verdict against the truth, especially if there be no one to support our cause. It is for these reasons that the laws, the oaths, and the solemnities in murder cases differ from those in all other cases. In this case of cases it is of the utmost importance that the issue be clear and the decisions correct. For, otherwise, either the murdered will be deprived of vengeance or an innocent man will suffer death unjustly. For their accusation is not decisive, the result depends on you. Decide, then, justly; for your decision, if wrong, admits of no remedy.

But how, you may ask, will you decide justly? By compelling my accusers to take the customary solemn oath before they put me upon my defense against an indictment for murder. And how are you to accomplish this? By acquitting me now. And remember that, even though you acquit me now, I shall not escape your judgment, since in the other trial, too, you will be my judges. By an acquittal now you make it possible to deal with me hereafter as you will, but, if you condemn me now, my case will not be open to reconsideration. If, then, you must make any mistake, an undeserved acquittal is less serious than an unjust condemnation. For the former is a mistake only; the latter an eternal disgrace. Take care, then, that you do no irreparable wrong. Some of you in the past have actually repented of condemning innocent men, but not one of you has ever repented of making an undeserved acquittal. Moreover, involuntary mistakes are pardonable, voluntary unpardonable. The former we attribute to chance; the latter to design. Of two risks, then, run the lesser; commit the involuntary mistake; acquit me.

Now, gentlemen, if my conscience were guilty, I should never have come into this city. But I did come—with an abiding faith in the justice of my cause, and strong in conscious innocence. For not once alone has a clear conscience raised up and supported a failing body in the hour of trial and tribulation. A guilty conscience, on the other hand, is a source of weakness to the strongest body. The confidence, therefore, with which I appear before you, is the confidence of innocence.

To conclude, gentlemen, I have only to say that I am not surprised that my accusers slander me. That is their part; yours is not to credit their slander. If, on the other hand, you listen to me, you can afterwards repent, if you like, and punish me by way of remedy, but, if you listen to my accusers, and do what they wish, no remedy will then be admissible. Moreover, no long time will intervene before you can decide lawfully what the prosecution now asks you to decide unlawfully. Matters like these require not haste, but deliberation. On the present occasion, then, take a survey of the case; on the next, sit in judgment on the witnesses; form, now, an opinion; later, decide the facts.

It is very easy, indeed, to testify falsely against a man charged with murder. For, if he be immediately condemned to death, his false accusers have nothing to fear, since all danger of retribution is removed on the day of execution. And, even if the friends of the condemned man cared to exact satisfaction for malicious prosecution, of what advantage would it be to him after his death?

Acquit me, then, on this issue, and compel my accusers to indict me according to law. Your judgment will then be strictly legal, and, if condemned, I cannot complain that itwas contrary to law. This request I make of you with due regard to your conscience as well as to my own right. For upon your oath depends my safety. By whichever of these considerations you are influenced, you must acquit me.

PERICLES

Pericles is considered by many historians to have been the greatest statesman and orator that Athens produced, but the truth regarding his oratorical ability cannot be verified by his orations, because not one of them, in its entirety, has come down to us. We are indebted to the historian Thucydides for what speeches of Pericles we possess, and he has this to say regarding their authenticity: "I have found it difficult to retain a memory of the precise words that I had heard spoken, and so it was with those who brought me report. I have made the persons say what it seemed to me most opportune for them to say, in light of the situation; at the same time I have adhered as closely as possible to the general sense of what was actually said." Pericles was born about 495 b. c., and died in 429.

In Favor of the Peloponnesian War (432 b. c.). I always adhere to the same opinion, Athenians, that we should make no concessions to the Lacedaemonians; although I know that men are not persuaded to go to war, and act when engaged in it, with the same temper; but that, according to results, they also change their views. Still I see that the same advice, or nearly the same, must be given by me now as before; and I claim from those of you who are being persuaded to war, that you will support the common resolutions, should we ever meet with any reverse; or not, on theother hand, to lay any claim to intelligence, if successful. For it frequently happens that the results of measures proceed no less incomprehensively than the counsels of man; and therefore we are accustomed to regard fortune as the author of all things that turn out contrary to our expectation.

Now the Lacedaemonians were both evidently plotting against us before, and now especially are doing so. For whereas it is expressed in the treaty, that we should give and accept judicial decisions of our differences, and each side [in the meantime] keep what we have; they have neither themselves hitherto asked for such a decision, nor do they accept it when we offer it; but wish our complaints to be settled by war rather than by words; and are now come dictating, and no longer expostulating. For they command us to raise the siege of Potidaea, and to leave Aegina independent, and to rescind the decree respecting the Megareans; while these last envoys that have come charge us also to leave the Greeks independent. But let none of you think we would be going to war for a trifle, if we did not rescind the decree respecting the Megareans, which they principally put forward [saying] that if it were rescinded, the war would not take place: nor leave it in your mind any room for self-accusation hereafter, as though you had gone to war for a trivial thing. For this trifle involves the whole confirmation, as well as trial, of your purpose. If you yield to these demands, you will soon also be ordered to do something greater, as having in this instance obeyed through fear: but by resolutely refusing you would prove clearly to them that they must treat with you more on an equal footing.

Henceforth then make up your minds, either to submit before you are hurt, or, if we go to war, as I think is better, alike to make no concession on important or trivial grounds, nor to keep with fear what we have not acquired; for both the greatest and the least demand from equals, imperiously urgedon their neighbors previous to a judicial decision, amounts to the same degree of subjugation.

Now with regards to the war, and the means possessed by both parties, that we shall not be the weaker side, be convinced of hearing the particulars. The Peloponnesians are men who cultivate their land themselves; and they have no money either in private or public funds. Then they are inexperienced in long and transmarine wars, as they only wage them with each other for a short time, owing to their poverty. And men of this description can neither man fleets nor often send out land armaments; being at the same time absent from their private business, and spending from their own resources; and, moreover, being also shut out from the sea: but it is superabundant revenues that support wars, rather than compulsory contributions. And men who till the land themselves are more ready to wage war with their persons than with their money: feeling confident, with regard to the former, that they will escape from dangers; but not being sure, with regard to the latter, that they will not spend it before they have done; especially should the war be prolonged beyond their expectations, as [in this case] it probably may. For in one battle the Peloponnesians and their allies might cope with all the Greeks together; but they could not carry on a war against resources of a different description to their own; since they have no one board of council, so as to execute any measure with vigor; and all having equal votes, and not being of the same races, each forwards his own interest; for which reasons nothing generally is brought to completion.

Most of all will they be impeded by scarcity of money, while, through their slowness in providing it, they continue to delay their operations; whereas the opportunities of war wait for no one. Neither, again, is their raising works against us worth fearing, or their fleet. With regard tothe former, it were difficult even in time of peace to set up a rival city; much more in a hostile country, and when we should have raised works no less against them: and if they build [only] a fort, they might perhaps hurt some part of our land by incursions and desertions; it will not, however, be possible for them to prevent our sailing to their country and raising forts, and retaliating with our ships, in which we are so strong. For we have more advantage for land-service from our naval skill, than they have for naval matters from their skill by land.

But to become skilful at sea will not easily be acquired by them. For not even have you, though practicing from the very time of the Median War, brought it to perfection as yet; how then shall men who are agriculturists and not mariners, and, moreover, will not even be permitted to practice, from being always observed by us with many ships, achieve anything worth speaking of? Against a few ships observing them they might run the risk, encouraging their ignorance by their numbers; but when kept in check by many, they will remain quiet; and through not practicing will be the less skilful, and therefore the more afraid. For naval service is a matter of art, like anything else; and does not admit of being practiced just when it may happen, as a bywork; but rather does not even allow of anything else being a bywork to it.

Even if they should take some of the funds at Olympia or Delphi, and endeavor, by higher pay, to rob us of our foreign sailors, that would be alarming, if we were not a match for them, by going on board ourselves and our resident aliens; but now this is the case; and, what is best of all, we have native steersmen, and crews at large, more numerous and better than all the rest of Greece. And with the danger before them, none of the foreigners would consent to fly his country, and at the same time with less hope of success to join them in the struggle, for the sake of a few days' higher pay.

The circumstances of the Peloponnesians then seem, to me at least, to be of such or nearly such a character; while ours seem both to be free from the faults I have found in theirs, and to have other great advantages in more than an equal degree. Again, should they come by land against our country, we will sail against theirs; and the loss will be greater for even a part of the Peloponnese to be ravaged, than for the whole of Attica. For they will not be able to obtain any land in its stead without fighting for it; while we have abundance, both in islands and on the mainland. Moreover, consider it [in this point of view]: if we have been islanders, who would have been more impregnable? And we ought, as it is, with views as near as possible to those of islanders, to give up all thought of our land and houses, and keep watch over the sea and the city; and not, though being enraged on their account, to come to an engagement with the Peloponnesians, who are much more numerous: (for if we defeat them, we shall have to fight again with no fewer of them; and if we meet with a reverse, our allies are lost also; for they will not remain quiet if we are not able to lead our forces against them); and we should make lamentation, not for the houses and land, but for the lives [that are lost]; for it is not these things that gain men, but men that gain these things. And if I thought that I should persuade you, I would bid you go out yourselves and ravage them, and show the Peloponnesians that you will not submit to them for these things, at any rate.

I have also many other grounds for hoping that we shall conquer, if you will avoid gaining additional dominion at the time of your being engaged in the war, and bringing on yourselves dangers of your own choosing; for I am more afraid of our own mistakes than of the enemy's plans. But those points shall be explained in another speech at the time of the events. At the present time let us send these men away with this answer: that with regard to the Megareans, we will also allow them to use our ports and markets, if the Lacedaemonians also abstain from expelling foreigners, whether ourselves or our allies (for it forbids neither the one nor the other in the treaty): with regard to the states, that we will leave them independent, if we also hold them as independent when we made the treaty; and when they, too, restore to the states a permission to be independent suitably to the interests, not of the Lacedaemonians themselves, but of the several states as they wish: that we are willing to submit to judicial decision, according to the treaty: and that we will not commence hostilities, but will defend ourselves against those who do. For this is both a right answer and a becoming one for the state to give.

But you should know that go to war we must; and if we accept it willingly rather than not, we shall find the enemy less disposed to press us hard; and, moreover, that it is from the greatest hazards that the greatest honours also are gained, both by state and by individual. Our fathers, at any rate, by withstanding the Medes—though they did not begin with such resources [as we have], but had even abandoned what they had and by counsel, more than by fortune, and by daring, more than by strength, beat off the barbarian, and advanced their resources to their present height. And we must not fall short of them; but must repel our enemies in every way, and endeavor to bequeath our power to our posterity no less [than we received it].

ANDOCIDES

Andocides, a Greek orator, diplomatist, and politician, was born at Athens about 467 b. c., and died about 391 b. c. His speeches disclose the possession of practical common sense rather than deep learning, he being one who gained his proficiency of speech by practice in the public assemblies, and not, as most of the orators of his time, in schools of rhetoric. Few authentic speeches of his are in existence, the one here given being his speech "On the Mysteries," which is considered his best. He delivered it in his own defense against the charge of having mutilated the busts of Hermes.

Speech on the Mysteries. The preparation and zeal of my enemies, gentlemen, to do me harm in every way, justly or unjustly, from the very time I arrived in this city, are by no means unknown to you. It is therefore unnecessary for me to speak at length on this matter. I shall make of you, however, a request that is both just and easy for you to grant as it is important for me to obtain. I ask you to bear in mind that I have come here now, when there was no necessity of my remaining in the city, and although I did not offer bail, and was not committed to prison. I have appeared before you simply because I have confidence in the justice of my cause, and firmly believe that you will decide fairly, and will rather justly acquit me in accordance with your laws and your oaths, than suffer me to be unjustly destroyed by my enemies.

It is only natural, gentlemen, that you should have the same opinion of a man that he has of himself. If he is unwilling to undergo trial and thus condemns himself, it is only reasonable that you, too,

108

should condemn him. But if, confident in his innocence, he awaits your judgment, you should be predisposed to acquit him. At least you ought not to condemn him by a premature verdict of guilty.

My enemies are reported to have said that I would not dare to undergo trial, but would seek safety in flight. "For what object," they say, "can Andocides have in submitting to trial when it is possible for him to leave the city and have all the necessaries and convenience of life elsewhere? In Cyprus, where he formerly lived, he has a large amount of good land, bestowed on him as a gift. Can he, then, be willing to put his life in jeopardy? For what purpose? Does he not perceive the feeling of our city towards him?"

My feeling in this matter, gentlemen, is very different from what my enemies suppose. Even though I do not, as these men assert, share the good will of my countrymen, I am unwilling to live elsewhere in affluence—an exile from my native land. I should much prefer to be a citizen of this commonwealth than of all others, however prosperous they may now seem to be. It is with such a feeling of patriotism that I entrust my life to your decision.

I ask you, then, gentlemen, to accord me in my defense a preponderance of your good will, since you know that, even if you grant both parties in the suit an impartial hearing, I, the defendant, must necessarily be at a disadvantage. For the prosecution, after long preparation, bring this indictment against me without danger to themselves. But I must make my defense in fear and trembling for my life, and weighed down by the obloquy that has been heaped upon me. It is, therefore, only reasonable that you should favor me rather than the prosecution. There is a further consideration to dispose you in my favor. Prosecutors have frequently been found to bring charges so palpably false that you could not but convict and punish them. Witnesses, too, who have been instrumental in bringing about the condemnation of innocent men, have been convicted only after it was too late to save the guiltless victims of their false testimony. Guided, then, and warned by the experience of the past, you will not take for granted the truth of what my accusers say. The magnitudeof the charges against me you can learn from the prosecution; but the truth or falseness of that charge you cannot know until you have heard my defense.

Now, how to begin my defense, gentlemen, perplexes me not a little. I feel considerable doubt whether I ought first to show you that the prosecution have brought the wrong form of action against me; or that the decree of Isotimidas is null and void; or that certain laws and oaths forbid this action; or whether I ought to tell you all the facts from beginning to end. But what most perplexes me is the fact that you do not all perhaps regard as equally serious the same points in the charge against me. Each one of you, I suppose, has in mind some point about which he would like to have me speak first. Since, however, it is impossible to speak of all points at one and the same time, I shall set before you all the facts in order from beginning to end, omitting nothing. For if you get a right understanding of the facts you will readily perceive how false a charge the prosecution have brought against me.

I think, then, that you will feel disposed of your own accord to pronounce a just sentence. And I am led to this conclusion because I have observed that you always consider it a matter of the greatest importance, both in private and public affairs, to vote according to your oaths. It is this very thing that holds the state together, much against the will of those who would have it otherwise. Confiding, then, in your sense of justice, I ask you to hear my defense with good will, and not to act the part of adversaries in this suit. Suspect not the truth of my statements, and ensnare not my words. Hear me patiently to the end, and then pronounce whatever judgment you deem best and most in accordance with your oaths. . . .

Now with regard to the information laid on account of the mutilation of the images, I will tell you everything from thebeginning. When, then, Teucrus came from Megara, having obtained special permission, he gave what information he had about the mysteries and images, and denounced eighteen men. Of the men thus denounced, some fled, and others were arrested and put to death on the strength of this information. Those who fled have returned and are now here. Many relatives of those who were put to death are likewise present. I ask, then, any one of these, who will, to interrupt me in the course of my argument and show, if he can, that I was the cause of exile or death in a single case.

After this had taken place, Pisander and Charicles, who were members of the commission of inquiry, and had the reputation at that time of being loyal to the people, declared that what had been done was not the work of merely a few men, but part of a conspiracy to overthrow the commonwealth, and that they ought, therefore, to continue the investigation.

The city was then in a sorry plight. When the herald made proclamation for the Senate to enter the council chamber and hauled down the signal, the trouble began. Then it was that the conspirators fled from the market-place in fear of arrest. Then, too, Diocleides, elated with hope over the misfortunes of the city, brought an impeachment before the Senate, declaring that he knew the men who had mutilated the Hermae, and that they were thirty in number. He told how he chanced to be an eye-witness of the affair. Now I ask you, judges, to give your attention to this matter, and recall whether I speak the truth, refreshing each other's memories; for Diocleides spoke in your midst. To that fact you yourselves can testify.

Diocleides, you will remember, said that he had a slave at Laurium, and that he had occasion to go for a payment due to him. "He

110

rose early in the morning, mistaking the hour, and started on his way. The moon was full. When he got near the gateway of Dionysus, he saw several men going down from the Odeum into the orchestra of the theater. Afraid of them, he drew into the shade, and crouched down between the pillar and the column with the bronze statue of the general. He saw the men, about three hundred in number, standing around in groups of fifteen and twenty. Most of them he recognized in the light of the moon." Thus, in the first place, judges, he assumed this story—a most extraordinary one—in order, I fancy, that it might rest with him to include in this list any Athenian he pleased, or at pleasure to exempt him. After he had seen all this he went, he said, to Laurium, where he learned on the following day that the Hermae had been mutilated. He knew at once that it was the work of the men he had seen in the night. Returning to the city he learned that a commission of inquiry had been appointed and that a reward of a hundred minae had been offered for information. Seeing Euphemus, the brother of Callias, the son of Telecles, setting in his smithy, he brought him into the Hephaesteum and told him how he had seen us on that night. Now, he said, he did not desire to receive a reward from the city rather than from us, if he could have us for friends. Euphemus said that he did well to tell him, and asked him to come to the house of Leogoras, that they might there confer with Andocides and the other needful persons. He came, he declared, on the following day, and knocked at the door. He met my father going out, who said to him: "Are you the visitor whom the company here expect? Well, you ought not to reject such friends," and with these words he was gone. In this way he sought to ruin my father, denouncing him as a confederate. He then stated that we told him we had decided to give him two talents instead of a hundred minae, as offered by the state for information, and that we pledged ourselves, in the event of our success, to make him one of us. His reply, he said, was that he would think it over. We then asked him, he maintained, to come to the house of Callias, the son of Telecles, that he, too, might be present. Thus he sought to ruin also my kinsman. He came, he said, to the home of Callias, concluded an agreement with us, and gave us pledges on the Acropolis, but we failed to pay him, as agreed, the following month. He came, therefore, he said, to give information about what had been done. Such, judges, was his impeachment. . . .

Now, after we were all arrested and the prison doors were shut at night, there came the mother of one man, the sister of another, and the wife and children of another. Then they wept and bewailed their misfortunes. And Charmides, a cousin of my own age, who had been brought up in our home from childhood, said to me: "Andocides, you see how great our calamity is. Although, then, heretofore, I had no wish to speak or to give you pain, yet I am now constrained to do so by our present evil. For all your friends and associates, except us, your

111

relations, have either been put to death of the reasons on account of which we now perish, or have gone into exile, thereby condemning themselves. If, then, you know anything of this matter, tell it, and save first yourself, then your father, whom you ought to love exceedingly, then your brother-in-law, who married your only sister, then the rest of your numerous kinsmen and relatives, and finally me, who never grieved you in my whole life, but have ever been most eager to do whatever was for your interest."

Now when Charmides had said this, judges, and each of the others besought and supplicated me, I reflected how unhappy I was to have fallen into such misfortune. Was I to see my kinsman put to death unjustly and their property confiscated, and see those who were in no sense to blame for what had been done have their names inscribed on columnsas impious sinners against the gods? Was I further to see three hundred Athenians perish undeservedly, the city involved in calamity, and the citizens suspicious of one another? Was I, I ask, to sit by idly, and see all this, or was it my place to tell the people of Athens what I had heard from Euphiletus himself, the man who committed the outrage? I further reflected, judges, that of those who had wrought the deed of shame some had been put to death on the information of Teucrus, and others, having gone into exile, had sentence of death passed upon them in their absence. Four remained, who had not been informed against by Teucrus,—Panaetius, Chaeredamus, Diacritus, and Lysistratus. These men above all seemed likely to have been confederates of those against whom Diocleides had informed, since they were their intimate friends. For these men, then, safety was never secure; but over my own relatives hung certain destruction, unless some one told the people of Athens the actual facts. It seemed to me, therefore, better to deprive these four men of their country, who are still alive and have returned to enjoy their patrimony, than to see my own suffer an unjust death. Such were my reflections.

If now any of you, judges, had a preconceived idea that I have information to ruin these men and save myself—an assertion that my enemies make in their attempt to asperse my character—examine that idea in the light of the facts. For I must now give a truthful account of my doings in the presence of the very men who perpetrated the crime and then fled. They know best whether I lie or speak the truth, and may confute me, if they can, in the course of my speech; for I appeal to them. But you must learn the facts. For in this trial, judges, nothing is so important for me as that, if acquitted, I should be acquitted with honor; and, further, that the general public should understand my whole conduct to have been absolutely free from baseness or cowardice.I told what I had heard from Euphiletus through solicitude for my friends and kinsmen, through solicitude for the whole city, with courage and not cowardice. If, then, this is so, I ask you to acquit me and not to think me base.

Now consider—for a judge ought to examine the facts by a human standard, as if the misfortune had been his own—what would any one of you have done? If it had been a question of death with honor or life with shame, you might condemn my conduct as cowardice. And yet many would have chosen life in preference to an honorable death. But here the case was the very reverse: by keeping silent I must have perished ignominiously in my innocence, and must also have permitted the destruction of my father, of my brother-in-law, of all my cousins and relations, whom I and no one else threatened with death, by concealing the guilt of others. The falsehoods of Diocleides had sent them to prison; their only hope of deliverance lay in the Athenians learning the whole truth. I was in danger, therefore, of becoming their murderer, if I failed to tell you what I had heard. I was also in danger of destroying three hundred Athenians, and of involving Athens in the most serious evils. This, then, was the prospect, if I were silent.

How different the prospect if I had made known the truth! Then I should save myself, my father, and my kinsmen, and should deliver the city from dangers and misfortunes. Accordingly four men who participated in the crime were driven into exile through me. I had nothing, however, to do with the death or exile of the men against whom Teucrus had laid information. Considering all this, judges, I concluded that the least of the pressing evils was to tell the whole truth, and, by convicting Diocleides of falsifying, to have him punished—a man who sought to ruin us unjustly by deceiving the city, and who, for so doing, was proclaimed a public benefactor and received money from the state. I therefore told the Senate that I knew the men who did the act; that, while we were at a banquet, Euphiletus suggested this scheme, which was not carried out then on account of my opposition; but that later, when I had fallen from my horse in the Cynosarges, and had broken my collar-bone and cut my head, so that I had to be carried home on a stretcher, Euphiletus, seeing my condition, told his confederates that I had agreed to coöperate with them and would mutilate the Hermes by the Phorbanteum. Thus did he deceive them. Yet on that very account the Hermes near my father's house, dedicated by the Aegean tribe, is, as you all know, the only one in Athens not mutilated; for that task, as Euphiletus told his companions, was assigned to me. When they found this out, they were furious, because I knew of the deed without having had a hand in it. On the following day Meletus and Euphiletus came to me and said: "We have done the deed, Andocides. And if you think fit to remain silent, you will have our friendship as heretofore; otherwise our enmity will be more effectual than any friendship you can make by betraying us." Thereupon I told them that I considered Euphiletus a villain, and that they ought to feel furious, not because I knew it, but because they had done the abominable deed. In support of this statement I gave my own slave for the torture, to prove that I had been ill and unable even to leave my bed; and the Presidents received the female slaves for examination in the house from which the conspirators set forth to begin their work. After the Senate and the commission of inquiry found out that everything was just as I had stated, they summoned Diocleides. No words were wasted. He at once admitted that he had lied, and asked to be spared on condition of revealing the men who had put him up to it. He said they were Alcibaides of the deme of Phegeus and Amiantus from Aegina; both of whom fled in fear. After you had heard this you imprisoned Diocleidesand put him to death, but delivered my relatives from destruction—all on my account. Moreover you allowed the exiles to return; and you yourselves were freed from great dangers and evils.

Wherefore, judges, you ought to pity me in my misfortune; nay, you ought to hold me in honor for what I have done. When Euphiletus proposed the most traitorous of all compacts, I opposed him, and upbraided him as he deserved. Yet I concealed the crime of the conspirators, even when some were put to death and others driven into exile through the information laid by Teucrus. Only after we were imprisoned and on the point of being put to death through the instrumentality of Diocleides, did I denounce the four conspirators—Panaetius, Diacritus, Lysistratus, and Chaeredemus. These men, I admit, were driven into exile on my account. But my act saved my father, my brother-in-law, three cousins, and seven other relatives, all of whom were about to suffer an unjust death. These now behold the light of day on my account, and they frankly admit it. Moreover, the man who threw the whole city into confusion and involved it in the greatest dangers has been convicted. Finally you have been delivered from great dangers and freed from suspicion, one against another.

Recall, now, judges, whether I speak the truth, and do those of you who know, enlighten the rest. And do you, clerk, call the persons themselves who were released through me; for they know and can tell you best. This is so, judges; as they will come up and testify as long as you care to listen. . . .

And now, gentlemen, when you are about to pronounce final judgment, there are certain things you should call to mind. Remember that you now enjoy among all the Greeks the enviable reputation of being not only brave on the field of battle, but wise in the council chamber, since you attend not so much to the punishment of past misdeeds as to the future security of the State and the concord of its citizens. Other States as well as ours have had their share of evils. But the peaceful settlement of civil discord is the triumph of the best and wisest peoples. Since, then, you have the admiration of all nations, hostile as well as friendly, take care that you do not deprive your city of its fair fame, or create the impression that your success is due rather to chance than deliberation.

I ask you further to have the same opinion of me that you have of my ancestors. Give me the chance to follow their example. They occupy a place in the memory of their countrymen by the side of the greatest benefactors of the State. They served their country nobly and well, chiefly through good will to you, and with the further purpose that, if ever they or their descendants should fall into misfortune, they might find favor and pardon with you. Forget them not; for once their meritorious deeds served our city in a time of need. When our navy was annihilated at Aegospotami, and many were bent on the destruction of Athens, the Spartans decided to save the city through respect for the memory of those men who had fought for the liberty of all Greece. Since, then, our city was saved through the merits of my ancestors; for to the deeds that saved our city my ancestors contributed no small part. Share with me, then, the salvation that you received from the Greeks.

Consider, also, if you save me, what manner of citizen you will have in me. Once rich and affluent, I have been reduced to penury and want through no fault of mine, but through calamities that befell our city. Since then I have earned my livelihood in an honest way, toiling with my hands and brain. Many friends, I have, too; among them kings and great men of the world, whose friendship you will share with me.

If, on the other hand, you destroy me, there will be no one left to perpetuate our name and family. And yet the home of Andocides and Leogoras is no disgrace to Athens. But great will be the disgrace if I am in exile, and Cleophon, the lyremaker, dwells in the house of my fathers—a house whose walls are decked with trophies taken by my ancestors from the enemies of their country.

Though my ancestors be dead, let their memory still live, and fancy that you see their shades solemnly pleading in my behalf. For whom else have I to plead for me? My father? He is dead. Brothers? I have none. Children? None have yet been born to me.

Do you, then, be to me father, brother, children. To you I flee for refuge; you I supplicate and beseech. Turn then, in supplication to yourselves, and grant me life and safety.

LYSIAS

Lysias, while he never attained Athenian citizenship, resided most of his life at Athens, and took an important and intimate part in the affairs of that city while it was a democracy. The ancient historians place his birth at 459 b. c., and his death at 378 b. c., but modern critics would place his birth at about 440 b. c., and his death at 380 b. c. Thirty-four orations are ascribed to Lysias, but the authenticity of several of them is questionable. His style is simple and clear, at the same time possessing force and vividness of expression.

The oration here given was delivered in Athens in 403 b. c., and is considered the best of his speeches that have come down to us.

Eratosthenes was one of the Thirty Tyrants who decreed the death of the brother of Lysias.

Against Eratosthenes (403 b. c.). It is an easy matter, O Athenians, to begin this accusation. But to end it without doing injustice to the cause will be attended with no small difficulty. For the crimes of Eratosthenes are not only too atrocious to describe, but too many to enumerate. No exaggeration can exceed, and within the time assigned for this discourse it is impossible fully to represent them. This trial, too, is attended with another singularity. In other causes it is usual to ask the accusers: "What is your resentment against the defendants?" But here you must ask the defendant: "What was your resentment against your country? What malice did you bear your fellow citizens? Why did you rage with unbridled fury against the state itself?"

The time has now indeed come, Athenians, when, insensible to pity and tenderness, you must be armed with just severity against Eratosthenes and his associates. What avails it to have conquered them in the field, if you be overcome by them in your councils? Do not show them more favor for what they boast they will perform, than resentment for what they have already committed. Nor, after having been at so much pains to become masters of their persons, allow them to escape without suffering that punishment which you once sought to inflict; but prove yourselves worthy of that good fortune which has given you power over your enemies.

The contest is very unequal between Eratosthenes and you. Formerly he was both judge and accuser; but we, even while we accuse, must at the same time make our defense. Those who were innocent he put to death without trial. To those who are guilty we allow the benefit of law, even though no adequate punishment can ever be inflicted. For should we sacrifice them and their children, would this compensate for the murder of your fathers, your sons, and your brothers? Should we deprive them of their property, would this indemnify the individuals whom they have beggared, or the Statewhich they have plundered? Though they can not suffer a punishment adequate to their demerit, they ought not, surely, on this account, to escape. Yet how matchless is the effrontery of Eratosthenes, who, being now judged by the very persons whom he formerly injured, still ventures to make his defense before the witnesses of his crimes. What can show more evidently the contempt in which he holds you, or the confidence which he reposes in others?

Let me now conclude with laying before you the miseries to which you were reduced, that you may see the necessity of taking punishment on the authors of them. And first, you who remained in the city, consider the severity of their government. You were reduced to such a situation as to be forced to carry on a war, in which, if you were conquered, you partook indeed of the same liberty with the conquerors; but if you proved victorious, you remained under the slavery of your magistrates. As to you of the Piraeus, you will remember that though you never lost your arms in the battles which you fought, yet you suffered by these men what your foreign enemies could never accomplish, and at home, in times of peace, were disarmed by your fellow citizens. By them you were banished from the country left you by your fathers. Their rage, knowing no abatement, pursued you abroad, and drove you from one territory to another. Recall the cruel indignities which you suffered; how you were dragged from the tribunal and the altars; how no place, however sacred, could shelter you against their violence. Others, torn from their wives, their children, their parents, after putting an end to their miserable lives, were deprived of funeral rites; for these tyrants imagined their government so firmly established that even the vengeance of the gods was unable to shake it.

But it is impossible for one, or in the course of one trial, to enumerate the means which were employed to underminethe power of this state, the arsenals which were demolished, the temples sold or profaned, the citizens banished or murdered, and those whose dead bodies were impiously left uninterred. Those citizens now watch your decree, uncertain whether you will prove accomplices of their death or avengers of their murder. I shall desist from any further accusations. You have heard, you have seen, you have experienced. Decide then!

ISOCRATES

Isocrates, one of the greatest of the great men who lived between 500 and 300 b. c., and made Greece famous for literary and oratorical preëminence, owes his renown not to his ability as a deliverer of speeches, but as a constructor of them, and as a teacher of rhetoric and oratory. He understood the principles of vocal expression perfectly, but he was of a retiring nature and lacked volume of voice, the latter being a particularly serious drawback because of the necessity of speaking in the open before vast concourses of people. He withdrew from active participation in the public life of Athens, and opened a school in that city for the training of orators. Isaeus, the teacher of Demosthenes, was one of his pupils. Isocrates was born in 436 b. c., and died at the age of ninety-eight.

Encomium on Evagoras. When I saw, O Nicocles, that you were honoring the tomb of your father, not only with numerous and magnificent offerings, according to custom, but also with dances, musical exhibitions, and athletic contests, as well as with horse races and trireme races, on a scale that left no possibility of their being surpassed, I thought that Evagoras, if the dead have any feeling of whathappens on earth, while accepting this offering favorably, and beholding with joy your filial regard for him and your magnificence, would feel far greater gratitude to any one who could show himself capable of worthily describing his mode of life and the dangers he had undergone than to any one else; for we shall find that ambitious and high-souled men not only prefer praise to such honors, but choose a glorious death in preference to life, and are more jealous of their reputation than of their existence, shrinking from nothing in order to leave behind a remembrance of themselves that shall never die.

Now, expensive displays produce none of these results, but are merely an indication of wealth; those who are engaged in liberal pursuits and other branches of rivalry, by displaying, some their strength, and others their skill, increase their reputation; but a discourse that could worthily describe the acts of Evagoras would cause his noble qualities to be ever remembered amongst all mankind.

Other writers ought accordingly to have praised those who showed themselves distinguished in their own days, in order that both those who are able to embellish the deeds of others by their eloquence, speaking in the presence of those who were acquainted with the facts, might have adhered to the truth concerning them, and that the younger generation might be more eagerly disposed to virtue, feeling convinced that they will be more highly praised than those to whom they show themselves superior.

At the present time, who could help being disheartened at seeing those who lived in the times of the Trojan wars, and even earlier, celebrated in songs and tragedies, when he knows beforehand that he himself, even if he surpass their noble deeds, will never be deemed worthy of such eulogies? The cause of this is jealousy, the only good of which is that it is the greatest curse to those who are actuated by it. Forsome men are naturally so peevish that they would rather hear men praised, as to whom they do not feel sure that they ever existed, than those at whose hands they themselves have received benefits.

Men of sense ought not to be the slaves of the folly of such men, but, while despising them, they ought at the same time to accustom others to listen to matters which ought to be spoken of, especially since we know that the arts and everything else are advanced, not by those who abide by established customs, but by those who correct and, from time to time, venture to alter anything that is unsatisfactory.

I know that the task I am proposing to myself is a difficult one— to eulogize the good qualities of a man in prose. A most convincing proof of this is that, while those who are engaged in the study of philosophy are ever ready to speak about many other subjects of various kinds, none of them has ever yet attempted to compose a treatise on a subject like this.

When a boy, he was distinguished for beauty, strength, and modesty, the most becoming qualities at such an age. In proof of which witnesses could be produced: of his modesty, those of the citizens who were brought up with him; of his beauty, all who saw him; of his strength, the contests in which he surpassed his compeers.

When he grew to man's estate, all these qualities were proportionately enhanced, and in addition to them he acquired courage, wisdom, and uprightness, and these in no small measure, as is the case with some others, but each of them in the highest degree.

For he was so distinguished for his bodily and mental excellence, that, whenever any of the reigning princes of the time saw him, they were amazed and became alarmed for their rule, thinking it impossible that a man of such talents would continue to live in the position of a private individual,and whenever they considered his character they felt such confidence in him, that they were convinced that he would assist them if any one ventured to attack them.

In spite of such changes of opinion concerning him, they were in neither case mistaken; for he neither remained a private individual, nor, on the other hand, did them injury, but the Deity watched over him so carefully in order that he might gain the kingdom honorably, that everything which could not be done without involving impiety was carried out by another's hands, while all the means by which it was possible to acquire the kingdom without impiety or injustice he reserved for Evagoras. For one of the nobles plotted against and slew the tyrant, and afterwards attempted to seize Evagoras, feeling convinced that he would not be able to secure his authority unless he got him out of the way.

Evagoras, however, escaped this peril and, having got safe to Soli in Cilicia, did not show the same feeling as those who are overtaken by like misfortunes. Others, even those who have been driven from sovereign power, have their spirits broken by the weight of their misfortunes; but Evagoras rose to such greatness of soul, that, although he had all along lived as a private individual, at the moment when he was compelled to flee, he felt that he was destined to rule.

Despising vagabond exiles, unwilling to attempt to secure his return by means of strangers, and to be under the necessity of courting those inferior to himself, he seized this opportunity, as befits all who desire to act in a spirit of piety and to act in self-defense rather than to be the first to inflict an injury, and made up his mind either to succeed in acquiring the kingdom or to die in the attempt if he failed. Accordingly, having got together fifty men (on the highest estimate), he made preparations to return to his country in company with them.

From this it would be easy to recognize his natural forceof character and the reputation he enjoyed amongst others; for, when he was on the point of setting sail with so small a force on so vast an undertaking, and when all kinds of perils stared him in the face, he did not lose heart himself, nor did any of those whom he had invited to assist him think fit to shrink from dangers, but, as if they were following a god, all stood by their promises, while he showed himself as

119

confident as if he had a stronger force at his command than his adversaries, or knew the result beforehand.

This is evident from what he did; for, after he had landed on the island, he did not think it necessary to occupy any strong position, and, after providing for the safety of his person, to wait and see whether any of the citizens would come to his assistance; but, without delay, just as he was, on that eventful night he broke open a gate in the wall, and leading his companions through the gap, attacked the royal residence.

There is no need to waste time in telling of the confusion that ensues at such moments, the terror of the assaulted, and his exhortations to his comrades; but, when the supporters of the tyrant resisted him, while the rest of the citizens looked on and kept quiet, fearing, on the one hand, the authority of their rule, and, on the other, the valor of Evagoras; he did not abandon the conflict, engaging either in single combat against numbers, or with few supporters against the whole of the enemy's forces, until he had captured the palace, punished his enemies, succored his friends, and finally recovered for his family its ancestral honors, and made himself ruler of the city.

I think, even if I were to mention nothing else, but were to break off my discourse at this point, it would be easy to appreciate the valor of Evagoras and the greatness of his achievements; however, I hope that I shall be able to present both even more clearly in what I am going to say.

For while, in all ages, wo many have acquired sovereign power, no one will be shown to have gained this high position more honorably than Evagoras. If we were to compare the deeds of Evagoras with those of each of his predecessors individually, such details would perhaps be unsuitable to the occasion, while time would be insufficient for their recital; but if, selecting the most famous of these men, we examine them in the light of his actions, we shall be able to investigate the matter equally well, and at the same time to discuss it more briefly.

Who would not prefer the perils of Evagoras to the lot of those who inherited kingdoms from their fathers? For no one is so indifferent to fame that he would choose to receive such power from his ancestors rather than to acquire it, as he did, and to bequeath it to his children. Further, amongst the returns of princes to their thrones that took place in old times, those are most famous which we hear of from the poets; for they not only inform us of the most renowned of all that have taken place, but add new ones out of their own imaginations. None of them, however, has invented the story of a prince who, after having undergone such fearful and terrible dangers, has returned to his own country; but most of them are represented as having regained possession of their kingdoms by chance, others as having overcome their enemies by perfidy and intrigue.

Amongst those who lived afterwards (and perhaps more than all) Cyrus, who deprived the Medes of their rule and acquired it for the

Persians, is the object of most general admiration. But, whereas, Cyrus conquered the army of the Medes with that of the Persians, an achievement which many (whether Hellenes or barbarians) could easily accomplish, Evagoras undoubtedly carried out the greater part of what has been mentioned by his own unaided energy and valor.

In the next place, it is not yet certain, from the expedition of Cyrus, that he would have faced the perils of Evagoras, while it is obvious, from the achievements of the latter, that he would readily have attempted the same undertakings as Cyrus. Further, while Evagoras acted in everything in accordance with rectitude and justice, several of the acts of Cyrus were not in accordance with religion; for the former merely destroyed his enemies, the latter slew his mother's father. Wherefore, if any were content to judge, not the greatness of events, but the good qualities of each, they would rightly praise Evagoras more than Cyrus.

But—if I am to speak briefly and without reserve, without fear of jealousy, and with the utmost frankness—no one, whether mortal, demigod, or immortal, will be found to have acquired his kingdom more honorably, more gloriously, or more piously than he did. One would feel still more confident of this if, disbelieving what I have said, he were to attempt to investigate how each obtained supreme power. For it will be manifest that I am not in any way desirous of exaggerating, but that I have spoken with such assurance concerning him because the facts which I state are true.

Even if he had gained distinction only for unimportant enterprises, it were fitting that he should be considered worthy of praise in proportion; but, as it is, all would allow that supreme power is the greatest, the most august, and most coveted of all blessings, human and divine. Who then, whether poet, orator, or inventor of words, could extol in a manner worthy of his achievements one who has gained the most glorious prize that exists by most glorious deeds?

However, while superior in these respects, he will not be found to have been inferior in others, but, in the first place, although naturally gifted with most admirable judgment, and able to carry out his undertakings most successfully, he did not think it right to act carelessly or on the spur of the moment in the conduct of affairs, but occupied most of his time in acquiring information, in reflection, and deliberation, thinking that, if he thoroughly developed his intellect, his rule would be in like manner glorious, and looking with surprise upon those who, while exercising care in everything else for the sake of the mind, took no thought for the intelligence itself.

In the next place, his opinion of events was consistent; for, since he saw that those who look best after realities suffer the least annoyance, and that true recreation consists not in idleness, but in success that is due to continuous toil, he left nothing unexamined, but had such thorough acquaintance with the condition of affairs, and the character of each of the citizens, that neither did those who plotted against him take him unawares, nor were the respectable citizens unknown to him, but all were treated as they deserved; for he neither punished nor rewarded them in accordance with what he heard from others, but formed his judgment of them from his own personal knowledge.

But, while he busied himself in the care of such matters, he never made a single mistake in regard to any of the events of everyday life, but carried on the administration of the city in such a spirit of piety and humanity that those who visited the island envied the power of Evagoras less than those who were subject to his rule; for he consistently avoided treating any one with injustice, but honored the virtuous, and, while ruling all vigorously, punished the wrongdoers in strict accordance with justice; having no need of counsellors, but, nevertheless, consulting his friends; often making concessions to his intimates, but in everything showing himself superior to his enemies; preserving his dignity, not by knitted brows, but by his manner of life; not behaving irregularly or capriciously in anything, but preserving consistency in word as well as in deed; priding himself, not onthe successes that were due to chance, but those due to his own efforts; bringing his friends under his influence by kindness, and subduing the rest by his greatness of soul; terrible, not by the number of his punishments, but by the superiority of his intellect over that of the rest; controlling his pleasures, but not led by them; gaining much leisure by little labor, but never neglecting important business for the sake of short-lived ease; and, in general, omitting none of the fitting attributes of kings, he selected the best from each form of political activity; a popular champion by reason of his care for the interests of the people, an able administrator in his management of the state generally, a thorough general in his resourcefulness in the face of danger, and a thorough monarch from his pre-eminence in all these qualities. That such were his attributes, and even more than these, it is easy to learn from his acts themselves.

HYPERIDES

Hyperides, born in 396 b. c., and died in 322 b. c., was a pupil in philosophy of Plato, and studied oratory under Isocrates. He was at one time a close associate and follower of Demosthenes, but later disagreed with him on matters pertaining to the state, and took part in the prosecution that finally drove Demosthenes into exile. Hyperides was famed for the charm of his delivery, being esteemed by many equal to Demosthenes in this respect, and for the brilliancy and quickness of his wit.

Speech Against Athenogenes. [Hyperides' client, whose name

122

does not appear, desired to obtain a boy slave, who, with his father and brother, was the property of Athenogenes. The plaintiff proposed to purchase the liberty of the boy in question, while Athenogenes, aided by Antigona,lured the purchaser, by false representations, into buying all three slaves with their liabilities, which he pretended were but trifling. After the bargain was completed the plaintiff found that the slaves had brought him debts enough to compass his ruin; he therefore brought suit against Athenogenes and engaged Hyperides as counsel. The following speech, of which some fragments are missing, presents a satisfactory example of the orator's style. The opening sentences are lost. What is here given is but an extract from the speech]:

Gentlemen, you have heard the whole story in all its details. Possibly, however, Athenogenes will plead, when his turn comes, that the law declares all agreements between man and man to be binding. Just agreements, my dear sir. Unjust ones, on the contrary, it declares shall not be binding. I will make this clearer to you from the actual words of the laws. You need not be surprised at my acquaintance with them. You have brought me to such a pass and have filled me with such a fear of being ruined by you and your cleverness that I made it my first and main duty to search and study the laws night and day.

Now one law forbids falsehood in the market-place, and a very excellent injunction it is, in my opinion; yet you have, in open market, concluded a contract with me to my detriment by means of falsehoods. For if you can show that you told me beforehand of all the loans and debts, or that you mentioned in the contract the full amount of them, as I have since found it to be, I will abandon the prosecution and confess that I have done you an injustice.

There is, however, also a second law bearing on this point, which relates to bargains between individuals by verbal agreements. It provides that "when a party sells a slave he shall declare beforehand if he has any blemish; if he omit to do so, he shall be compelled to make restitution." If, then, the vendor of a slave can be compelled to make restitutionbecause he has omitted to mention some chance infirmity, is it possible that you should be free to refuse responsibility for the fraudulent bargain which you have deliberately devised? Moreover, an epileptic slave does not involve in ruin all the rest of his owner's property, whereas Midas, whom you sold to me, has ruined, not me alone, but even my friends as well.

And now, Athenogenes, proceed to consider how the law stands, not only with respect to slaves, but also concerning free men. Even you, I suppose, know that children born of a lawfully betrothed wife are legitimate. The lawgiver, however, was not content with merely providing that a wife should be betrothed by her father or brother, in order to establish legitimacy. On the contrary, he expressly enacts that "if a man shall give a woman in betrothal justly and equitably, the children born of such marriage shall be legitimate," but not if he betroths her on false representations and inequitable terms. Thus the law makes just betrothals valid, and unjust ones it declares invalid.

Again, the law relating to testaments is of a similar nature. It enacts that a man may dispose of his own property as he pleases, "provided that he be not disqualified by old age or disease or insanity, or by influenced by a woman's persuasions, and that he be not in bonds or under any other constraint." In circumstances, then, in which marriages and testaments relating solely to a man's own property are invalidated, how can it be right to maintain the validity of such an agreement as I have described, which was drawn up by Athenogenes in order to steal property belonging to me?

Can it be right that the disposition of one's property by will should be nullified if it is made under the persuasions of a woman, while, if I am persuaded by Athenogenes' mistress and am entrapped by them into making this agreement, I am thereby to be ruined, in spite of the express support which is given me by the law? Can you actually dare to rest yourcase on the contract of which you and your mistress procured the signature by fraud, which is also the very ground on which I am now charging you with conspiracy, since my belief in your good faith induced me to accept the conditions which you proposed? You are not content with having got the forty minas which I paid for the slaves, but you must needs plunder me of five talents in addition, plucking me like a bird taken in a snare. To this end you have the face to say that you could not inform me of the amount of the debts which Midas had contracted, because you had not the time to ascertain it. Why, gentlemen, I, who brought absolute inexperience into the arrangement of commercial matters, had not the slightest difficulty in learning the whole amount of the debts and the loans within three months; but he, with an hereditary experience of three generations in the business of perfumery; he, who was at his place in the market every day of this life; he, who owned three shops and had his accounts made up every month, he, forsooth, was not aware of the debts! He is no fool in other matters, but in his dealings with his slave it appears he at once became a mere idiot, knowing of some of the debts, while others, he says, he did not know of—those, I take it, which he did not want to know of. Such a contention, gentlemen, is not a defense, but an admission that he has no sound defense to offer. If he states that he was not aware of the debts, it is plain that he cannot at the same time plead that he told me all about them; and it is palpably unjust to require me to discharge debts of the existence of which the vendor never informed me.

Well, then, Athenogenes, I think it is tolerably plain on many grounds, that you knew of Midas' debts, and not the least from that fact that you demanded....[18]

---

[18] The rest of the column is hopelessly mutilated.

If, however, you did not inform me of the total amountof the debts simply because you did not know it yourself, and I entered into the contract under the belief that what I had heard from you was the full sum of them, which of us ought in fairness to be liable for them—I, who purchased the property after their contraction, or you who originally received the sums borrowed? In my opinion it should be you; but if we differ on this point let the law be our arbiter. The law was not made either by infatuated lovers or by men engaged in conspiracy against their neighbor's property, but by the most public-spirited of statesmen, Solon. Solon, knowing that sales of property are common in the city, enacted a law—and one universally admitted to be just—to the effect that fines and expenditures incurred by slaves should be discharged by the master for whom they work. And this is only reasonable; for if a slave effect a good stroke of business or establish a flourishing industry, it is his master who reaps the profit of it. You, however, pass over the law in silence, and are eloquent about the iniquity of breaking contracts. Whereas Solon held that a law was more valid than a temporary ordinance, however just that ordinance might be, you demand that a fraudulent contract should outweigh all laws and all justice alike.

I am told, however, that the defendant has another plea in reserve, and will argue that I brought all this mischief on my own head by disregarding his advice. He will declare that he offered to let me take the two boys, but that he urged me to leave Midas to him and not to buy him. I, however, he says, refused and insisted on buying all three. And this, they say, he intends to plead before a court such as the present! His object, of course, is to assume the appearance of fair dealing, but he must have forgotten that he will not be addressing an audience of fools, but one quite capable of seeing through his shameless effrontery. Let me tell you the actual facts, and you will see that they are of a piecewith the rest of the conduct of himself and his confederate. He sent the boy, whom I mentioned just now, to me, to say that he could not be mine unless I bought his father and his brother as well as himself. I had actually assented to this and promised to pay the price for all three of them, when Athenogenes, thinking that he now had the upper hand and wishing me to have as much trouble as possible, came to some of my friends. . . .[19]

Now I am no professional perfume-seller, neither have I learned any other trade. I simply till the land which my father gave me. It was solely by this man's craft that I was entrapped into the sale. Which is more probable on the face of things, Athenogenes, that I was coveting your business (a business of which I had no sort of experience), or that

---

[19] The rest of the column is mutilated.

you and your mistress were plotting to get my money? I certainly think the design was on your side. . . .[20]

Further, at the time of the war against Philip he left the city shortly before the battle, and instead of marching out with us to Chaeronea he migrated to Troezen. By so doing he broke the law which enacts that if a man migrates from the city during time of war he shall be liable to impeachment and summary arrest whenever he returns. His action shows that he had made up his mind that the city would escape peril, while he laid ours under sentence of death; and he corroborated this by not marrying his daughters here in Athens, but giving them to husbands in Troezen. . . .[21]

So while he has broken the general covenant which every citizen makes with his state, he lays stress on the private covenant which he made with me, apparently expecting people to believe that a man who is indifferent to justice in his dealings with you would have been careful to observe it in his dealings with me! Why, so universal and impartial was he in his want of principle that, when he had gone to Troezen, and the people of Troezen had conferred their citizenship upon him, he put himself under the directions of Mnesias of Argos, and having been appointed archon by his means, expelled the citizens from their own city. They will prove this to you themselves, since they are living here in exile. You, gentlemen, gave them an asylum when they were expelled from their country, you gave them your citizenship, who shared with them every privilege that you possess. You remembered the service which they had rendered to you more than a hundred and fifty years ago, during the war with Persia, and you recognized the duty of helping in the hour of their misfortune those who had aided you in the hour of your peril. But this scoundrel, this deserter from Athens who had procured admission as a citizen of Troezen, when once his position was thus secured, cared nothing for either the State or the welfare of the citizens, but behaved with the utmost barbarity towards the city which had granted him its hospitality. . . .[22]

To prove the truth of these assertions the clerk shall read to you, first, the law which forbids resident aliens to migrate in time of war; secondly, the evidence of the Troezenians; and finally the ordinance which these same Troezenians passed in your honor, in return for which you gave them asylum here and conferred your citizenship upon them. Read.

[The law, the evidence, and the ordinance are read.]

Now take the deposition of his own relative. . . .

---

[20] The remainder of this column and the whole of the next are either lost or so mutilated as to be unintelligible.

[21] When the next continuous passage is reached the speaker has quitted the direct issue and is attacking the political conduct of his adversary.

[22] Half a column is hopelessly mutilated here.

You know of what manner he conspired against me, and how he has been found a traitor against your state; how hedespaired of your safety and abandoned the commonweal in the hour of danger; and how he has made homeless many of those to whom he migrated. Will you not then punish this scoundrel, now that you have him in your power? And for myself, gentlemen, I implore you not to refuse me your protection. Reflect that your decision in this case is a matter of life or death for me, while an adverse verdict will inflect no very serious loss upon him. . . . Remember, gentlemen, the oath that you have taken and the laws that have been read in your ears, and give sentence against him in accordance with the justice that you have been sworn to observe.

ISAEUS

Isaeus, the pupil of Isocrates and the teacher of Demosthenes, was born about 420 b. c., but it is disputed as to whether he was born a Chalcidian or an Athenian. He is famous for his mastery of argumentative oratory, and appears to have studied Lysias attentively, because of the similarity of their styles. Lysias, however, used closely the divisions of a speech, such as introduction, argument, and epilogue, whereas Isaeus avoided formal arrangement of his matter and depended on his argumentative skill for convincing his hearers. He died about the year 370 b. c. Eleven of his speeches, dealing mainly with the law of inheritance, have come down to us.

Menexenus and Others Against Dicaeogenes and Leochares. [Dicaeogenes, whose estate was in dispute, had four sisters, all of whom were married and had issue. When he died without children, his uncle, Proxenus, produced a will by which the deceased appeared to have left a third part of his estate to his cousin, Dicaeogenes. This cousin, not content with a share, insisted that he had a right to the whole, and, having set up another will in his own favor, took possession of the remaining two-thirds of the property. This belonged to the sisters of the deceased, who proved the second will to be a forgery; upon this Dicaeogenes undertook to restore the two-thirds without diminution, and one Leochares was his surety; but on their refusal to perform their promise, the nephews of the elder Dicaeogenes began a suit against them for the performance of their agreement.]

We had imagined, judges, that all agreements made in court concerning this dispute would have been specifically performed; for when Dicaeogenes disclaimed the remaining two-thirds of this estate, and was bound, together with his surety, to restore them without any controversy, on the faith of this assurance we gave a release of our demands; but now, since he refuses to perform his engagement, we bring our complaint, conformably to the oath which we have taken, against both him and his surety, Leochares.

[The Oath]

That we swore truly, both Cephisodotus, who stands near me, perfectly knows, and the evidence, which we shall adduce, will clearly demonstrate. Read the depositions.

[Evidence]

You have heard the testimony of these witnesses, and I am persuaded that even Leochares himself will not venture to assert that they are perjured; but he will have recourse perhaps to this defense, that Dicaeogenes has fully performed his agreement, and that his own office of surety is completely satisfied. If he allege this, he will speak untruly and will easily be confuted; for the clerk shall read to you a schedule of all the effects which Dicaeogenes, the son of Menexenus, left behind him, together with an inventory of those which the defendant unjustly took; and if he affirms that our uncle neither had them in his lifetime nor left them to us at his death, let him prove his assertion; or if he insists that the goods were indeed ours, but that we had them returned to us, let him call a single witness to that fact; as we have produced evidence on our part that Dicaeogenes promised to give us back the two-thirds of what the son of Menexenus possessed, and that Leochares undertook to see him perform his promise. This is the ground of our action, and this we have sworn to be true. Let the oath be read.

[The Oath]

Now, judges, if the defendants intended only to clear themselves of this charge, what has already been said would be sufficient to ensure my success; but, since they are prepared to enter once more into the merits of the question concerning the inheritance, I am desirous to inform you on our side of all the transactions in our family; that, being apprised of the truth, and not deluded by their artifices, you may give a sentence agreeable to reason and justice.

Menexenus our grandfather had one son named Dicaeogenes, and four daughters, of whom Polyaratus my father married one; another was taken by Democles of Phrearrhi; a third by Cephisophon of Paeania; and the fourth was espoused by Theopompus the father of Cephisodotus. Our uncle Dicaeogenes, having sailed to Cnidos in the Parhalian galley, was slain in a sea fight; and, as he left no children, Proxenus the defendant's father brought a will to our parents, in which his son was adopted by the deceased and appointed heir to a third part of his fortune; this part our parents, unable at that time to contest the validity of the will permitted him to take; and each of the daughters of

Menexenus,as we shall prove by the testimony of persons then present, had a decree for her share of the residue.

When they had thus divided the inheritance and had bound themselves by oath to acquiesce in the division, each person possessed his allotment for twelve years; in which time, though the courts were frequently open for the administration of justice, not one of these men thought of alleging any unfairness in the transaction; until, when the state was afflicted with troubles and seditions, this Dicaeogenes was persuaded by Melas the Egyptian, to whom he used to submit on other occasions, to demand from us all our uncle's fortune and to assert that he was appointed heir to the whole.

When he began his litigation we thought he was deprived of his senses; never imagining that the same man, who at one time claimed to be heir to a third part, and at another time an hear to the whole, could gain any credit before this tribunal; but when we came into court, although we urged more arguments than our adversary and spoke with justice on our side, yet we lost our cause; not through any fault of the jury, but through the villainy of Melas and his associates, who, taking advantage of the public disorders, assumed a power of seizing possessions to which they had no right, by swearing falsely for each other. By such men, therefore, were the jury deceived; and we, overcome by this abominable iniquity, were stripped of our effects; for my father died not long after the trial and before he could prosecute, as he intended, the perjured witnesses of his antagonist.

On the very day when Dicaeogenes had thus infamously prevailed against us, he ejected the daughter of Cephisophon, the niece of him who left the estate, from the portion allotted to her; took from the wife of Democles what her brother had given her as co-heiress; and deprived both the mother of Cephisodotus and the unfortunate youth himself of theirwhole fortune. Of all these he was at the same time guardian and spoiler, next of kin, and cruelest enemy; nor did the relation which he bore them excite in the least degree his compassion; but the unhappy orphans, deserted and indigent, became destitute even of daily necessities.

Such was the guardianship of Dicaeogenes their nearest kinsman! who gave to their avowed foes what their father Theopompus had left them, illegally possesses himself of the property which they had from their maternal uncle and their grandfather; and (what was the most open act of cruelty) having purchased the house of their father and demolished it, he dug up the ground on which it stood, and made that handsome garden for his own house in the city.

Still further; although he receives an annual rent of eighty minas from the estate of our uncle, yet such are his insolence and profligacy that he sent my cousin, Cephisodotus, to Corinth as a service attendant on his brother Harmodius; and adds to his other injuries this cruel reproach, that he wears ragged clothes and coarse buskins; but is not this unjust, since it was his own violence which reduced the boy to poverty?

On this point enough has been said, I now return to the narration from which I have thus digressed. Menexenus then, the son of Cephisophon, and cousin both to this young man and to me, having a claim to an equal portion of the inheritance, began a prosecution against those who had perjured themselves in the former cause, and convicted Lycon, whom he had first brought to justice, of having falsely sworn that our uncle appointed this Dicaeogenes heir to his whole estate; when, therefore, this pretended heir was disappointed in his hopes of deluding you, he persuaded Menexenus, who was acting both for our interest and his own, to make a compromise, which, though I blush to tell it, his baseness compels me to disclose.

What was their agreement?

That Menexenus should receive a competent share of the effects on condition of his betraying us, and releasing the other false witnesses, whom he had not yet convicted; then, injured by our enemies, and by our friends, we remained with silent indignation; but you shall hear the whole transaction from the mouths of witnesses.

[Evidence]

Nor did Menexenus lose the reward of his perfidy; for, when he had dismissed the persons accused, and given up our cause, we could not recover the promised bribe from his seducer whose deceit he so highly resented, that he came over again to our side.

We, therefore, justly thinking that Dicaeogenes had no right to any part of the inheritance, since his principal witness had been actually convicted of perjury, claimed the whole estate as next of kin to the deceased; nor will it be difficult to prove the justice of our claim; for, since two wills have been produced, one of an ancient date, and the other more recent; since by the first, which Proxenus brought with him, our uncle made the defendant heir to a third part of his fortune, which will Dicaeogenes himself prevailed upon the jury to set aside; and since the second, under which he claims the whole has been proved invalid by the conviction of the perjured witnesses, who swore to its validity; since, I say, both will have been shown to be forged, and no other testament existed, it was impossible for any man to claim the property as heir by appointment, but the sisters of the deceased, whose daughters we married, were entitled to it as heirs by birth.

These reasons induced us to sue for the whole as next of kin, and each of us claimed a share; but when we were on the point of taking the usual oaths on both sides, this Leochares put in a protestation that the inheritance was not controvertible; to this protestation we took exceptions, and having begun to prosecute Leochares for perjury, we discontinued the former case. After we had appeared in court, and urged the same arguments on which we have now insisted, and after

Leochares had been very loquacious in making his defense, the judges were of opinion that he was perjured, and as soon as this appeared by the number of pellets, which were taken out of the urns, it is needless to inform you what entreaties he used both to the court and to us, or what an advantage we might then have taken; but attend to the argument which we have made, and upon our consenting that the Archon should mix the pellets together without counting them, Dicaeogenes undertook to surrender two-thirds of the inheritance, and to resign them without any dispute to the sisters of the deceased, and for the full performance of this undertaking, Leochares was his surety, together with Mnesiptolemus the Plotian; all which my witnesses will prove.

[Evidence]

Although we had been thus injured by Leochares, and had it in our power, after he was convicted of perjury, to mark him with infamy, yet we consented that judgment should not be given, and were willing to drop the prosecution upon condition of recovering our inheritance; but after all this mildness and forbearance we were deceived, judges, by these faithless men; for neither has Dicaeogenes restored to us the two-thirds of his estate, conformably to his agreement in court; nor will Leochares confess that he was bound for the performance of that agreement. Now if these promises had not been made before five hundred jurymen and a crowd of hearers, one cannot tell how far this denial might have availed him; but, to show how falselythey speak, I will call some witnesses who were present both when Dicaeogenes disclaimed two-thirds of the succession and undertook to restore them undisputed to the sisters of our uncle, and when Leochares engaged that he should punctually perform what he had undertaken; to confirm his evidence, judges, we entreat you, if any of you were then in court, to recollect what passed, and, if our allegations are true, to give us the benefit of your testimony, for, if Dicaeogenes speaks the truth, what advantage did we reap from gaining the cause, or what inconvenience did he sustain by losing it?

If, as he asserts, he only disclaimed the two-thirds without agreeing to restore them unencumbered, what has he lost by relinquishing his present claim to an estate the value of which he has received? For he was not in possession of the two third parts, even before we succeeded in our suit, but had either sold or mortgaged them; it was his duty, however, to return the money to the purchasers and to give us back our share of the land; since it was with a view to this that we, not relying singly upon his own engagement, instead upon his finding a surety. Yet, except two small houses without the walls of the city, and about sixty acres of land in the plain, we have received no part of our inheritance; nor did we care to eject the purchasers of the rest lest we should involve ourselves in litigation; for when, by the

131

advice of Dicaeogenes, and on his promise not to oppose our title, we turned Micio out of a bath which he had purchased, he brought an action against us and recovered forty minas.

This loss, judges, we incurred through the perfidy of Dicaeogenes; for we, not imagining that he would recede from an agreement so solemnly made, assured the court that we would suffer any evil if Dicaeogenes should warrant the bath to Micio; not that we depended on his own word, but we could not conceive that he would betray the sureties whohad undertaken for him; yet this very man, who disavowed all pretensions to these two-thirds, and even now admits his disavowal, had the baseness, when he was vouched by Micio, to acknowledge his warranty; while I, unhappy man, who had not received a particle of my share, was condemned to pay forty minas for having ousted a fair purchaser and left the court oppressed by the insults of this Dicaeogenes. To prove the transaction I shall call my witnesses.

[Evidence]

Thus have we been injured, judges, by this man; whilst Leochares, who was bound for him and has been the cause of all our misfortunes, is confident enough to deny what has been proved against him; because his undertaking was not entered in the register of the court; now, judges, as we were then in great haste, we had time to enter part only of what had been agreed on, and took care to provide faithful witnesses of all the rest; but these men have a convenient subterfuge: what is advantageous to them they allow to be valid although it be not written, but deny the validity of what may be prejudicial to their interests unless it be in writing; nor am I surprised that they refuse to perform their verbal promises since they will not act conformably to their written agreements.

That we speak truly, an undeniable proof shall be produced: Dicaeogenes gave my sister in marriage with a portion of forty minas to Protarchides of Potamos; but, instead of paying her fortune in money he gave her husband a house which belonged to him in Ceramicus; now she had the same right with my mother to a share of the estate; when Dicaeogenes, therefore, had resigned to the women two-thirds of the inheritance, Leochares told Protarchides in what manner he had booomo a surety, and promised in writing to give him his wife's allotment if he would surrender to him the housewhich he had taken instead of the portion; Protarchides, whose evidence you shall now hear, consented; but Leochares took possession of his house and never gave him any part of the allotment.

[Evidence]

As to the repairs of the bath and the expenses of building, Dicaeogenes has already said, and will probably say again, that we have

132

not reimbursed him, according to our engagement, for the sum which he expended on that account, for which reason he cannot satisfy his creditors nor give us the shares to which we are entitled. To answer this, I must inform you that, when we compelled him in open court to disclaim this part of the inheritance, we permitted him, by the advice of the jury, to retain the products of the estate, which he had enjoyed for so long, by way of compensation for his expense in repairs and for his public charges; and some time after, not by compulsion, but of our own free will, we gave him a house in the city, which we separated from our own estate and added to this third part.

This he had as an additional recompense for the materials which he had bought for his building; and he sold the house to Philonicus for fifty minas; nor did we make him this present as a reward of his probity, but as a proof that our own relatives, how dishonest soever, are not undervalued by us for the sake of lucre; and even before, when it was in our power to take ample revenge of him by depriving him of all his possession, we could not act with the rigor of justice, but were contented with obtaining a decree for part of our own property; whilst he, when he had procured an unjust advantage over us, plundered us with all possible violence, and now strives to ruin us, as if we were not his kinsmen, but his inveterate foes.

We will now produce a striking instance of our candor and of his knavery. When, in the month of December, judges,the prosecution against Leochares was carried on with firmness, both he and Dicaeogenes entreated me to postpone the trial and refer all matters in dispute to arbitration; to which proposal, as if we had sustained only a slight injury, we consented; and four arbitrators were chosen, two by us, and as many by them; we then swore, in their presence, that we would abide by their award; and they told us that they would settle our controversy, if possible, without being sworn; but that, if they found it impossible to agree, they would severally declare upon oath what they thought the merits of the case. After they had interrogated us for a long time, and inquired minutely into the whole transaction, Diotamus and Melanopus the two arbitrators, whom we had brought, expressed their readiness to make their award, either upon oath or otherwise, according to their opinion of the truth from the testimony of both parties; but the other two, whom Leochares had chosen, refused to join in any award at all; though one of them, Diopithes, was a kinsman of Leochares, and an enemy to me on account of some former disputes, and his companion, Demaratus, was a brother of that Mnesiptolemus whom I mentioned before as one of the sureties for Dicaeogenes; these two decided against giving any opinion, although they had obliged us to swear that we would submit to their decision.

[Evidence]

It is abominable, then, that Leochares should request you to

133

pronounce a sentence in his favor which his own relation, Diopithes, refused to pronounce; and how can you, judges, with propriety decree for this man, when even his friends have virtually decreed against him? For all these reasons I entreat you, unless you think my request inconsistent with justice, to decide this case against Leochares.

As for Dicaeogenes, he deserves neither your compassion as an indigent and unfortunate man, nor your indulgence as a benefactor in any degree to the state; I shall convince you, judges, that neither of these characters belongs to him; shall prove him to be both a wealthy and a profligate citizen, and shall produce instances of his base conduct towards his friends, his kinsmen, and the public. First, though he took from us an estate from which he annually received eighty minas, and although he enjoyed the profits of it for ten years, yet he is neither in possession of the money nor will declare in what manner he has employed it. It is also worthy of your consideration, that, when he presided over the games of his tribe at the feast of Bacchus he obtained only the fourth prize, and was the last of all in the theatrical exhibitions and the Pyrrhic dances: these were the only offices that he has served, and these, too, by compulsion; and see how liberally he behaved with so large an income! Let me add that in a time of the greatest public calamity, when so many citizens furnished vessels of war, he would not equip a single galley at his own expense, nor even joined with another; whilst others, whose entire fortune was not equal to his yearly rents, bore that expensive office with alacrity; he ought to have remembered that it was not his father who gave him his estate, but you, judges, who established it by your decree; so that, even if he had not been a citizen, gratitude should have prompted him to consult the welfare of the city.

Again, when contributions were continually brought by all who loved their country, to support the war and provide for the safety of the state, nothing came from Dicaeogenes; when Lechaeum indeed was taken, and when he was pressed by others to contribute, he promised publicly that he would give three minas, a sum less than that which Cleonymus the Cretan voluntarily offered; yet even this promise he never performed; but his name was hung up on the statues of the Eponymi with an inscription asserting, to his eternal dishonor, that he had not paid the contribution, which he promised in public, for his country's service. Who can now wonder, judges, that he deceived me, a private individual, when he so notoriously deluded you all in your common assembly? Of this transaction you shall now hear the proof.

[Evidence]

Such and so splendid have been the services which Dicaeogenes, possessed of so large a fortune, has performed for the city! You perceive, too, in what manner he conducts himself towards his relatives, some of whom he has deprived, as far as he was able, of their property; others he has basely neglected, and forced, through the want

134

of mere necessaries, to enter into the service of some foreign power. All Athens saw his mother sitting in the temple of Illithyia, and heard her accuse him of a crime which I blush to relate, but which he blushed not to commit. As to his friends, he has now incurred the violent hatred of Melas the Egyptian, who had been fond of him from his early youth, by refusing to pay him a sum of money which he had borrowed; his other companions he had either defrauded of sums which they lent him, or has failed to perform his promise of giving them part of his plunder if he succeeded in his cause.

Yet our ancestors, judges, who first acquired this estate, and left it to their descendants, conducted all the public games, contributed liberally toward the expense of the war, and continually had the command of galleys, which they equipped: of these noble acts the presents with which they were able, from what remained of their fortune after their necessary charges, to decorate the temples, are no less undeniable proofs, than they are lasting monuments of their virtue; for they dedicated to Bacchus the tripods which they won by their magnificence in their games; they gave new ornaments to the temple of the Pythian Apollo, and adornedthe shrine of the goddess in the citadel, where they offered the first fruits of their estate, with a great number, if we consider that they were only private men, of statues both in brass and stone. They died fighting resolutely in defense of their country; for Dicaeogenes, the father of my grandfather, Menexenus, fell at the head of the Olysian legion in Spartolus; and his son, my uncle, lost his life at Cnidos, where he commanded the Parhalian galley.

His estate, O Dicaeogenes, thou hast unjustly seized and shamefully wasted, and, having converted it into money, hast the assurance to complain of poverty. How hast thou spent that money? Not for the use of the state or of your friends; since it is apparent that no part of it has been employed for those purposes; not in breeding fine horses, for thou never wast in possession of a horse worth more than three minas; not in chariots, for, with so many farms and so great a fortune, that never hadst a single carriage even drawn by mules; nor hast thou redeemed any citizen from captivity; nor hast thou conveyed to the citadel those statues which Menexenus had order to be made for the price of three talents, but was prevented by his death from consecrating in the temple; and, through thy avarice, they lie to this day in the shop of the statuary; thus hast thou presumed to claim an estate to which thou hast no color of right, and hast not restored to the gods the statues, which were truly their own. On what ground, Dicaeogenes, canst thou ask the jury to give a sentence in thy favor? Is it because thou hast frequently served the public offices; expended large sums of money to make the city more respectable, and greatly benefited the State by contributing bountifully towards supporting the war? Nothing of this sort can be alleged with truth. Is it because thou

135

art a valiant soldier? But thou never once could be persuaded to serve in so violent and so formidable a war, in which even the Olynthians and the islanders losetheir lives with eagerness, since they fight for this country; while thou, who art a citizen, wouldst never take arms for the city.

Perhaps the dignity of thy ancestors, who slew the tyrant, emboldens thee to triumph over us; as for them, indeed, I honor and applaud them, but cannot think that a spark of their virtue animates thy bosom; for thou hast preferred the plunder of our inheritance to the glory of being their descendant, and wouldst rather be called the son of Dicaeogenes than of Harmodius; not regarding the right of being entertained in the Prytaneum, nor setting any value on the precedence and immunities which the posterity of those heroes enjoy; yet it was not for noble birth that Harmonius and Aristogiton were so transcendently honored, but for their valor and probity; of which thou, Dicaeogenes, hast not the smallest share.

LYCURGUS

Lycurgus, a pupil both of Plato and Isocrates, was born at Athens about the year 396 b. c., and died in 323 b. c. During the great struggle with Philip of Macedon, he allied himself with Demosthenes and became one of the leaders of the national party. He was a man of refined and artistic tastes, a patriot, and an orator. Only the conclusion of his speech is here given.

Oration Against Leocrates. Gentlemen, you have heard the witnesses. It may well be that what I now declare will rouse your indignation and your scorn of this Leocrates. Not content to abscond alone with his wretched self and his money, he must needs drag with him the ancestral faith, today become your law because your ancestors kept it, the establishment of the fathers and the heritage of him their child, drag this to Megara, filch it from the land. He hallowednot that sacred name of old, would tear it from its home, make it forsake with him the temples and the country once its own, as if in the land of the stranger it could rise again, for him. Athena, with no Athens there! in Megara! their land and their laws to be here! Why did your fathers give to the land her name? Because her land was here. In the name of Athena did they put their trust; she abandons not her own. Leocrates, recreant to law and tradition and religion, took from us all, as far as in him lay, the help that is ours from on high. And not content with all these grievous wrongs, he took the capital he had withdrawn here and with it made shipments of grain from Cleopatra in Epirus into Leucas and from there into Corinth; this in violation of your law which lays so severe a penalty on any man of Athens who shall ship grain to any port but ours. Here then is your man; traitor in war; lawbreaker in business;

false to the faith and the land and the law. Here he is in your jurisdiction: shall not his doom be death? shall he not serve warning to others? If not, then ye must be some listless men, whose wrath no crime can rouse.

And now in what strains did Homer voice this theme? To your fathers he was such a noble poet that they passed a law that at every pan-Athenian festival, as the five years came round, his epics alone should be delivered; thus bearing witness to the world of Greece that the greatest of works were the works for them. A salutary measure. Brevity is the nature of the law. It may not instruct; it must simply command. To the poets it must refer the life of man, to portray the human spirit in its loftiest achievement, and with the resistless argument of art our souls are swayed. It is Hector who speaks rousing the Trojans in their country's name:

When ye have reached the ships, fight onward, ceaselessly striving:
What though the stroke of fate shall call some man to his glory?
Where is the sting of death when a hero falls for his country?
Wife and child and home are safe in the hour that the Argives
Take to the ships once more and sail for the land of their fathers.

With strains like these, men of Athens, ringing in the ears of your sires, they could emulate the deeds of old; rising to such heights of valor that not for their own native State alone, but for all Hellas as a common fatherland, they stood ready to offer up their lives. There on Marathon they went into line in the face of the barbarians, bore down all Asia in arms, the stake their lives alone, winning security for Greece at large; not puffed up with the pride of renown, but glad their work was worthy of its fame; of Greece the champions, masters of the heathen worlds; letting their deeds proclaim aloud with glory. Such was the strenuous life they led in Athens in the great days of old that once when the Lacedaemonians, valiant of men, were at war with the Messinians, the god vouchsafed them a response that bade them take a leader from our people, and then they should conquer their enemies. If then divine judgment declared in favor of our leadership, even for the children of Hercules, lords for all time in Sparta, are we not justified in our faith that once Athenian valor was peerless? Who that is Greek does not know that they took one Tyrtaeus for their general? And with him they overthrew their enemies. And when the immediate peril was past, they (with an admirable wisdom) turned the episode to the advantage of their youth for all time. For when Tyrtaeus left them, his elegiacs were still theirs. While other poets have had no vogue among them,for him their enthusiasm has been so great that they passed a law that whenever a campaign was to open, all the man should be called to the tent of the king to hear the strains of Tyrtaeus. Nothing else, they thought, could make their men so ready to lay down their lives for their country. And now the day is come when we ourselves may need the sound of those elegiacs which could make their way to the souls of Spartans:

> Blest is the brave: how glorious is his prize,
> When at his country's call he dares and dies.
> And sad the sight when, envious of the dead,
> The man without a country begs his bread.
> His poor old parents feebly toil along,
> And little children who have done no wrong.
> Spurned by the glance he meets at every turn,
> He learns how hot the beggar's brand can burn.
> His name is shame: the human form divine
> Shows in its fall the soul's dishonored shrine.
> Deeds in the dust of ages swiftly root,
> And children's children reap the bitter fruit.
> Strike for our country, comrades: on, ye brave!
> Where is the man that dreads a patriot grave?
> And ye, my younger brethren, side by side,
> Shoulder to shoulder stand, whate'er betide.
> The surging thrill ye feel before your foe
> Swept o'er your father's heart-strings long ago.
> To those whose days are longer in the land
> Lend in the pride of youth the helping hand.
> For shame to see an old man fall in front
> When young men leave him there to bear the brunt:
> Low in the dust the hoary hair is trailed;
> And last is quenched a soul that never quailed,
> Youth in its bloom should pluck the glowing bough
> Whose leaves in glory wreathe a hero's brow.
> Welcome to man, and fair in woman's eye,
> The manly form that living dares to die.
> Fate hangs apoise, with gloom and triumph fraught:
> Up, hearts! and in the balance count we our lives as naught.

Noble sentiments, gentlemen, that sway the soul of him that hath ears to hear. The Spartans could hear them, and receive such an impulse into manhood that they engaged with us in a struggle for the hegemony. It was nature's rivalry; for the noblest achievements have been wrought on either side. Our ancestors had overthrown the barbarian who had set the first hostile foot upon Attic soil; in them was made manifest a manhood that no money could corrupt, a valor no host countervail. In Thermopylae the Lacedaemonians made their stand; and though the fate they met was not like ours, yet there the ideals of human devotion became reality.

And thus on the borne of life we can see the memorials of the valor of our race graven with the chisel of truth unto all Greek blood:

138

FOR THEIRS:

Go stranger, tell the Spartans where we lie,
True to the land that taught her sons to die.

FOR YOURS:

On Marathon when Athens fought alone,
Down to the dust the golden East was thrown.

These great memories, Athenians, are the glory of the men who bequeathed them and of Athens the undying renown. Not in this wise was Leocrates wrought. The fair fame of the city, flower of the ages, deliberately hath he defiled. If then he meet death at your hands, all Greece willfeel the abhorrence in which you hold such acts. If not, then are the fathers of their ancient fame bereft by the same fell stroke that wounds your brothers in citizenship. They who revere not the men of old will follow the footsteps of this man, quick to descry the path that shall lead them to favor with our enemies, quick to perceive that shamelessness, treachery, cowardice, need only a verdict from you to prove their native worth.

One word more and I am done. To your sovereign chastisement I commit the man who stands for Athenian annihilation. On your own honor and in the presence of the gods you are to give Leocrates his due. On the head of the criminal lies the crime; but in a miscarriage of justice the jurors delinquent become participant of guilt. Gentlemen, ye cast the secret ballot now; but be not deceived: not one man among you can deposit a vote that the eye of heaven does not see. In my opinion, gentlemen, your verdict today reaches all the greatest and most fearful crimes at once: we behold them in the person of Leocrates; treason, for he abandoned the city to subjugation by the enemy; apostasy, for he played a coward's part in freedom's cause; sacrilege for the groves might be felled, the temples razed, as far as he was concerned; abomination, for the memorials of our fathers might be swept away and the hallowed observance abolished; desertion, for the nidering did not report for duty in the line. Where then is the man who will vote to clear him? Who is he that will show his sympathy with crime that shows malice aforethought? Is there a man so bereft of sense that he will set Leocrates free and so place his own security at the mercy of men who would abandon him? that out of pity for Leocrates he will take no pity on himself, when his choice may mean death at the hands of the foe? that by extending clemency to a traitor he will lay himself open to the retribution of heaven?

In support of our country, religion and laws I have pleaded this case, in righteousness and in fairness, indulging in no irrelevant abuse of the man and making no charges extraneous to the case. You must all

139

be convinced that a vote for the acquittal of Leocrates is a vote for the conviction of the country; for in the life of nations subjugation is the death. Here stand the two urns; one for your undoing, one for your redemption: vote there for the disruption of the country, vote here for her security and prosperity. Think, men of Athens: the land and the trees are pleading, the harbors, the walls are entreating, the temples and shrines are in prayer. Save them. Make of Leocrates an example. One final declaration of my confidence: this pity that fills your hearts for the tears you look upon can never avail to pervert your loyalty to the law of the land, your devotion to the people of Athens.

AESCHINES

Aeschines, best known as an opponent of Demosthenes, was, in fact, a gallant solider, a man of much ability, and a really great orator. He was born in Attica, 389 b. c., five years before the birth of his famous rival, and died 314 b. c. His eloquence was of a high order, but his renown was tarnished by his defeat of Demosthenes in the contest on the proposition of Ctesiphon that Demosthenes should be awarded a golden crown for his patriotic services to the state. The speech delivered by Aeschines on that occasion was in many respects able, but he committed the grievous error of abusing his adversary and thus exposing his animosity.

Against Crowning Demosthenes. You see, Athenians, what preparations are on foot, what forces are arrayed, what appeals to the Assembly are being made by certain persons to prevent the proper and ordinary course of justice from having its effect in the city. For myself I came before you, first, with a firm belief in the immortal gods, next, with an abiding confidence in the laws and in you, convinced that intrigues will not more avail with you than these laws and the cause of justice.

I could indeed have fain desired that both in the Council of Five Hundred and in the Assembly the presiding officers had compelled conformity to established rules of debate, and that the laws had been enforced concerning the orderly deportment of public speakers which were laid down by Solon. It should thus have been permitted to the oldest citizens, as the laws prescribe, to ascend the platform decorously, and without tumult or annoyance, according to their experience, express their opinions upon what they regarded most advantageous to the city. Afterwards, each citizen in order of seniority should have in turn presented his independent views upon every question.

In this way it seems to me would the affairs of the city have been best conducted, and prosecutions have been reduced within the smallest compass. Since, however, the old recognized rules of procedure have been swept away, and certain men recklessly introduce illegal propositions, and certain others put them to the vote—men who have managed to secure the presidency, not by just and proper means, but taking possession of it by contrivance—it is brought to pass that if any other senator shall succeed in reaching the first place in due course of law and shall then attempt to obtain the result of your votes properly, such an one is denounced and impeached by the men who regard our government as no longer a common inheritance but as their own peculiar property. And when in this way, by reducing private citizens to servitude and by securing absolute power themselves, they have overthrown established legal judgments and have passed decrees according to the dictates of their passions, there shall be heard no longer that most beautiful and proper invitation of the herald, "Who desires to express his opinion, of citizens of fifty years of age and upwards, and afterwards, of all other in rotation?"

Thus neither the laws, nor the senators, nor the presidents, nor the presiding tribe itself a tenth part of the city, can control the indecent conduct of these orators.

Such being the case, and such the position in which the city is placed—and you must be convinced that this is so,—one part at least of the constitution, if I know anything of the matter, still survives—the right of prosecution for proposing unconstitutional measures. Should you destroy this right, or surrender it to those who will destroy it, I prophesy that you will have unconsciously given away to a few men almost our entire form of government. For you must surely know, Athenians, that but three forms of government exist, monarchy, oligarchy, and democracy: the two former are administered according to the feeling and opinions of those who are at the head of affairs, but republics repose upon the authority of law. Let no one of you, therefore, forget, but on the contrary let him lay it carefully to heart, that when he enters this tribunal for the trial of such an issue, on that day he is called upon to cast his vote upon his own right of free speech. Therefore was it that our old lawgivers placed in the forefront of the juror's oath these words, "I will render a verdict according to law," knowing well that when the laws were jealously observed by the city free institutions were safe.

Wherefore is it that, bearing these things in mind, you should hold in abhorrence all who commit unconstitutional acts, and that you should look upon no infraction of the constitution as small or unimportant, but treat all as of thegravest nature. Nor should you suffer any man to deprive you of this most vital right—neither the persuasions of the generals who for a long time past have been at work with certain of our orators to overthrow the constitution, nor the solicitations of strangers when those whose administration has been illegal have brought up hither to screen them from justice—but as each one of you would blush to quit the ranks in which he was stationed on

141

the day of battle, so you should now blush at the thought of abandoning the post in which you are placed by the laws which are today the guardians of our institutions.

You must further bear in mind that your fellow citizens have now entrusted to your keeping the city itself in thus confiding the constitution to your charge; not only those of them who are here present intent upon the course of this trial, but those also who are necessarily absent upon their private business. If, therefore, holding in due regard these your fellow citizens, and remembering the oaths you have sworn and the laws you are living under, you should convict Ctesiphon for having introduced an unconstitutional bill false in terms and injurious to the city, overturn, Athenians, such unconstitutional enactments, confirm our free institutions, and punish the men who have been advising against the law and against the interests both of the State and of yourselves. If in this frame of mind you listen to the words which are about to be spoken, I well know that your verdict will be in accordance with justice and right, and that it will redound to the credit of yourselves and of the whole community.

I have thus far spoken about the general nature of this prosecution, and, I hope, with sufficient fairness. I now desire to speak briefly about the laws which have been passed in regard to persons who are accountable to the state, against which the decree of Ctesiphon offends.

In former times it happened that men who had exercised the highest employment and had been entrusted with the management of the public revenues, although guilty therein of the grossest corruption, would, by conniving with certain orators both in the Senate and the General Assembly, anticipate all examination into their accounts by means of votes of condemnation and proclamations of thanks in their behalf. Not only were citizens who attempted to bring them to justice for the state of their accounts in this way much perplexed, but the jurors themselves who were to try the cause were reduced to a grave dilemma. And many of these officials, although clearly proved to have embezzled public moneys in the most flagrant way, were yet permitted to leave the judgment-seat unpunished. And not unreasonably. For the jurors were ashamed, it seems to me, that it should appear the same man in the same city, and perchance in the very same year, who had been proclaimed in the Assemblies as worthy of being honored with a golden crown by the people for his virtue and uprightness, should a short time afterwards be brought to trial, and go forth from our courts of justice convicted of fraud in his accounts. So that the jurors were compelled, as it were, to give their verdict not so much upon the crime which was proven, as in regard to the honor of the city itself. And hence it was that one of our lawgivers provided for this very emergency by propounding a law—and a most admirable one it was—by which the coronation of all persons liable to account was distinctly forbidden.

Notwithstanding the passage of this law, evasions of it more efficacious than the law itself have been invented, in ignorance of which, unless they be explained to you, you would be entirely deceived. This decree for the crowning of officials while they were still liable to account were introduced contrary to law by men not ill disposed by nature—if any one can be well-disposed whothus acts illegally—and by way of a slave to propriety they added to the propositions the words, "after they shall have rendered a correct account of their administration." The city, however, was injured in the same way by this evasion, since the accounting was equally forestalled by the panegyrics and votes of crowns; and the propounder of the decree, by thus qualifying it, admitted to his discredit that at the time of its proposal he was conscious of an intended infraction of the law. But this fellow Ctesiphon, men of Athens, at one bound clears both law and qualification; for by his decree he asks that Demosthenes, while actually in office, before he has furnished any explanations or delivered in any accounts, shall be crowned by the people! . . .

You have just heard, Athenians, that the law directs the proclamation of one who is crowned by the people to be made in the Pnyx at an Assembly of the people, and nowhere else. Ctesiphon, however, not only transgresses the law by directing it to be done in the theatre, thus changing the place from that where the Athenians hold their Assembly, but he commands it to take place, not before the people alone, but in presence of the assembled Greeks, that they may see along with us what manner of man it is whom we then honor. . . .

Since, then, it is directed that those honored with a crown by the Senate shall be proclaimed in the Senate Chamber, and those crowned by the people in the Assembly, and it is interdicted to those crowned by the tribes or demes to be so proclaimed in the theatre, that no one by mean solicitations for crowns and proclamations should thereby obtain a spurious honor, and it is moreover forbidden by the law that proclamation shall be made by any one unless by the Senate, the people, the tribes, and the demes; if all these be excepted, what remains but the case of crowns conferred by foreignstates? That this is manifestly so, I shall convince you by the laws themselves. . . .

Besides it is enjoined by law that the crown of gold which shall be proclaimed in the theatre in behalf of any one shall be taken from him and consecrated to Athens. Who would dare, however, from this, to accuse the people of Athens of a sordid economy? Never was there a city, never an individual, so destitute of generosity, as in the same moment to proclaim, take away, and consecrate a crown of their own bestowal! This consecration is doubtless directed to be made because the crown has been conferred by strangers, that no man may estimate a foreign honor as of greater value than his country, and may not be tempted in consequence to fail in his devotion to her. The crown conferred by the people and proclaimed in the Assembly is never consecrated, but on the contrary is permitted to be enjoyed, not only by its recipient, but by his descendants, that by preserving this memorial in their family they may never become ill-disposed to their country. And this is the reason why the lawmaker has prohibited the proclamation in the theatre of a crown conferred by strangers unless authorized by a decree of the people; the foreign city which may desire so to honor one of your citizens shall first through an embassy demand it of the people; and thus he who is crowned shall owe higher debt of gratitude to you who have permitted the proclamation than to those who have presented him with the crown itself. . . .

I may here foretell the part that he will play when he sees that you are in earnest in your endeavor to hold him to his true course. Ctesiphon will introduce that arch-impostor, that plunderer of the public, who has cut the constitution into shreds; the man who can weep more easily than others laugh, and from whom perjury flows in ready words!

He can, I doubt not, change his tone, and pass from tears to gross abuse, insult the citizens who are listening outside, and cry out that the partisans of oligarchical power, detested by the hand of truth, are pressing round the prosecutor to support him, while the friends of the constitution are rallying round the accused. And when he dares to speak so, answer thus his seditious menaces: "What, Demosthenes, had the heroes who brought back our fugitive citizens from Phyle been like you, our democratic form of government had ceased to exist! Those illustrious men saved the state exhausted by great civil disorders in pronouncing that wise and admirable sentence 'oblivion of all offenses.' But you, more careful of your rounded periods than of the city's safety, are willing to reopen all her wounds."

When this perjurer shall seek for credit by taking refuge in his oaths, remind him that to the foresworn man who asks belief in them from those he has deceived so often, of two things one is needful, neither of which exists for Demosthenes; he must either get new gods, or an audience not the same. And to his tears and wordy lamentations, when he shall ask, "Whither shall I fly, Athenians should you cast me out, I have not where to rest," reply "Where shall the people seek refuge, Demosthenes; what allies, what resources, what reserve have you prepared for us? We all see what you have provided for yourself. When you have left the city, you shall not stop, as you would seem, to dwell in Piraeus, but, quickly thence departing, you shall visit other lands with all the appointments for your journey provided through your corruption from Persian gold or public plunder."

But why at all these tears, these cries, this voice of lamentation? Is it not Ctesiphon who is accused, and even for him may not the penalty be moderated by you? Thou pleadest not, Demosthenes, either for thy life, thy fortune, or thy honor! Why is he then so disquieted? About crowns of gold and proclamations in the theatre against the

144

laws: the man who, were the people so insensate or so forgetful of the present as to wish to crown him in this time of public distress, should himself step forth and say, "Men of Athens, while I accept the crown, I disapprove the proclamation of the honor at a time like this: it should not be in regard to things for which the state is now mourning and while it is in the depth of grief." Would not a man whose life was really upright so speak out; only a knave who assumes the garb of virtue would talk as you do?

Let none of you, by Hercules, be apprehensive lest this high-souled citizen, this distinguished warrior, from loss of this reward should on his return home take his life. The man who rates so low your consideration as to make a thousand incisions on that impure and mortgaged head which Ctesiphon proposes against all law to honor with a crown, makes money of his wounds by bringing actions for the effects of his own premeditated blows. Yes, that crown of his so often battered, that perhaps even now it bears upon it the marks of Meidias' anger, that crown which brings its owner in an income, serves both for revenue and head! . . .

And can it be that he whom you have thought worthy by your decree, of the honor of this crown, is so unknown to the public which has been so largely benefited by him that you must procure assistance to speak in his behalf? Ask of the jurors whether they know Chabrias, Iphicrates and Timotheus, and learn from them why they have honored and erected statues to them? Will they not proclaim with one voice that they rendered honor to Chabrias for his naval victory near Naxos; to Iphicrates for having cut off a Spartan corps; to Timotheus for his expedition to Corcyra; to other heroes for their many glorious achievements? Ask them now why Demosthenes is to be rewarded. Is it for hisvenality, for his cowardice, for his base desertion of his post in the day of battle? In honoring such an one will you not dishonor yourselves and the gallant men who have laid down their lives for you in the field? whose plaintive remonstrances against the crowing of this man you may almost seem to hear. Strange, passing strange, does it seem, Athenians, that you banish from the limits of the state the stocks and stones the senseless implements which have unwittingly caused death by casualty; that the hand which has inflicted the wound of self-destruction is buried apart from the rest of the body; and that yet you can render honor to this Demosthenes, by whose counsels this last fatal expedition in which your troops were slaughtered and destroyed was planned! The victims of this massacre are thus insulted, in their graves, and the survivors outraged and discouraged when they behold the only reward of patriotic valor to be an unremembered death and a disregarded memory! And last and most important of all consequences, what answer shall you make to your children when they ask you after what examples they shall frame their lives? Is it not, men of Athens— you know it well—is it not the palaestra, the seminary, or the study of the liberal arts alone, which form and educate our youth. Of vastly greater value are the lessons taught by these honors publicly conferred. If a man proclaimed and crowned in the theatre for virtue, courage, and patriotism when his irregular and vicious life belies the honor, the young who witness this are perverted and corrupted! In a profligate and a pander, such as Ctesiphon, sentenced and punished, an instructive lesson is given to the rising generation. Has a citizen voted in opposition to justice and propriety, and does he, on his return to his house, attempt to instruct his son; disobedience surely follows, and the lesson is justly looked upon as importunate and out of place. Pronounce your verdict then, not as simplejurors, but as guardians of the State, whose decision can be justified in the eyes of their absent fellow citizens who shall demand a strict account of it. Know ye not, Athenians, that the people is judged by the ministers whom it honors; will it not be disgraceful, then, that you shall be thought to resemble the baseness of Demosthenes, and not the virtues of your ancestors?

How, then, is this reproach to be avoided? It must be to distrusting the men who usurp the character of upright and patriotic citizens, which their entire conduct gainsays. Good will and zeal for the public interest can be readily assumed in name: oftentimes those who have the smallest pretensions to them by their conduct seize upon and take refuge behind these honorable titles. When you find, then, an orator desirous of being crowned by strangers and of being proclaimed in presence of the Greeks, let him, as the law requires in other cases, prove the claim which he asserts by the evidence of a life free from reproach, and a wise and blameless course. If he be unable to do this, do not confirm to him the honors which he claims, and try at least to preserve the remnant of that public authority which is fast escaping from you. Even now, strange as it should seem, are not the Senate and the people passed over and neglected, and despatches and deputations received by private citizens, not from obscure individuals, but from the most important personages of Europe and Asia? Far from denying that for which under our laws the punishment is death, it is made the subject of open public boast; the correspondence is exhibited and read; and you are invited by some to look upon them as the guardians of the constitution, while others demand to be rewarded as the saviors of the country. The people, meanwhile, as if struck with the decrepitude of age and broken down by their misfortunes, preserve the republic only in name and abandon to others the reality of authority. You thus retire from the Assembly, not as from a public deliberation, but as from an entertainment given at common cost where each guest carries away with him a share of the remnants of the feast. That I speak forth the words of truth and soberness, hearken to which I am about to say.

It distresses me to recur so often to our public calamities, but when a private citizen undertook to sail only to Samos to get out of the way, he was condemned to death on the same day by the Council of

Areopagus as a traitor to his country. Another private citizen, unable to bear the fear which oppressed him, and sailing in consequence to Rhodes, was recently denounced for this and escaped punishment by an equal division of the votes. Had a single one been cast on the other side, he would have been either banished or put to death. Compare these instances with the present one. An orator, the cause of all our misfortunes, who abandons his post in time of war and flies from the city, proclaims himself worthy of crowns and proclamations. Will you not drive such a man from your midst as the common scourge of Greece; or will you not rather seize upon and punish him as a piratical braggart who steers his course through our government by dint of phrases?

Consider, moreover, the occasion on which you are called upon to record your verdict. In a few days the Pythian Games will be celebrated, and the assembled Greeks will all be reunited in your city. She has already suffered much disparagement from the policy of Demosthenes: should you now crown him by your votes you will seem to share the same opinion as the men who wish to break the common peace. By adopting the contrary course you will free the state from any such suspicion.

Let your deliberations, then, be in accord with the interests of the city: it is for her, and not a foreign community, you are now to decide. Do not throw away your honors, but confer them with discernment upon high-minded citizens and deserving men. Search with both eyes and ears as to who they are among you who are today standing forth in Demosthenes' behalf. Are they the companions of his youth who shared with him the manly toils of the chase or the robust exercises of the palaestra? No, by the Olympian Jove, he has passed not his life in hunting the wild boar or in the preparation of his body for fatigue and hardship, but in the exercise of chicane at the cost of the substance of men of wealth!

Examine well his vainglorious boasting when he shall dare to say that by his embassy he withdrew the Byzantines from the cause of Philip; that by his eloquence he detached from him the Acarnanians, and so transported the Thebans as to confirm them upon your side. He believes indeed that you have reached such a point of credulity that you are ready to be persuaded by him of anything he may choose to utter, as if you had here in your midst the goddess Persuasion herself, and not an artful demagogue.

And when, at the close of his harangue, Demosthenes shall invite the partakers of his corruption to press round and defend him, let there be present in your imagination upon the platform from which I am now speaking the venerable forms of the ancient benefactors of the state, arrayed in all their virtue, to oppose these men's insolence. I see among them the wise Solon, that upright lawgiver who founded our popular government upon the soundest principles of legislation, gently advising

147

you with his native moderation not to place your oaths and the law under the control of this man's discourse. And Aristides, by whose equity the imposts upon the Greeks were regulated, whose daughters, left in poverty through his incorruptible integrity, were endowed by the state, Aristides is seen complaining of this outrage upon justice, and demanding whether the descendantsof the men who fought worthy of death and actually banished from their city and country Arthmius the Zelian, then living in their midst and enjoying the sacred rights of hospitality for merely bringing Persian gold into Greece, are now going to cover themselves with disgrace by honoring with a crown of gold the man who has not simply brought higher the stranger's money, but is enjoying here the price of his treason. And Themistocles and the men who fell at Marathon and Plataea, think you that they are insensible to what is taking place? Do not their voices cry out from the very tombs in mournful protests against this perverse rendering of honor to one who has dared to proclaim his union with the barbarians against the Greeks?

As for me, O Earth and Sun, O Virtue, and thou, Intelligence, by whose light we are enabled to discern and to separate good from evil, as for me, I have directed my efforts against this wrong. I have lifted up my voice against this injustice! If I have spoken well and loftily against this crime, I have spoken as I should have wished; but if my utterances have been feeble and ill-directed, still they have been according to the measure of my strength. It is for you, men of Athens and jurors, to weigh carefully both what has been spoken and what has been left unsaid, and to render such a decision as shall not only be upright but for the advantage of the State.

DEMOSTHENES

Demosthenes, considered the greatest of the Greek orators, and consequently the greatest orator in the history of the world, as oratory flourished nowhere as it did in Greece between 500 and 300 b. c., was born about 383 b. c., and died by poison administered to himself, after being captured by Macedonian troops, 322 b. c.

"He [Demosthenes] seems to have lacked by nature all the physical qualifications of a great orator, and to have acquired them solely by indefatigable self-discipline and training. At about the age of thirty he made his first appearance as a politician; he continued to practice as a logographer (speech-writer) until he was about forty, by which time he had made a fortune sufficient to enable him to devote himself exclusively to political life until he died, at the age of sixty-one."

Demosthenes studied under Isaeus and profited by the work previously done by the great rhetoricians and orators, Lysias, Isocrates,

Antiphon, and others. Demosthenes' political morality was of the highest, and this was one of the main sources of his great strength.

Speech of Demosthenes in Defense of Ctesiphon, Commonly known as the "Oration on the Crown." I begin, men of Athens, by praying to every god and goddess that the same good-will, which I have ever cherished toward the commonwealth and all of you, may be requited to me on the present trial. I pray likewise—and this specially concerns yourselves, your religion, and your honor—that the gods may put it in your minds not to take counsel of my opponent touching the manner in which I am to be heard—that would, indeed, be cruel!—but of the laws and of your oath; wherein (besides the other obligations) it is prescribed that you shall hear both sides alike. This means, not only that you must pass no precondemnation, not only that you must extend your good-will equally to both, but also that you must allow the parties to adopt such order and course of defense as they severally choose and prefer.

Many advantages hath Aeschines over me on this trial; and two especially, men of Athens. First, my risk in the contest is not the same. It is assuredly not the same for me to forfeit your regard, as for my adversary not to succeed in his indictment. To me—but I will say nothing untoward at the outset of my address. The prosecution, however, is play to him. My second disadvantage is, that natural disposition of mankind to take pleasure in hearing invective and accusation, and to be annoyed by those who praise themselves. To Aeschines is assigned the part which gives pleasure; that which is (I may fairly say) offensive to all, is left for me. And if, to escape from this, I make no mention of what I have done, I shall appear to be without defense against his charges, without proof of my claims to honor; whereas, if I proceed to give an account of my conduct and measures, I shall be forced to speak frequently of myself. I will endeavor then to do so with all becoming modesty; what I am driven to by the necessity of the case will be fairly chargeable to my opponent, who has instituted such a prosecution.

I think, men of the jury, you will all agree that I, as well as Ctesiphon, am a party to this proceeding, and that it is a matter of no less concern to me. It is painful and grievous to be deprived of anything, especially by the act of one's enemy; but your good-will and affection are the heaviest loss, precisely as they are the greatest prize to gain.

Such being the matters at stake in this cause, I conjure and implore you all alike, to hear my defense to the charge in that fair manner which the laws prescribe—laws, to which their author, Solon, a man friendly to you and to popular rights, thought that validity should be given, not only by the recording of them, but by the oath of you, the jurors; not that he distrusted you, as it appears to me, but, seeing that the charges and calumnies, wherein the prosecutor is powerful by being the first speaker, cannot be gotover by the defendant, unless each of you jurors, observing his religious obligation, shall work with like favor receive the arguments of the last speaker, and lend an equal and impartial ear to both, before he determines upon the whole case.

As I am, it appears, on this day to render an account both of my private life and my public measures, I would fain, as in the outset, call upon the gods to my aid; and in your presence I implore them, first, that the good-will which I have ever cherished toward the commonwealth and all of you may be fully requited to me on the present trial; next, that they may direct you to such a decision upon this indictment as will conduce to your common honor, and to the good conscience of each individual.

Had Aeschines confined his charge to the subject of the prosecution, I, too, would have proceeded at once to my justification of the decree. But since he has wasted now fewer words in the discussion of other matters, in most of them calumniating me, I deem it both necessary and just, men of Athens, to begin by shortly adverting to these points, that none of you may be induced by extraneous arguments to shut your ears against my defense of the indictment.

To all his scandalous abuse of my private life, observe my plain and honest answer. If you know me to be such as he alleged—for I have lived nowhere else but among you—let not my voice be heard, however transcendent my statesmanship! Rise up this instant and condemn me! But if, in your opinion and judgment, I am far better and of better descent than my adversary; if (to speak without offense) I am not inferior, I or mine, to any respectable citizens; that give no credit to him for his other statements—it is plain they were all equally fictions— but to me let the same good-will, which you have uniformly exhibited upon many former trials, be manifested now. With all your malice, Aeschines, it was very simple to suppose that I shouldturn from the discussion of measures and policy to notice your scandal. I will do no such thing; I am not so crazed. Your lies and calumnies about my political life I will examine forthwith; for that loose ribaldry I shall have a word hereafter, if the jury desire to hear it.

The crimes whereof I am accused are many and grievous; for some of them the laws enact heavy—most severe penalties. The scheme of this present proceeding includes a combination of spiteful insolence, insult, railing, aspersion, and everything of the kind; while for the said charges and accusations, if they were true, the state has not the means of inflicting an adequate punishment, or anything like it. For it is not the right to debar another of access to the people and privilege of speech; moreover, to do so by way of malice and insult—by Heaven! is neither honest, nor constitutional, nor just. If the crimes which he saw me committing against the State were as heinous as he so tragically gave out, he ought to have enforced the penalties of the law against them at the time; if he saw me guilty of an impeachable offense, by impeaching and so bringing me to trial before you; if moving illegal decrees, by indicting me for them. For surely if he can prosecute Ctesiphon on my account, he would not have forborne to indict me myself, had he thought he could convict me. In short, whatever else he saw me doing to your prejudice, whether mentioned or not mentioned in his catalogue of slander, there are laws for such things, and punishments, and trials, and judgments, with sharp and severe penalties; all of which he might have enforced against me: and had he done so—had he thus pursued the proper method with me, his charges would have been consistent with his conduct. But now he has declined the straightforward and just course, avoided all proofs of guilt at the time, and after this long interval gets up, to play his part withal, a heap of accusation, ribaldry, and scandal. Then he arraignsme, but prosecutes the defendant. His hatred of me he makes the prominent part of the whole contest; yet, without having ever met me upon that ground, he openly seeks to deprive a third party of his privileges. Now, men of Athens, besides all the other arguments that may be urged in Ctesiphon's behalf, this, methinks, may very fairly be alleged—that we should all try our own quarrel by ourselves; not leave our private dispute, and look what third party we can damage. That surely were the height of injustice.

It may appear, from what has been said, that all his charges are alike unjust and unfounded in truth; yet I wish to examine them separately, and especially his calumnies about the peace and the embassy, where he attributed to me the acts of himself and Philocrates. It is necessary also, and perhaps proper, men of Athens, to remind you how affairs stood at those times, that you may consider every single measure in reference to the occasion.

When the Phocian war had broken out—not through me, for I had not then commenced public life—you were in this position: you wished the Phocians to be saved, though you saw they were not acting right; and would have been glad for the Thebans to suffer anything, with whom for a just reason you were angry; for they had not borne with moderation their good fortune at Leuctra. The whole of Peloponnesus was divided: they that hated the Lacedaemonians were not powerful enough to destroy them; and they that ruled before by Spartan influence were not masters of the states: among them, as among the rest of the Greeks, there was a sort of unsettled strife and confusion. Philip, seeing this—it was not difficult to see—lavished bribes upon the traitors in every state, embroiled and stirred them all up against each other; and so, by the errors and follies of the rest, he was strengthening himself, and growing up to the ruin of all. But when every one saw that the then overbearing,but now unfortunate, Thebans, harassed by so long a war, must of necessity have recourse to you, Philip, to prevent this, and obstruct the union of the states, offered to you peace, to them succor. What helped him then almost to surprise you in a voluntary snare? The cowardice, shall I call it? or ignorance—or both—of the other Greeks, who while you were waging a long and incessant war—and that, too, for their common benefit, as the event has shown—assisted you neither with money nor men, nor anything else whatsoever. You, being justly and naturally offended with them, lent a willing ear to Philip.

The peace then granted was through such means brought about, not through me, as Aeschines calumniously charged. The criminal and corrupt practice of these men during the treaty will be found, on fair examination, to be the cause of our present condition. The whole matter am I for truth's sake discussing and going through; for, let there appear to be ever so much criminality in these transactions, it is surely nothing to me. The first who spoke and mentioned the subject of peace was Aristodemus the actor; the seconder and mover, fellow-hireling for that purpose with the prosecutor, was Philocrates the Agnusian—your associate, Aeschines, not mine, though you should burst with lying. Their supporters—from whatever motives—I pass that by for the present—were Eubulus and Cephisophon. I had nothing to do with it.

Notwithstanding these facts, which I have stated exactly according to the truth, he ventured to assert—to such a pitch of impudence had he come—that I, besides being author of the peace, had prevented the country making it in a general council with the Greeks. Why, you—I know not what name you deserve!—when you saw me robbing the state of an advantage and connection so important as you described just now, did you ever express indignation? did you come forwardto punish and proclaim what you now charge me with? If, indeed, I had been bribed by Philip to prevent the conjunction of the Greeks, it was your business not to be silent, but to cry out, to protest, and inform the people. But you never did so—your voice was never heard to such a purpose, and no wonder; for at that time no embassy had been sent to any of the Greeks—they had all been tested long before; and not a word of truth upon the subject has Aeschines spoken.

Besides, it is the country that he most traduces by his falsehoods. For, if you were at the same time calling on the Greeks to take arms and sending your own ambassadors to treat with Philip for peace, you were performing the part of an Eurybatus, not the act of a commonwealth, or of honest men. But it is false, it is false. For what purpose could ye have sent for them at that period? For peace? They all had it. For war? You were yourselves deliberating about peace. It appears, therefore, I was not the adviser or the author of the original peace; and none of his other calumnies against me are shown to be true.

Observe again, after the state had concluded the peace, what line of conduct each of us adopted. Hence you will understand who it was that coöperated in everything with Philip, who that acted in your behalf, and sought the advantage of the commonwealth.

I moved in the council, that our ambassadors should sail

instantly for whatever place they heard Philip was in, and receive his oath: they would not, however, notwithstanding my resolution. What was the effect of this, men of Athens? I will explain. It was Philip's interest that the interval before the oaths should be as long as possible; yours, that it should be as short. Why? Because you discontinued all your warlike preparations, not only from the day of swearing peace, but from the day you conceived hopes of it; a thing which Philip was from the beginning studious to contrive, believing—rightly enough—that whatever of your possessions he might take before the oath of ratification he should hold securely; as none would break the peace on such account. I, men of Athens, foreseeing and weighing these consequences, moved the decree, to sail for whatever place Philip was in, and receive his oath without delay; so that your allies, the Thracians, might be in possession of the places which Aeschines ridiculed just now (Serrium, Myrtium, and Ergisce), at the time of swearing the oaths; and that Philip might not become master of Thrace by securing the post of vantage, nor provide himself with plenty of money and troops to facilitate his further designs. Yet this decree he neither mentions nor reads; but reproaches me, because, as Councillor, I thought it proper to introduce the ambassadors. Why, what should I have done? Moved not to introduce men who were come for the purpose of conferring with you? or ordered the Manager not to assign them places at the theatre? They might have had places for their two obols, if the resolution had not been moved. Was it my duty to guard the petty interests of the state, and have sold our main interests like these men? Surely not. Take and read me this decree, which the prosecutor, knowing it well, passed over. Read!

THE DECREE

"In the Archonship of Mnesiphilus, on the thirteenth of Hecatombaeon, in the presidency of the Pandionian tribe, Demosthenes, son of Demosthenes of Paeania, moved: Whereas, Philip hath sent ambassadors for peace, and hath agreed upon articles of treaty, it is resolved by the Council and people of Athens, in order that the peace voted in the first assembly may be ratified, to choose forthwith from the whole body of Athenians five ambassadors; and that the persons elected do repair, without any delay, wheresoever they shall ascertain that Philip is, and as speedily as may be exchange oaths with him, according to the articles agreed on between him and the Athenian people, comprehending the allies of either party. For ambassadors were chosen, Eubulus of Anaphlystus, Aeschines of Cothocidae, Cephisophon of Rhamnus, Democrates of Phyla, Cleon of Cothocidae."

Notwithstanding that I had passed this decree for the advantage

153

of Athens, not that of Philip, our worthy ambassadors so little regarded it as to sit down in Macedonia three whole months, until Philip returned from Thrace after entirely subjugating the country; although they might in ten days, or rather in three or four, have reached the Hellespont and saved the fortresses, by receiving his oath before he reduced them: for he would never have touched them on our presence, or we should not have sworn him; and thus he would have lost the peace, and not have obtained both the peace and the fortresses.

Such was the first trick of Philip, the first corrupt act of these accursed miscreants, in the embassy: for which I avow that I was and am and ever will be at war and variance with them. But mark another and still greater piece of villainy immediately after. When Philip had sworn to the peace, having secured Thrace through these men disobeying my decree, he again bribes them not to leave Macedonia until he had got all ready for his expedition against the Phocians. His fear was, if they reported to you his design and preparation for marching, you might sally forth, sail round with your galleys to Thermopylae as before, and block up the strait; his desire, that, the moment you received the intelligence from them, he should have passed Thermopylae, and you be unable to do anything. And in such terror and anxiety was Philip, lest, notwithstanding he had gained these advantages, if you voted succor before the destruction of thePhocians, his enterprise should fail, he hires this despicable fellow, no longer in common with the other ambassadors, but by himself individually, to make that statement and report to you, by which everything was lost.

I conjure and beseech you, men of Athens, throughout the trial to remember this: that, if Aeschines in his charge had not travelled out of the indictment, neither would I have spoken a word irrelevant; but since he has resorted to every species both of accusation and calumny, it is necessary for me to reply briefly to each of his charges.

What, then, were the statements made by Aeschines, through which everything was lost? That you should not be alarmed by Philip's having passed Thermopylae—that all would be as you desired, if you kept quiet; and in two or three days you would hear he as their friend to whom he had come as an enemy, and their enemy to whom he had come as a friend—it was not words that cemented attachments (such was his solemn phrase), but identity of interest; and it was the interest of all alike, Philip, the Phocians, and you, to be relieved from the harshness and insolence of the Thebans. His assertions were heard by some with pleasure, on account of the hatred which then subsisted against the Thebans. But what happened directly, almost immediately, afterwards? The wretched Phocians were destroyed, their cities demolished; you that kept quiet, and trusted to Aeschines, were shortly bringing in your effects out of the country, while Aeschines received gold; and yet more—while you got nothing but your enmity with the

Thebans and Thessalians, Philip won their gratitude for what he had done. To prove what I say, read me the decree of Callisthenes, and the letter of Philip, from both of which these particulars will be clear to you.

These and like measures, Aeschines, are what become anhonorable citizen (by their success—O earth and heaven! we should have been the greatest of people incontestably, and deserved to be so: even under their failure the result is glory, and no one blames Athens or her policy; all condemn fortune that so ordered things); but never will he desert the interests of the commonwealth, nor hire himself to her adversaries, and study the enemy's advantage, instead of his country's; nor on a man who has courage to advise and propose measures worthy of the state, and resolution to persevere in them, will he cast an evil eye, and, if any one privately offends him, remember and treasure it up; no, nor keep himself in a criminal and treacherous retirement, as you so often do. There is indeed a retirement just and beneficial to the state, such as you, the bulk of my countrymen, innocently enjoy; that, however, is not the retirement of Aeschines; far from it. Withdrawing himself from public life when he pleases (and that is often), he watches for the moment when you are tired of a constant speaker, or when some reverse of fortune has befallen you, or anything untoward has happened (and many are the casualties of human life); at such a crisis he springs up an orator, rising from his retreat like a wind; in full voice, with words and phrases collected, he rolls them out audibly and breathlessly, to no advantage or good purpose whatsoever, but to the detriment of some or other of his fellow-citizens and to the general disgrace.

Yet from this labor and diligence, Aeschines, if it proceeded from an honest heart, solicitous for your country's welfare, the fruits should have been rich and noble and profitable to all—alliances of states, supplies of money, conveniences of commerce, enactment of useful laws, opposition to our declared enemies. All such things were looked for in former times; and many opportunities did the past afford for a good man and true to show himself; during which timeyou are nowhere to be found, neither first, second, third, fourth, fifth, nor sixth—nor in any rank at all—certainly in no service by which your country was exalted. For what alliance has come to the state by your procurement? What succors, what acquisition of good will or credit? What embassy or agency is there of yours, by which the reputation of the country has been increased? What concern, domestic, Hellenic, or foreign, of which you have had the management, has improved under it? What galleys? what ammunition? what arsenals? what repair of walls? what cavalry? What in the world are you good for? What assistance in money have you ever given, either to the rich or the poor, out of public spirit or liberality? None. But, good sir, if there is nothing of this, there is at all events zeal and loyalty. Where? when? You infamous fellow! Even at a

155

time when all who ever spoke upon the platform gave something for the public safety, and last Aristonicus gave the sum which he had amassed to retrieve his franchise, you neither came forward nor contributed a mite—not from inability—no! for you have inherited above five talents from Philo, your wife's father, and you had a subscription of two talents from the chairmen of the Boards for what you did to cut up the navy law. But, that I may not go from one thing to another and lose sight of the question, I pass this by. That it was not poverty prevented your contributing, already appears: it was, in fact, your anxiety to do nothing against those to whom your political life is subservient. On what occasion, then, do you show your spirit? When do you shine out? When aught is to be spoken against your countrymen!—then it is you are splendid in voice, perfect in memory, an admirable actor, a tragic Theocrines.

You mention the good men of olden times; and you are right to do so. Yet it is hardly fair, O Athenians, that he should get the advantage of that respect which you have forthe dead, to compare and contrast me with them—me who am living among you; for what mortal is ignorant that toward the living there exists always more or less of ill will, whereas the dead are no longer hated even by an enemy? Such being human nature, am I to be tried and judged by the standard of my predecessors? Heaven forbid! It is not just or equitable, Aeschines. Let me be compared with you, or any persons you like of your party who are still alive. And consider this—whether it is more honorable and better for the state, that because of the services of a former age, prodigious though they are beyond all power of expression, these of the present generation should be unrequited and spurned, or that all who give proof of their good intentions should have their share of honor and regard from the people? Yet indeed—if I must say so much—my politics and principles, if considered fairly, will be found to resemble those of the illustrious ancients, and to have had the same objects in view, while yours resemble those of their calumniators: for it is certain there were persons in those times who ran down the living, and praised people dead and gone, with a malignant purpose like yourself.

Two things, men of Athens, are characteristic of a well-disposed citizen: so may I speak of myself and give the least offense: In authority, his constant aim should be the dignity and pre-eminence of the commonwealth; in all times and circumstances his spirit should be loyal. This depends upon nature; power and might upon other things. Such a spirit, you will find, I have ever sincerely cherished. Only see, when my person was demanded—when they brought Amphictyonic suits against me—when they menaced—when they promised—when they set these miscreants like wild beasts upon me—never in any way have I abandoned my affection for you. From the very beginning I chose an honest and straightforward course in politics, to support thehonor, the power, the glory of my fatherland, these to exalt, in these

156

to have my being. I do not walk about the market place gay and cheerful because the stranger has prospered, holding out my right hand and congratulating those who I think will report it yonder, and on any news of our own success shudder and groan and stoop to the earth, like these impious men, who rail at Athens, as if in so doing they did not rail at themselves; who look abroad, and if the foreigner thrives by the distress of Greece, are thankful for it, and say we should keep him so thriving all the time.

Never, O ye gods, may those wishes be confirmed by you! If possible, inspire even in these men a better sense and feeling! But if they are indeed incurable, destroy them by themselves; exterminate them on land and sea; and for the rest of us, grant that we may speedily be released from our present fears, and enjoy a lasting deliverance.

CHAPTER VIII

THE LATIN ORATORS

THEIR STYLE AND MEANS

The Latin temperament being practical, whereas the Grecian was highly imaginative, it was a long time before Roman oratory escaped from the hardness of competition and delivery that pervaded it for many centuries, and it was not until the conquest of Greece that the classic style of oratory made its deep impress upon the work of the Roman orators.

The elder Cato was austere in matter and manner, and the younger Cato, dying 103 years after the death of his great-grandfather, inherited many of his characteristics, and although his oratory displayed candor, truth, and courage, it lacked the finish, smoothness, and grace of the Grecian school, which qualities were, to a great extent, possessed by Cicero, Caesar, Crassus, and Marc Antony. Caius Gracchus and his brother Tiberius had a marked influence upon the Roman style of oratory by softening and smoothing it, but this influence was not strongly felt until the coming of Cicero, and that marvellous group of statesmen, politicians, and orators which embraced Pompey, Crassus, Caesar, Cato, Antonius (Marc Antony), andHortensius. The Latin oratory had been candid but hard, and lacked all the grace that made the Grecian oratory so bewitching; but Cicero, by combining the candor of the Roman style with the beauty of the Grecian, produced a form of oratory that has not been surpassed by any other orator.

Crassus was undoubtedly an orator of the first rank. Plutarch said of him: "As for learning, he chiefly cared for rhetoric, and what would be serviceable with large numbers; he became one of the best speakers at Rome, and by his pains and industry outdid the best natural orators." Little of his matter has come down to us.

Julius Caesar, among his other powers, possessed that of oratory, and were it not for his transcendent abilities as a solider, which overshadowed his other talents, his oratorical ability would have insured him a place in history.

Marc Antony was another great orator of the Ciceronian period, but nothing very authentic of his has come down to us. Shakespeare was indebted to Plutarch for his idea of the oration over the body of Caesar, and this matchless oration no doubt gives us a just conception of Antony's style. History tells us that Antony possessed almost unnatural influence over his soldiers through his eloquence, and that when they were discouraged over long marches, hardships, and privations, he would go the rounds of his encampment, addressing his troops; that he would so enthuse them that they would forget their fears and miseries, and rush with him to victory. The speechdelivered over the body of Caesar by Marc Antony is reported by Dion Cassius in his History of Rome, but how much of it was spoken by Antony is problematical.

The selections here given will convey a clear and comprehensive idea of the scope and style of Roman oratory in its palmiest days.

CATO THE CENSOR

Marcus Porcius Cato, surnamed Censorius, or Major, Roman statesman, general, and orator, bas born at Tusculum, 234 b. c., and died in 149 b. c. He was scrupulously honest himself, and demanded honesty in all who would serve the state. He opposed the influence of Greek civilization over the Romans, and conceived it to be his duty to prevent new ideas being taught to the younger men of his generation. He was a maintainer of primitive discipline, and it was for this reason he gained the title of the Censor. The speech here given displays his character and style to perfection. It was delivered in the Roman Forum in 215 b. c.

Speech in Support of the Oppian Law. If, Romans, every individual among us had made it a rule to maintain the prerogative and authority of a hundred with respect to his own wife, we should have less trouble with the whole sex. But now our privileges, overpowered at home by female contumacy, are, even here in the Forum, spurned and trodden under foot; and because we are unable to withstand each separately, we now dread their collective body. I was accustomed to think it a fabulous and fictitious tale that in a certain island the whole race of males was utterly extirpated by a conspiracy of the women.

But the utmost danger may be apprehended equally from either sex if you suffer cabals and secret consultations to be held: scarcely indeed can I determine, in my own mind, whether the act itself, or the precedent that it affords, is of more pernicious tendency. The latter of these more particularly concerns us consuls and the other magistrates; the former, you, my fellow-citizens: for, whether the measure proposed to your consideration be profitable to the state or not, is to be determined by you, who are to vote on the occasion.

As to the outrageous behavior of these women, whether it be merely an act of their own, or owing to your instigations, Marcus Fundanius and Lucius Valerius, it unquestionably implies culpable conduct in magistrates. I know not whether it reflects greater disgrace on you, tribunes, or on the consul: on you certainly, if you have brought these women hither for the purpose of raising tribunician seditions; on

159

us, if we suffer laws to be imposed on us by a secession of women, as was done formerly by that of the common people. It was not without painful emotions of shame that I, just now, made my way into the Forum through the midst of a band of women.

Had I not been restrained by respect for the modesty and dignity of some individuals among them, rather than of the whole number, and been unwilling that they should be seen rebuked by a consul, I should not have refrained from saying to them, "What sort of practice is this, of running out into the public, besetting the streets, and addressing other women's husbands? Could not each have made the same request to her husband at home? Are your blandishments more seducing in public than in private, and with other women's husbands than with your own? Although if females would let their modesty confine them within the limits of their own right, it did not become you, even at home, to concern yourselves about any laws that might be passed or repealed here." Our ancestors thought it not proper that women should perform any, even private, business, without a director, but that they should be ever under the control of parents, brothers, or husbands. We, it seems, suffer them, now, to interfere in the management of state affairs, and to thrust themselves into the Forum, into general assemblies, and into assemblies of election: for what are they doing at this moment in your streets and lanes? What, but arguing, some in support of the motion of tribunes; others contending for the repeal of the law?

Will you give the reins to their intractable nature, and then expect that themselves should set bounds to their licentiousness, and without your interference? This is the smallest of the injunctions laid on them by usage or the laws, all of which women bear with impatience: they long for entire liberty; nay, to speak the truth, not for liberty, but for unbounded freedom in every particular: for what will they not attempt if they now come off victorious? Recollect all the institutions respecting the sex, by which our forefathers restrained their profligacy and subjected them to their husbands; and yet, even with the help of all these restrictions, they can scarcely be kept within bounds. If, then, you suffer them to throw these off one by one, to tear them all asunder, and, at last, to be set on an equal footing with yourselves, can you imagine that they will be any longer tolerable? Suffer them once to arrive at an equality with you, and they will from that moment become your superiors.

But, indeed, they only object to any new law being made against them; they mean to deprecate, not justice, but severity. Nay, their wish is that a law which you have admitted, established by your suffrages, and found in the practice and experience of so many years to be beneficial, should now be repealed; and that by abolishing one law you should weakenall the rest. No law perfectly suits the convenience of every member of the community; the only consideration is, whether, on

160

the whole, it is profitable to the greater part. If, because a law proves obnoxious to a private individual, it must therefore be cancelled and annulled, to what purpose is it for the community to enact laws, which those, whom they were particularly intended to comprehend, could presently repeal? Let us, however, inquire what this important affair is which has induced the matrons thus to run out into public in this indecorous manner, scarcely restraining from pushing into the Forum and the assembly of the people.

Is it to solicit that their parents, their husbands, children, and brothers may be ransomed from captivity under Hannibal?

By no means: and far be ever from the commonwealth so unfortunate a situation. Yet, when such was the case, you refused this to the prayers which, on that occasion, their duty dictated. But it is not duty, nor solicitude for their friends; it is religion that has collected them together. They are about to receive the Idaean Mother, coming out of Phrygia from Pessinus.

What motive, that even common decency will not allow to be mentioned, is pretended for this female insurrection? Hear the answer:

That we may shine in gold and purple; that both on festival and common days, we may ride through the city in our chariots, triumphing over vanquished and abrogated law, after having captured and wrested from your suffrages; and that there may be no bounds to our expenses and our luxury.

Often have you heard me complain of the profuse expenses of the women—often of these of the man; and that not only of men in private stations, but of the magistrates; and that the state was endangered by two opposite vices, luxury and avarice; these pests which have ever been the ruin of every great state. These I dread the more, as the circumstances of the commonwealth grow daily more prosperous and happy; as the empire increases; as we have passed over into Greece and Asia, places abounding with every kind of temptation that can inflame the passions; and as we have begun to handle even royal treasures; for I greatly fear that these matters will rather bring us into captivity than we them.

Believe me, those statues from Syracuse made their way into this city with hostile effect. I already hear too many commending and admiring the decorations of Athens and Corinth, and ridiculing the earthen images of our Roman gods that stand on the fronts of their temples. For my part, I prefer these gods—propitious as they are, and I hope will continue, if we allow them to remain in their own mansions.

In the memory of our fathers, Pyrrhus, by his ambassador Cineas, made trial of the dispositions, not only of our men, but of our women also, by offers of presents: at that time the Oppian law, for restraining female luxury, had not been made; and yet not one woman accepted a present. What, think you, was the reason? That for which

161

our ancestors made no provision by law on this subject: there was no luxury existing which might be restrained.

As diseases must necessarily be known before their remedies, so passions come into being before the laws which prescribe limits to them. What called forth the Licinian law, restricting estates to five hundred acres, but the unbounded desire of enlarging estates? What the Cineian law, concerning gifts and presents, but that the plebeians had become vassals and tributaries to the senate? It is not, therefore, in any degree surprising that no want of the Oppian Law, or of any other, to limit the expenses of the women, was felt at that time, when they refused to receive gold andpurple that was thrown in their way and offered to their acceptance. If Cineas were now to go round the city with his presents, he would find numbers of women standing in the public streets ready to receive them.

There are some passions the causes or motives of which I can no way account for. To be debarred of a liberty in which another is indulged may perhaps naturally excite some degree of shame or indignation; yet, when the dress of all is alike, what inferiority in appearance can any one be ashamed of? Of all kinds of shame, the worst, surely, is the being ashamed of frugality or of poverty; but the law relieves you with regard to both; you want only that which it is unlawful for you to have.

This equalization, says the rich matron, is the very thing that I cannot endure. Why do I not make a figure, distinguished with gold and purple? Why is the poverty of others concealed under this cover of law, so that it should be thought that, if the law permitted, they would have such things as they are not now able to procure? Romans, do you wish to excite among your wives an emulation of this sort, that the rich should wish to have what no other can have; and that the poor, lest they should be despised as such, should extend their expenses beyond their abilities? Be assured that when a woman once begins to be ashamed of what she ought not to be ashamed of, she will not be ashamed of what she ought. She who can, will purchase out of her own purse; she who cannot, will ask her husband.

Unhappy is the husband, both he who complies with the request and he who does not; for what he will not give himself, another will. Now they openly solicit favors from other women's husbands: and, what is more, solicit a law and votes. From some they obtain them; although, with regard to you, your property, or your children, you would find it hard to obtain anything from them. If the law ceasesto limit the expenses of your wife, you yourself will never be able to limit them. Do not suppose that the matter will hereafter be in the same state in which it was before the law was made on the subject. It is safer that a wicked man should never be accused than he should be acquitted; and luxury, if it had never been meddled with, would be more tolerable than it will be, now, like a wild beast, irritated by having been chained and then let loose. My opinion is that the Oppian law ought on no account to be repealed. Whatever determination you may come to, I pray all the gods to prosper it.

CATO THE YOUNGER

Marcus Porcius Cato, great-grandson of Cato the Censor, and distinguished from him by being called Uticensis, from the city of Utica, where he met his death, was born 95 b. c., and died by his own hand in 46 b. c. He resembled his great ancestor in the severity of his opposition to views entertained by others that differed from his own, yet this was somewhat softened by his Greek training, which modified greatly the hard and stubborn spirit of the old Latin race. He was a brave man, a lover of his country, and a great orator.

On the Punishment of the Catiline Conspirators (63 b. c.). My feelings, Conscript Fathers, are extremely different when I contemplate our circumstances and dangers, and when I revolve in my mind the sentiments of some who have spoken before me. Those speakers, as it seems to me, have considered only how to punish the traitors who have raised war against their country, their parents, their altars, and their homes; but the state of affairs warns us rather to secure ourselves against them, than to take counsel as to whatsentence we should pass upon them. Other crimes you may punish after they have been committed; but as to this, unless you prevent its commission, you will, when it has once taken effect, in vain appeal to justice. When the city is taken, no power is left to the vanquished.

But, in the name of the immortal gods, I call upon you who have always valued your mansions and villas, your statues and pictures, at a higher price than the welfare of your country, if you wish to preserve those possessions, of whatever kind they are, to which you are attached; if you wish to secure quiet for the enjoyment of your pleasures, arouse yourselves and act in defense of your country. We are not now debating on the revenues, or on injuries done to our allies, but our liberty and our life are at stake.

Often, Conscript Fathers, have I spoken at great length in this assembly; often have I complained of the luxury and avarice of our citizens, and, by that very means, have incurred the displeasure of many. I, who never excused to myself, or to my own conscience, the commission of any fault, could not easily pardon the misconduct, or indulge the licentiousness, of others. But though you little regarded my remonstrances, yet the republic remained secure; its own strength was proof against your remissness. The question, however, at present under discussion, is not whether we live in a good or bad state of morals; nor how great, nor how splendid, the empire of the Roman people is; but whether these things around us, of whatever value they are, are to

163

continue our own, or to fall, with ourselves, into the hands of the enemy.

In such a case, does any one talk to me of gentleness and compassion? For some time past, it is true, we have lost the real names of things; for to lavish the property of others is called generosity, and audacity in wickedness is called heroism, and hence the state is reduced to the brink of ruin.But let those who thus misname things be liberal, since such is the practice, out of the property of our allies; let them be merciful to the robbers of the treasury; but let them not lavish our blood, and, while they spare a few criminals, bring destruction on all the guiltless.

Caius Caesar, a short time ago, spoke in fair and elegant language, before this assembly, on the subject of life and death; considering as false, I suppose, what is told of the dead—that the bad, going a different way from the good, inhabit places gloomy, desolate, dreary, and full of horror. He accordingly proposes that the property of the conspirators should be confiscated, and themselves kept in custody in the municipal towns; fearing, it seems, that, if they remained at Rome, they might be rescued either by their accomplices in the conspiracy, or by a hired mob; as if, forsooth, the mischievous and profligate were to be found only in the city, and not through the whole of Italy, or as if desperate attempts would not be more likely to succeed where there is less power to resist them. His proposal, therefore, if he fears any danger from them, is absurd; but if, amid such universal terror, he alone is free from alarm, it the more concerns me to fear for you and myself.[23]

Be assured, then, that when you decide on the fate of Lentulus and the other prisoners, you at the same time determine that of the army of Catiline, and of all the conspirators. The more spirit you display in your decision, the more will their confidence be diminished; but if they shall perceive you in the smallest degree irresolute, they will advance upon you with fury.

Do not suppose that our ancestors, from so small a commencement, raised the republic to greatness merely by force of arms. If such had been the case, we should enjoy it ina most excellent condition; for of allies and citizens, as well as arms and horses, we have a much greater abundance than they had. But there were other things which made them great, but which among us have no existence—such as industry at home, equitable government abroad, and minds impartial in council, uninfluenced by any immoral or improper feeling. Instead of such virtues, we have luxury and avarice, public distress and private superfluity; we extol wealth, and yield to indolence; no distinction is made between good men and bad; and ambition usurps

---

[23] This is the famous passage in which Cato intimated that Caesar was in some manner allied with the conspirators.

164

the honors due to virtue. Nor is this wonderful; since you study each his individual interest, and since at home you are slaves to pleasure, and here to money or favor; and hence it happens that an attack is made on the defenseless state.

But on these subjects I shall say no more. Certain citizens of the highest rank, have conspired to ruin their country; they are engaging the Gauls, the bitterest foes of the Roman name, to join in a war against us; the leader of the enemy is ready to make a descent upon us; and do you hesitate, even in such circumstances, how to treat armed incendiaries arrested within your walls? I advise you to have mercy upon them; they are young men who have been led astray by ambition; send them away, even with arms in their hands. But such mercy, and such clemency, if they turn those arms against you, will end in misery to yourselves. The case is, assuredly, dangerous, but you do not fear it; yes, you fear it greatly, but you hesitate now to act, through weakness and want of spirit, waiting one for another, and trusting to the immortal gods, who have so often preserved your country in the greatest dangers. But the protection of the gods is not obtained by vows and effeminate supplications; it is by vigilance, activity, and prudent measures, that general welfare is secured. Whenyou are once resigned to sloth and indolence, it is in vain that you implore the gods; for they are then indignant and threaten vengeance.

In the days of our forefathers, Titus Manlius Torquatus, during a war with the Gauls, ordered his own son to be put to death because he had fought with an enemy contrary to orders. That noble youth suffered for excess of bravery; and do you hesitate what sentence to pass on the most inhuman of traitors? Perhaps their former life is at variance with their present crime. Spare, then, the dignity of Lentulus, if he has ever spared his own honor or character, or had any regard for the gods or for men. Pardon the youth of Cethegus, unless this be the second time that he has made war upon his country. As to Gabinius, Statilius, Coeparius, why should I make any remark upon them? Had they ever possessed the smallest share of discretion they would never have engaged in such a plot against their country.

In conclusion, Conscript Fathers, if there were time to amend an error, I might easily suffer you, since you disregard words, to be corrected by experience of consequences. But we are beset by dangers on all sides; Catiline, with his army, is ready to devour us; while there are other enemies within the walls, and in the heart of the city; nor can any measures be taken, or any plans arranged, without their knowledge. The more necessary is it, therefore, to act with promptitude. What I advise, then, is this: That, since the state, by a treasonable combination of abandoned citizens, has been brought into the greatest peril; and since the conspirators have been convicted on the evidence of Titus Volturcius, and the deputies of the Allobroges, and on their own confession, of having concerted massacres, conflagrations, and other horrible and cruel outrages, against their fellow citizen and their country, punishment be inflicted, according to the usage of our ancestors, on the prisoners who have confessed their guilt, as on the men convicted of capital crimes.[24]

JULIUS CAESAR

Caius Julius Caesar was born about 100 b. c., and died at the hands of Brutus, Cassius, and their fellow-conspirators in 44 b. c. He was a marvellous man in every respect, achieving almost equal eminence as a solider, a statesman, a man of letters and an orator. He advised against putting to death those who were engaged with Catiline in his conspiracy, and had Cicero listened to his advice, and refrained from executing Lentulus, Cethegus, Statilius, Gabinius, and others, he would have escaped the humiliation of banishment on the charge of unlawfully putting to death a Roman citizen.

Speech Delivered in the Roman Senate on the Treatment of the Catiline Conspirators. It becomes all men, Conscript Fathers, who deliberate on dubious matters, to be influenced neither by hatred, affection, anger, nor pity. The mind, when such feelings obstruct its view, cannot easily see what is right; nor has any human being consulted, at the same moment, his passions and his interest. When the mind is freely exerted, its reasoning is sound; but passion, if it gain possession of it, becomes its tyrant, and reason is powerless.

I could easily mention, Conscript Fathers, numerous examples of kings and nations, who, swayed by resentment or compassion, have adopted injudicious courses of conduct; but I had rather speak of those instances in which our ancestors, in opposition to the impulse of passion, acted with wisdom and sound policy.

In the Macedonian war, which we carried on against King Perses, the great and powerful state of Rhodes, which had risen by the aid of the Roman people, was faithless and hostile to us; yet, when the war was ended, and the conduct of the Rhodians was taken into consideration, our forefathers left them unmolested, lest any should say that war was made upon them for the sake of seizing their wealth, rather than of punishing their faithlessness. Throughout the Punic wars, too, through the Carthaginians, both during peace and in suspension of arms, were guilty of many acts of injustice, yet our ancestors never took occasion to retaliate, but considered rather what was worthy of themselves than what might justly be inflicted on their enemies.

Similar caution, Conscript Fathers, is to be observed by yourselves, that the guilt of Lentulus, and the other conspirators, may

---

[24] A decree of the Senate was made in accordance with this advice.

not have greater weight with you than your own dignity, and that you may not regard your indignation more than your character. If indeed, a punishment adequate to their crimes be discovered, I consent to extraordinary measures; but if the enormity of their crime exceeds whatever can be devised, I think that we should inflict only such penalties as the laws have provided.

Most of those who have given their opinions before me have deplored, in studied and impressive language, the sad fate that threatens the republic; they have recounted the barbarities of war, and the afflictions that would fall on the vanquished; they have told us that maidens would be dishonored, and youths abused; that children would be torn from the embraces of their parents; that matrons would be subjected to the pleasure of the conquerors; that temples anddwelling-houses would be plundered; that massacres and fires would follow; and that every place would be filled with arms, corpses, blood, and lamentations. But to what end, in the name of the eternal gods! was such eloquence directed? Was it intended to render you indignant at the conspiracy? A speech, no doubt, will inflame him whom so frightful and monstrous a reality has not provoked! Far from it: for to no man does evil, directly against himself, appear a light matter; many, on the contrary, have felt it more seriously than was right.

But to different persons, Conscript Fathers, different degrees of license are allowed. If those who pass a life sunk in obscurity commit any error, through excessive anger, few become aware of it, for their fame is as limited as their fortune; but of those who live invested with extensive power, and in an exalted station, the whole world knows the proceedings. Thus in the highest position there is the least liberty of action; and it becomes us to indulge neither partiality nor aversion, but least of all animosity; for what in others is called resentment is in the powerful termed violence and cruelty.

I am, indeed, of opinion, Conscript Fathers, that the utmost degree of torture is inadequate to punish their crime; but the generality of mankind dwell on that which happens last, and, in the case of malefactors, forget their guilt, and talk of their punishment, should that punishment have been inordinately severe. I feel assured, too, that Decimus Silanus, a man of spirit and resolution, made the suggestions which he offered, from zeal for the state, and that he had no view, in so important a matter, to favor or to enmity; such I know to be his character, and such his discretion. Yet his proposal appears to me, I will not say cruel (for what can be cruel that is directed against such characters?), but foreign to our policy. For, assuredly, Silanus, either your fears,or their treason, must have induced you, a consul-elect, to propose this new kind of punishment. Of fear it is unnecessary to speak, when, by the prompt activity of that distinguished man our consul, such numerous forces are under arms; and as to the punishment, we may say, what is, indeed, the truth, that in trouble and distress death is a relief from suffering, and not a torment; that it puts an end to all human woes; and that, beyond it, there is no place either for sorrow or joy.

But why, in the name of the immortal gods, did you not add to your proposal, Silanus, that, before they were put to death they should be punished with the scourge? Was it because the Porcian law forbids it? But other laws forbid condemned citizens to be deprived of life, and allow them to go into exile. Or was it because scourging is a severer penalty than death? Yet what can be too severe, or too harsh, toward men convicted of such an offence? But if scourging be a milder punishment than death, how is it consistent to observe the law as to the smaller point, when you disregard it as to the greater?

But who, it may be asked, will blame any severity that shall be decreed against these parricides of their country? I answer that time, the course of events, and fortune, whose caprice governs nations, may blame it. Whatever shall fall on the traitors, will fall on them justly; but it is for you, Conscript Fathers, to consider well what you resolve to inflict on others. All precedents productive of evil effects had their origin from what was good; but when a government passes into the hands of the ignorant and unprincipled, any new example of severity, inflicted on deserving and suitable objects, is extended to those that are improper and undeserving of it. The Lacedaemonians, when they had conquered the Athenians, appointed thirty men to govern their state. These thirty began their administration by puttingto death, even without a trial, all who were notoriously wicked, or publicly detestable; acts at which the people rejoiced, and extolled their justice. But afterward, when their lawless power gradually increased, they proceeded, at their pleasure, to kill the good and bad indiscriminately, and to strike terror into all; and thus the state, overpowered and enslaved, paid a heavy penalty for its imprudent exultation.

Within our own memory, too, when the victorious Sylla ordered Damasippus, and others of similar character, who had risen by distressing their country, to be put to death, who did not commend the proceeding? All exclaimed that wicked and factious men, who had troubled the state with their seditious practices, had justly forfeited their lives. Yet this proceeding was the commencement of great bloodshed. For whenever any one coveted the mansion or villa, or even the plate or apparel of another, he exerted his influence to have him numbered among the proscribed. Thus they, to whom the death of Damasippus had been a subject of joy, were soon after dragged to death themselves; nor was there any cessation of slaughter, until Sylla had glutted all his partisans with riches.

Such excesses, indeed, I do not fear from Marcus Tullius, or in these times. But in a large state there arise many men of various dispositions. At some other period, and under another consul, who, like the present, may have an army at his command, some false accusation may be credited as true; and when, with our example for a precedent, the consul shall have drawn the sword on the authority of the senate, who shall stay its progress, or moderate its fury?

Our ancestors, Conscript Fathers, were never deficient in conduct or courage; nor did pride prevent them from imitating the customs of other nations, if they appeared deserving of regard. Their armor, and weapons of war, they borrowedfrom the Samnites; their ensigns of authority, for the most part, from the Etrurians; and, in short, whatever appeared eligible to them, whether among allies or among enemies, they adopted at home with the greatest readiness, being more inclined to emulate merit than to be jealous of it. But at the same time, adopting a practice from Greece, they punished their citizens with the scourge, and inflicted capital punishment on such as were condemned. When the republic, however, became powerful, and faction grew strong from the vast number of citizens, men began to involve the innocent in condemnation, and other like abuses were practiced; and it was then that the Porcian and other laws were provided, by which condemned citizens were allowed to go into exile. This lenity of our ancestors, Conscript Fathers, I regard as a very strong reason why we should not adopt any new measures of severity. For assuredly there was greater merit and wisdom in those, who raised so mighty an empire from humble means than in us, who can scarcely preserve what they so honorably acquired. Am I of opinion, then, you will ask, that the conspirators should be set free, and that the army of Catiline should thus be increased? Far from it; my recommendation is, that their property be confiscated, and that they themselves be kept in custody in such of the municipal towns as are best able to bear the expense; that no one hereafter bring their case before the senate, or speak on it to the people; and that the senate now give their opinion that he who shall act contrary to this, will act against the republic and general safety.

CATILINE

Lucius Sergius Catilina (Catiline), who is best known for his conspiracy against the government of Rome, was born about the year 108 b. c., and was killed in the battleof Faesulae, Italy, in 62 b. c. He was a man of dissolute habits, devoid of any moral sense, a murderer, and a traitor, yet he was a brave soldier and an able orator. In Catiline's time the lower classes were in a wretched state of poverty and had strong reasons for discontent with the government. This fact Catiline seized upon with masterly effect, for through it a free pardon and large rewards were offered to all who would desert his cause and testify regarding the conspiracy, not one of Catiline's followers betrayed him.

Catiline failed, not through the weakness of his cause, nor for his lack of ability, but because of the utter worthlessness of his character.

Speech to the Conspirators. If your courage and fidelity has not been sufficiently proved by me, this favorable opportunity would have occurred to no purpose; mighty hopes, absolute power, would in vain be within our grasp; nor should I, depending on irresolution or fickle-mindedness, pursue contingencies instead of certainties. But as I have, on so many remarkable occasions, experienced your bravery and attachment to me, I have ventured to engage in a most important and glorious enterprise. I am aware, too, that whatever advantages or evils affect you, the same affect me; and to have the same desires and the same aversions is assuredly a firm bond of friendship.

What I have been meditating you have already heard separately. But my ardor for action is daily more and more excited when I consider what our future condition of life must be unless we ourselves assert our claims to liberty. For, since the government has fallen under the power and jurisdiction of a few, kings and princes have constantly been their tributaries; nations and states have paid themtaxes; but all the rest of us, however brave and worthy, whether noble or plebeian, have been regarded as a mere mob, without interest or authority, and subject to those to whom, if the state were in a sound condition, we should be a terror. Hence all influence, power, honor, and wealth, are in their hands, or where they dispose of them; to us, they have left only insults, dangers, persecutions, and poverty. To such indignities, O bravest of men, how long will you submit? Is it not better to die in a glorious attempt, than, after having been the derision of other men's insolence, to resign a wretched and degraded existence with ignominy?

But success (I call gods and men to witness) is in our own hands. Our years are fresh, our spirit is unbroken; among our oppressors, on the contrary, through age and wealth a general debility has been produced. We have, therefore, only to make a beginning; the course of events will accomplish the rest.

Who in the world, indeed, that has the feelings of a man, can endure that they should have a superfluity of riches, to squander in building over seas and levelling mountains, and that means should be wanting to us even for the necessaries of life; that they should join together two houses or more, and that we should not have a hearth to call our own? They, though they purchase pictures, statues, and embossed plate; though they pull down new buildings and erect others, and lavish and abuse their wealth in every possible method, yet cannot, with the utmost efforts of caprice, exhaust it. But for us there is poverty at home, debts abroad; our present circumstances are bad, our prospects much worse; and what, in a word, have we left, but a miserable existence?

Will you not, then, awake to action? Behold that liberty, that liberty for which you have so often wished, with wealth, honor, and glory, are set before your eyes. Allthese prizes fortune offers to the victorious. Let the enterprise itself, then, let the opportunity, let your property, your dangers, and the glorious spoils of war, animate you far more than my words. Use me either as your leader or your fellow solider; neither my heart nor my hand shall be wanting to you. These objects I hope to effect, in concert with you, in the character of consul; unless, indeed, my expectation deceives me, and you prefer to be slaves rather than masters.

Speech to His Troops. I am well aware, soldiers, that words cannot inspire courage, and that a spiritless army cannot be rendered active, or a timid army valiant, by the speech of its commander. Whatever courage is in the heart of a man, whether from nature or from habit, so much will be shown by him in the field; and on him whom neither glory nor danger can move, exhortation is bestowed in vain; for the terror in his breast stops his ears.

I have called you together, however, to give you a few instructions, and to explain to you, at the same time, my reasons for the course which I have adopted. You all know, soldiers, how severe a penalty the inactivity and cowardice of Lentulus has brought upon himself and us; and how, while awaiting reinforcements from the city, I was unable to march into Gaul. In what situation our affairs now are, you will understand as well as myself. Two armies of the enemy, one on the side of Rome and the other on that of Gaul, oppose our progress; while the want of corn and of other necessaries prevents us from remaining, however strongly we may desire to remain, in our present position. Whithersoever we would go, we must open a passage with our swords. I conjure you, therefore, to maintain a brave and resolute spirit; and to remember, when you advance to battle, that on your own right hands depend riches, honor, and glory, with the enjoyment of your liberty and ofyour country. If we conquer, all will be safe, we shall have possessions in abundance; and the colonies and corporate towns will open their gates to us. But if we lose the victory through want of courage, those same places will turn against us, for neither place nor friend will protect him whom his arms have not protected. Besides, soldiers, the same exigency does not press upon our adversaries as presses upon us; we fight for our country, for our liberty, for our life; they contend for what but little concerns them, the power of a small party. Attack them, therefore, with so much the greater confidence, and call to mind your achievements of old.

We might, with the utmost ignominy, have passed the rest of our days in exile. Some of you, after losing your property, might have waited at Rome for assistance from others. But because such a life, to men of spirit, was disgusting and unendurable, you resolved upon your present course. If you wish to quit it, you must exert all your resolution, for none but conquerors have exchanged war for peace. To hope for safety in flight when you have turned away from the enemy the arms by which the body is defended is indeed madness. In battle those who are most afraid are always in most danger; but courage is equivalent to a rampart.

When I contemplate you, soldiers, and when I consider your past exploits, a strong hope of victory animates me. Your spirit, your age, your valor, give me confidence; to say nothing of necessity, which makes even cowards brave. To prevent the numbers of the enemy from surrounding us, our confined situation is sufficient. But should Fortune be unjust to your valor, take care not to lose your lives unavenged; take care not to be taken and butchered like cattle, rather than, fighting like men, to leave to your enemies a bloody and mournful victory.

CICERO

Marcus Tullius Cicero, the greatest of the Roman orators, and one of the foremost orators of all times, was born at Arpinum, on the northern border of the Volscian territory, 106 b. c., and was killed by order of Marc Antony at the close of the year 43 b. c. Thus passed away, at the age of sixty-three, one of the most illustrious statesmen and the most eloquent orator that the vast empire of Rome produced.

Cicero lived in a venal age, yet he escaped contamination. He was a politician, yet he rarely stooped to the trickery of the ancient politicians. Only in two instances did he fall below the high standard of manliness up to which all must measure who would be esteemed patriots: once, when he combined with Catiline, a notoriously corrupt and ruined character, for the consulship; and again, in turning from Pompey and crooking "the pregnant hinges of the knee" to Caesar when that warrior's star commenced to climb toward the zenith of his fame. A weak trait in Cicero's character was shown in his behavior during banishment. Instead of bearing up bravely against the injustice of his enemies, strong in the consciousness of his own rectitude, he cringingly besought clemency and begged to be permitted to return to Rome, thus tacitly admitting that there had been just grounds for his banishment. Despite these failings, he was a truly great man who did much for his country and the world. Much of his spoken and written matter has come down to us and authentic information concerning his education, his style of oratory, the manner of his life, and his views of men and questions are to be had at first hand. He is not shrouded in mystery, as are many great men of a much nearer period, but he can be as clearly perceived by the student of today as he was by his contemporaries—in fact, clearer, because the picture is not now, as it was then, blurred by the excessive praise of friends nor the calumnies of enemies.

All through his life Cicero worked to fit himself for adequately filling such positions of honor and renown as he sought, and he finally became the most perfect specimen of the Roman of the governing class.

As a youth he was under the instruction of the famous orator Crassus, and he read the poets and orators of Greece under the guidance of the Greek poet Archias, then a teacher at Rome, during the early period of his schooling. He studied the Roman national law and ritual under the two Scaevolas, as he desired a thorough knowledge of these things in order that he might become a successful advocate. He also studied under Philo, the chief of the Academics, Diodotus the Stoic, and Milo the philosopher. He commenced his career as an advocate when twenty-six years of age by a civil cause in the speech Pro Quinctio, and in the following year he undertook a criminal cause in the action brought against Roscius Amerinus. Soon after this he went to Athens and diligently studied the art of declamation under the best masters. Some claim that Cicero was not original in his matter nor his manner;that he spent too much time studying the works and methods of others; but be this as it may, he certainly became wonderfully proficient in gathering the matter and presenting it in a manner that was marvelously impressive and successful. He was undoubtedly the best prepared orator that the world has ever known; and as a speaker he was always master of himself, his subject, and his audience.

The First Oration Against Verres (70 b. c.). That which was above all things to be desired, O judges, and which above all things was calculated to have the greatest influence toward allaying the unpopularity of your order, and putting an end to the discredit into which your judicial decisions have fallen, appears to have been thrown in your way, and given to you not by any human contrivance, but almost by the interposition of the gods, at a most important crisis of the republic. For an opinion has now become established, pernicious to us and pernicious to the public, which has been the common talk of every one, not only at Rome, but among foreign nations also—that in the courts of law as they exist at present, no wealthy man, however guilty he may be, can possibly be convicted.

Now at this time of peril to your order and to your tribunal, when men are ready to attempt by harangues, and by the proposal of new laws, to increase the existing unpopularity of the senate, Caius Verres is brought to trial as a criminal—a man condemned in the opinion of every one by his life and actions, but acquitted by the enormousness of his wealth according to his own hope and boast. I, O judges, have undertaken this cause as prosecutor with the greatest good wishes and expectation on the part of the Roman people, not in order to increase the unpopularity ofthe senate, but to relieve it from the discredit which I share with it. For I have brought before you a man, by acting justly in whose case you have an opportunity of retrieving the lost credit of your judicial proceedings, of regaining your credit with the Roman people, and of giving satisfaction to foreign nations; a man, the embezzler of public funds, the petty tyrant of Asia and Pamphylia, the robber who deprived the city of its rights, the disgrace and ruin of the province of

Sicily. And if you come to a decision about this man with severity and a due regard to your oaths, that authority which ought to remain in you will cling to you still; but if that man's vast riches shall break down the sanctity and honesty of the courts of justice, at least I shall achieve this, that it shall be plain that it was rather honest judgment that was wanting to the republic, than a criminal to the judges or an accuser to the criminal.

I, indeed, that I may confess to you the truth about myself, O judges, though many snares were laid for me by Caius Verres, both by land and sea, which I partly avoided by my own vigilance, and partly warded off by the zeal and kindness of my friends, yet I never seemed to be incurring so much danger, and I never was in such a state of great apprehension as I am now in this very court of law. Nor does the expectation which people have formed of my conduct of this prosecution, nor this concourse of so vast a magnitude as is here assembled, influence me (though indeed I am greatly agitated by these circumstances) so much as his nefarious plots which he is endeavoring to lay at one and the same time against me, against you, against Marcus Glabrio, the praetor, and against the allies, against foreign nations, against the senate, and even against the very name of senator; whose favorite saying it is that they have got to fear who have stolen only as much as is enough for themselves, but that he has stolen so much that it may easilybe plenty for many; that nothing is so holy that it can not be corrupted, or so strongly fortified that it can not be stormed by money. But if he were as secret in acting as he is audacious in attempting; perhaps in some particular he might some time or other have escaped our notice.

But it happens very fortunately that to his incredible audacity there is joined a most unexampled folly. For as he was unconcealed in committing his robberies of money, so in his hope of corrupting the judges he has made his intentions and endeavors visible to every one. He says that only once in his life has he felt fear at the time when he was first impeached as a criminal by me; because he was only lately arrived from his province, and was branded with unpopularity and infamy, not modern but ancient and of long standing; and, besides that, the time was unlucky, being very ill suited for corrupting the judges. Therefore, when I had demanded a very short time to prosecute my inquiries in Sicily, he found a man to ask for two days less to make investigations in Achaia; not with any real intention of doing the same with his diligence and industry, that I have accomplished by my labor, and daily and nightly investigations. For the Achaean inquisitor never even arrived at Brundusium. I in fifty days so traveled over the whole of Sicily that I examined into the records and injuries of all the tribes and of all private individuals, so that it was easily visible to every one that he had been seeking out a man not really for the purpose of bringing

174

the defendant whom he accused to trial, but merely to occupy the time which ought to belong to me.

Now that most audacious and most senseless man thinks this. He is aware that I am come into court so thoroughly prepared and armed that I shall fix all his thefts and crimes not only in your ears, but in the very eyes of all men. He sees that many senators are witnesses of his audacity; hesees that many Roman knights are so, too, and many citizens, and many of the allies besides to whom he has done unmistakable injuries. He sees also that very numerous and very important deputations have come here at the same time from friendly cities, armed with the public authority and evidence collected by their states.

In truth, what genius is there so powerful, what faculty of speaking, what eloquence so mighty, as to be in any particular able to defend the life of that man convicted as it is of so many vices and crimes, and long since condemned by the inclinations and private sentiments of every one. And, to say nothing of the stains and disgraces of his youth, what other remarkable event is there in his questorship, that first step to honor, except that Cnaeus Carbo was robbed by his questor of the public money? that the consul was plundered and betrayed? his army deserted? his province abandoned? the holy nature and obligations imposed on him by lot violated? whose lieutenancy was the ruin of all Asia and Pamphylia, in which provinces he plundered many houses, very many cities, all the shrines and temples; when he renewed and repeated against Cnaeus Dolabella his ancient wicked tricks when he had been questor, and did not only in his danger desert, but even attack and betray the man to whom he had been lieutenant, and proquaestor, and whom he had brought into odium by his crimes; whose city praetorship was the destruction of the sacred temples and the public works, and, as to his legal decisions, was the adjudging and awarding of property contrary to all established rules and precedents. But now he has established great and numerous monuments and proofs of all his vices in the province of Sicily, which he for three years so harassed and ruined that it can by no possibility be restored to its former condition, and appears scarcely able to be at all recovered after a long series of years, and a long successionof virtuous praetors. While this man was praetor the Sicilians enjoyed neither their own laws nor the decrees of our senate, nor the common rights of every nation. Every one in Sicily has only so much left as either escaped the notice or was disregarded by the satiety of that most avaricious and licentious man.

No legal decision for three years was given on any other ground but his will; no property was so secure to any man, even if it had descended to him from his father and grandfather, but he was deprived of it at his command; enormous sums of money were exacted from the property of the cultivators of the soil by a new and nefarious system. The most faithful of the allies were classed in the number of enemies.

Roman citizens were tortured and put to death like slaves; the greatest criminals were acquitted in the courts of justice through bribery; the most upright and honorable men, being prosecuted while absent, were condemned and banished without being heard in their own defense; the most fortified harbors, the greatest and strongest cities, were laid open to pirates and robbers; the sailors and soldiers of the Sicilians, our own allies and friends, died of hunger; the best built fleets on the most important stations were lost and destroyed, to the great disgrace of the Roman people. This same man while praetor plundered and stripped those most ancient monuments, some erected by wealthy monarchs and intended by them as ornaments for their cities; some, too, the work of our own generals, which they either gave or restored as conquerors to the different states in Sicily. And he did this not only in the case of public statues and ornaments, but he also plundered all the temples consecrated in the deepest religious feelings of the people. He did not leave, in short, one god to the Sicilians which appeared to him to be made in a tolerableworkmanlike manner, and with any of the skill of the ancients.

I am prevented by actual shame from speaking of his nefarious licentiousness as shown in rapes and other such enormities; and I am unwilling also to increase the distress of those men who have been unable to preserve their children and their wives unpolluted by his wanton lust. But, you will say, these things were done by him in such a manner as not to be notorious to all men. I think there is no man who has heard his name who cannot also relate wicked actions of his; so that I ought rather to be afraid of being thought to omit many of his crimes, than to invent any charges against him. And, indeed, I do not think that this multitude which has collected to listen to me wishes so much to learn of me what the facts of the case are, as to go over it with me, refreshing its recollection of what it knows already.

And as this is the case, that senseless and profligate man attempts to combat me in another manner. He does not seek to oppose the eloquence of any one else to me; he does not rely on the popularity, or influence, or authority, of any one. He pretends that he trusts to those things; but I see what he is really aiming at (and indeed he is not acting with any concealment). He sets before me empty titles of nobility—that is to say, the names of arrogant men, who do not hinder me so much by being noble, as assist me by being notorious; he pretends to rely on their protection, when he has in reality been contriving something else this long time. What hope he now has, and what he is endeavoring to do, I will now briefly explain to you, O judges.

But first of all, remark, I beg you, how the matter has been arranged by him from the beginning. When he first returned from the province he endeavored to get rid of hisprosecution by corrupting the judges at a great expense; and this object he continued to keep in view

176

till the conclusion of the appointment of the judges. After the judges were appointed, because in drawing lots for them the fortune of the Roman people had defeated his hopes, and in the rejecting some my diligence had defeated his impudence, the whole attempt at bribery was abandoned. The affair was now going on admirably; lists of your names and of the whole tribunal were in every one's hands. It did not seem possible to mark the votes of these men with any distinguishing mark or color or spot of dirt; and that fellow, from having been brisk and in high spirits, became on a sudden so downcast and humbled that he seemed to be condemned not only by the Roman people but even by himself. But lo! all of a sudden, within these few days, since the consular comitia have taken place, he has gone back to his original plan with more money, and the same plots are now laid against your reputation and against the fortunes of every one, by the instrumentality of the same people; which fact at first, O judges, was pointed out by me by a very slight hint and indication; but afterward, when my suspicions were once aroused, I arrived at the knowledge of all the most secret counsels of that party without any mistake.

For as Hortensius, the consul-elect, was being attended home again from the Campus by a great concourse and multitude of people, Caius Curio fell in with that multitude by chance—a man whom I wish to name by way of honor rather than disparagement. I will tell you what if he had been unwilling to have it mentioned, he would not have spoken of in so large an assembly so openly and undisguisedly; which, however, shall be mentioned by me deliberately and cautiously, that it may be seen that I pay due regard to our friendship and to his dignity. He sees Verresin the crowd by the arch of Fabius,[25] he speaks to the man, and with a loud voice congratulates him on his victory. He does not say a word to Hortensius himself, who had been made consul, or to his friends and relations who were present attending on him; but he stops to speak to this man, embraces him, and bids him cast off all anxiety. "I give you notice," said he, "that you have been acquitted by this day's comitia." And as many most honorable men heard this, it is immediately reported to me the first thing. To some it appeared scandalous, to others, again, ridiculous—ridiculous to those who thought that this case depended on the credibility of the witnesses, on the importance of the charges, and on the power of the judges, and not on the consular comitia; scandalous to those who looked deeper, and who thought and this congratulation had reference to the corruption of the judges.

In truth, they argued in this manner—the most honorable men spoke to one another and to me in this manner—that there were now

---

[25] This arch, as explained in a note to Mr. Yonge's translation, had been erected to commemorate the victory obtained by Fabius over the Allobroges; and it was erected in the Via Sacra, as Cicero mentions in his speech Pro Plancio.

manifestly and undeniably no courts of justice at all. The very criminal who the day before thought that he was already condemned, is acquitted, now that his defender has been made consul. What are we to think then? Will it avail nothing at all Sicily, all the Sicilians, that all the merchants who have business in that country, that if the consul-elect wills it otherwise. What! will not the judges be influenced by the accusation, by the evidence, by the universal opinion of the Roman people? No. Everything will be governed by the power and authority of one man.

In the meantime my comitia began to be held; of which that fellow thought himself the master, as he had been of all the other comitia this year. He began to run about, that influential man, with his son, a youth of engaging and popular manners, among the tribes. The son began to address and to call on all the friends of his father—that is to say, all his agents—for bribery; and when this was noticed and perceived, the Roman people took care with the most earnest good will that I should not be deprived of my honor through the money of that man, whose riches had not been able to make me violate my good faith. After that I was released from the great anxiety about my canvass, I began, with a mind much more unoccupied and much more at ease, to think of nothing and to do nothing except what related to this trial. I find, O judges, these plans formed and begun to be put in execution by them to protract the matter, whatever steps it might be necessary to take in order to do so, so that the cause might be pleaded before Marcus Metellus as praetor. That by doing so they would have these advantages: firstly, that Marcus Metellus was most friendly to them; secondly, that not only would Hortensius be consul, but Quintus Metellus also; and listen while I show you how a great a friend he is to them. For he gave him a token of his good will of such a sort that he seemed to be giving it as a return for the suffrages of the tribes which he had secured to him. Did you think that I would say nothing of such serious matters as these? and that, at a crisis of such danger to the republic and my own character, I would consult anything rather than my duty and my dignity? The other consul-elect sent for the Sicilians; some came, because Lucius Metellus was praetor in Sicily. To them he speaks in this manner: that he is the consul; that one of his brothers has Sicily for a province; that the other is to be judge in all prosecutions for extortion; and that care had been taken in many ways that there should be no possibility of Verres being injured.

I ask you, Metellus, what is corrupting the course of justice, if this is not—to seek to frighten witnesses, and especially Sicilians, timid and oppressed men, not only by your own private influence, but by their fear of the consul, and by the power of two praetors? What could you do for an innocent man or for a relation, when for the sake of a most guilty one, entirely unconnected with you, you depart from your duty and your dignity, and allow what he is constantly saying to appear

178

true to any one who is not acquainted with you? For they said that Verres said that you had not been made consul by destiny, as the rest of your family had been, but by his assistance. Two consuls, therefore, and the judge are to be such because of his will. We shall not only, says he, avoid having a man too scrupulous in investigating, too subservient to the opinion of the people, Marcus Glabrio, but we shall have this advantage also: Marcus Caesonius is the judge, the colleague of your accuser, a man of tried and proved experience in the decision of actions. It will never do for us to have such a man as that on the bench, which we are endeavoring to corrupt by some means or other; for before, when he was one of the judges on the tribunal of which Junius was president, he was not only very indignant at the shameful transaction, but he even betrayed and denounced it.

But as for what I had begun to say—namely, that the contest is between you and me, this is it—I, when I had undertaken this cause at the request of the Sicilians, and had thought it a very honorable and glorious thing for me that they were willing to make experiment of my integrity and diligence, who already knew by experience my innocence and temperance: then, when I had undertaken this business, I proposed to myself some greater action also by which theRoman people should be able to see my good will toward the republic. For that seemed to me to be by no means worthy of my industry and efforts, for that man to be brought to trial by me who had already condemned by the judgment of all men, unless that intolerable influence of yours, and that grasping nature which you have displayed for some years in many trials, were interposed also in the case of that desperate man. But now, since all this dominion and sovereignty of yours over the courts of justice delights you so much, and since there are some men who are neither ashamed of their licentiousness and their infamy, nor weary of it, and who, as if on purpose, seem to wish to encounter hatred and unpopularity from the Roman people, I profess that I have undertaken this, a great burden perhaps, and one dangerous to myself, but still worthy of my applying myself to it with all the vigor of my age, and all diligence.

And since the whole order of the senate is weighed down by the discredit brought on it by the wickedness and audacity of a few, and is overwhelmed by the infamy of the tribunals, I profess myself an enemy to this race of men, an accuser worthy of their hatred, a persevering, a bitter adversary. I arrogate this to myself, I claim this for myself, and I will carry out this enmity in my magistracy, and from that post in which the Roman people have willed that from the next first of January I shall act in concert with it in matters concerning the republic, and concerning wicked men. I promise the Roman people that this shall be the most honorable and the fairest employment of my aedileship. I warn, I forewarn, I give notice beforehand to those men who are wont either to put money down, to undertake for others, to receive money, or to promise money, or to act as agents in bribery, or as go-betweens in corrupting the seat of judgment, and who have promised their influence or their impudencein aid of such a business, in this trial to keep their hands and inclination from this nefarious wickedness.

And what do you suppose will be my thoughts, if I find in this very trial any violation of the laws committed in any similar manner? especially when I can prove by many witnesses that Caius Verres often said in Sicily, in the hearing of many persons, "that he had a powerful friend, in confidence with whom he was plundering the province; and that he had so distributed the three years of his Sicilian praetorship that should say he did exceedingly well, if he appropriated the gains of one year to the augmentation of his own property, those of the second year to his patrons and defenders, and reserved the whole of the third year, the most productive and gainful of all, for the judges."

From which it came into my mind to say that which, when I had said lately before Marcus Glabrio at the time of striking the list of judges, I perceived the Roman people greatly moved by: that I thought that foreign nations would send ambassadors to the Roman people to procure the abrogation of the law, and of all trials, about extortion; for if there were no trials, they think that each man would only plunder them of as much as he would think sufficient for himself and his children; but now, because there are trials of that sort, every one carries off as much as it will take to satisfy himself, his patrons, his advocates, the praetor, and the judges; and that this is an enormous sum; that they may be able to satisfy the cupidity of one most avaricious man, but are quite unable to incur the expense of his most guilty victory over the laws. O trials worthy of being recorded! O splendid reputation of our order! when the allies of the Roman people are unwilling that trials for extortion should take place, which were instituted by our ancestors for thesake of all allies. Would that man ever have had a favorable hope of his own safety, if he had not conceived in his mind a bad opinion of you? on which account, he ought, if possible, to be still more hated by you than he is by the Roman people, because he considers you like himself in avarice and wickedness and perjury.

And I beg you, in the name of the immortal gods, O judges, think of and guard against this; I warn you, I give notice to you of what I am well assured, that this most seasonable opportunity has been given to you by the favor of the gods, for the purpose of delivering your whole order from hatred, from unpopularity, from infamy, and from disgrace. There is no severity believed to exist in the tribunals, nor any scruples with regard to religion; in short, there are not believed to be any tribunals at all. Therefore we are despised and scorned by the Roman people; we are branded with a heavy and now long standing infamy. Nor, in fact, is there any other reason for which the Roman people has with so much earnestness sought the restoration of the tribunician

180

power: but when it was demanding that in words, it seemed to be asking for that, but in reality it was asking for tribunals which it could trust.

But now men on the watch-towers; they observe how every one of you behaves himself in respecting religion and observing the laws. They see that, ever since the passing of the law for restoring the power of the tribunes, only one senator, and he, too, a very insignificant one, has been condemned. And though they do not blame this, yet they have nothing which they can very much command. For there is no credit in being upright in a case where there is no one who is either able or who endeavors to corrupt one. This is a trial in which you will be deciding about the defendant, the Roman people about you; by the example of what happens to this man it will be determined whether, when senatorsare the judges, a very guilty and a very rich man can be condemned.

On which account, in the first place, I beg this of the immortal gods, which I seem to myself to have hopes of, too—that in this trial no one may be found to be wicked except he who has long since been found to be such; secondly, if there are many wicked men, I promise this to you, O judges, I promise this to the Roman people, that my life shall fail rather than my vigor and perseverance in prosecuting their iniquity. But that iniquity, which if it should be committed, I promise to prosecute severely, with however much trouble and danger to myself, and whatever enmities I may bring on myself by doing so, you, O Marcus Glabrio, can guard against ever taking place by your wisdom, and authority, and diligence. Do you undertake the cause of the tribunals? Do you undertake the cause of impartiality, of integrity, of good faith and religion? Do you undertake the cause of the senate, that, being proved worthy by its conduct in this trial, it may come into favor and popularity with the Roman people? Think who you are and in what a situation you are placed; what you ought to give to the Roman people and what you ought to repay to your ancestors. Let the recollection of the Acilian Law passed by your father occur to your mind, owing to which law the Roman people has had this advantage of most admirable decisions and very strict judges in cases of extortion.

I am resolved not to permit the praetor or the judges to be changed in this cause. I will not permit the matter to be delayed till the lictors of the consuls can go and summon the Sicilians, whom the servants of the consuls-elect did not influence before, when by an unprecedented course of proceeding they sent for them all; I will not permit these miserable men, formerly the allies and friends of the Roman people, now their slaves and supplicants, to lose not onlytheir rights and fortunes by their tyranny, but to be deprived of even the power of bewailing their condition; I will not, I say, when the cause has been summed up by me, permit them after a delay of forty days has intervened, then at last to reply to me when my accusation has already fallen into oblivion through lapse of time; I will not permit the decision to be given when this crowd collected from all Italy has departed from Rome, which has assembled from all quarters at the same time on account of the comitia, of the games, and of the census.

The reward of the credit gained by your decision, or the danger arising from the unpopularity which will accrue to you if you decide unjustly, I think ought to belong to you; the labor and anxiety to me; the knowledge of what is done and the recollection of what has been said by every one, to all. I will adopt this course, not an unprecedented one, but one that has been adopted before, by this who are now the chief men of our state—the course, I mean, of at once producing the witnesses.

What you will find novel, O judges, is this, that I will so marshal my witnesses as to unfold the whole of my accusation; that when I have established it by examining my witnesses, by arguments, and by my speech, then I shall show the agreement of the evidence with my accusation: so that there shall be no difference between the established mode of prosecuting, and this new one, except that, according to the established mode, when everything has been said which is to be said, then the witnesses are produced; here they shall be produced as each count is brought forward, so that the other side shall have the same opportunity of examining them, of arguing and making speeches on their evidence. If there be any one who prefers an uninterrupted speech and the old mode of conducting a prosecution without any break, he shall have it in some other trial. But for this time lethim understand that what we do is done by us on compulsion (for we only do it with the design of opposing the artifice of the opposite party by our prudence). This will be the first part of the prosecution. We say that Caius Verres has not only done many licentious acts, many cruel ones, toward Roman citizens, and toward some of the allies, many wicked acts against both gods and man; but especially that he has taken away four hundred thousand sesterces out of Sicily contrary to the laws. We will make this so plain to you by witnesses, by private documents, and by public records, that you shall decide that, even if we had abundant space and leisure days for making a long speech without any inconvenience, still there was no need at all of a long speech in this matter.

CHAPTER IX

THE MODERN ORATORS

The need of orators is as great today as when John Hampden spoke against the exactions of Charles I, James Otis argued against writs of assistance, or Daniel Webster expounded the Constitution of his country. The need is here, but where are the orators? Questions of great moment now confront America and the world, but there is no Demosthenes to arouse men to the necessity of action, no Cicero to drive out the traitor Injustice, no Patrick Henry to consolidate the forces of Liberty. The power of the newspaper is great, and today it is doing noble work for progress; but this power can be used, and is being used, for evil as well as for good. A subsidized press is as dangerous as a Catiline or an Aeschines, and government by newspapers is as tyrannous as was the rule of Nero, Louis XI, or George III. The questions of the tariff, the trusts, finance, religion, education, and civic justice are burning, vital ones that closely affect the well-being of man on earth and his preparation for a larger existence in a hopeful spiritual future, and they should be plainly and honestly presented, clearly discussed, and justly settled. These results cannot be reached through papers that are owned by the great financiers and trustmagnates, and where the complaints and demands of the people receive scant consideration. Wherein, then, lie the hopes of the masses? In the power of the spoken word. All great reforms, through all ages, have been brought about by the voiced thoughts of men who not only knew their rights but had the courage that gave them the ability to enforce them. A band of noble missionaries should be created, composed of men and women who not only have ideas concerning the questions of today but who know how to express those ideas by word of mouth.

The eighteenth century produced oratorical giants that were undoubtedly equal in many cases to the orators of Greece and Rome in their palmiest days. Such men as the Earl of Chatham, Charles James Fox, Henry Grattan, Lord Brougham, Thomas Erskine, and William C. Plunket of Great Britain, and James Otis, Samuel Adams, Alexander Hamilton, Patrick Henry, and Richard Henry Lee of America, compare favorably with any group of ancient orators existing within a like period of time; while in behalf of the nineteenth century, America boasts of Pinckney, Prentiss, Wirt, Clay, Calhoun, Everett, Choate, Phillips, Lincoln, and Webster, and Great Britain points to Gladstone, Cobden, Curran, O'Connell, and Bright. The great rhetorician Burke is not placed among the foremost orators for the reason that he was a great constructor of speeches but not equally great in the art of delivery. His speeches are masterpieces of composition, and live today as such, but he was a poor speaker, and consequently should not be called an orator, because an orator, in the true sense of the word, is primarily a speaker, whereas Burke's genius consisted of his masterly logic and his marvellous power of composition.

Today, America has many beautiful writers and clever constructors of speeches, but not one really great orator. Theodore Roosevelt and William J. Bryan are two representatives of the best this country can offer in the way of orators, but neither of them measures up to the standard of Edward Everett, Wendell Phillips, or Daniel Webster. The main reason for the dearth of real orators is the lack of training in the art of delivery. Much attention is given to gaining a knowledge of the matter that is to be spoken, but little consideration is given to the delivery of that matter to the listener after once it has been gathered by the speaker. It is unfortunate that men like John Mitchell and Dr. Washington Gladden, who are standing up so nobly for the rights of labor, should be poorly equipped as speakers. Both these men possess noble thoughts which read impressively, but, when spoken, lack much force and power, on account of the poor delivery.

This point can be illustrated further by citing the manner and delivery of two men well known to the public of today—Andrew Carnegie and John H. Finley. Both have done considerable public speaking, and one is the president of a college.

On a night in 1911, the members of the Young Men's Bible Class of the Fifth Avenue Baptist Church of New York were addressed by these gentlemen. Both were at a considerable disadvantage from the fact that they had been invited to address a "Young Men's Bible Class," and as they naturally concluded the class would be composed of young men, they arranged their speeches accordingly; consequently, their plans of address were upset on finding that the majority of the class was composed of men close to the half-century mark, and many beyond it; or, as Mr. Carnegie wittily stated it, "with parts in their hair a lot wider than my own."

However, no exception could be taken to the matter of either speaker, although both changed their themes on finding the audience more matured in years than they had expected, and both had to pocket their notes on the subjects upon which they had intended to talk, and to speak extemporaneously. Both speakers cleverly switched to matters upon which they were thoroughly informed—Mr. Carnegie narrating events in his busy and influential life, and Dr. Finley discussing how to get the most benefit out of a twenty-four hour day. The matter of both was good, but the manner was unsatisfactory. Mr. Carnegie talked in a pleasant, conversational way which would have been most enjoyable had it not been that his delivery was slow. His utterance was often so slow as to mar the expressive force of his good language. He also leaned on the reading desk in front of him, not because he needed physical

184

support, he looked strong and rugged on the eve of his seventy-sixth birthday, but from the force of a bad habit.

He was perfectly at home before the audience, spoke in clear tones, at times with considerable force, particularly when quoting from Rev. John Home's tragedy of "Douglas," was winning in manner, took immediate hold of his audience, was witty in appropriate places, and would have been altogether delightful but for length and attitude. Mr. Carnegie was perfectly at home while facing the audience, and had his delivery equaled his matter, the speech would have been a most happy and effective one.

From Dr. Finley, because of his being President of the College of the City of New York, one might reasonably expect much in the way of delivery, but on this occasion the assembly received less than from the other speaker. He stood on the platform awkwardly, hands in pockets most of the time, and seldom did he utter a really smooth sentence, but separated his words in a manner to irritate the audience. He would say, for instance, "We—have—been—progressing—upward—and—onward—for—millions—of—years—," as though he had only one word in his mind at a time, whereas the learned President's head was full of grand and glorious thoughts that only needed to be spoken in phrases and sentences, instead of single words, in order to make him a most instructive and entertaining speaker. Dr. Finley's matter was well arranged, his diction excellent, but his delivery was unfortunate.

The orators of old, with few exceptions, studied the art of delivery as faithfully as they studied rhetoric, asdid the British and American orators of the eighteenth and nineteenth centuries, but the public speakers of the twentieth century sadly neglect this most important part of the speaker's art. Dr. Arthur T. Hadley, President of Yale University, is an able and learned man whose compositions are chaste and effective but whose delivery mars the force of his matter. He looks down on the floor immediately in front of him, instead of sweeping his glance over his audience, awkwardly swings his arms, and speaks his lines as though he were wound up and compelled to utter his matter within the given time. This is said with all respect to the famous educator, but his style of delivery should be avoided. Educators, more than most professional men, should be entertaining and convincing speakers, but, as a rule, they are woefully deficient in the qualities necessary to the making of orators. They, of all men, should set an example to the generation that is soon to take up the duties of life, and if college presidents improved their delivery, a long step would be taken toward making them oratorical beacons for the guidance of their students.

William J. Bryan, one of the best orators, if not the best, of today, owes his success mainly to his delivery. It is not so much what he says but how he says it that makes him a successful speaker. He possesses a rich, strong, and flexible voice that adds greatly to the effectiveness of his matter, and his speeches invariably sound better than they read. He will hold an audience absolutely in hand, sway it at his will, and force it against itsinclination momentarily to agree with him, even though, after mature deliberation, his reasoning may be disputed and his conclusions rejected. Mr. Bryan's power lies not in the beauty or force of his composition but in his mastery over the spoken word.

Theodore Roosevelt, contrary to the views of many, is, in the opinion of the author, an orator. He is not merely a speaker, because his speeches possess him as much as he possesses his speeches. He impresses an audience by his sincerity, convinces it by his reasoning, and persuades it by his earnestness. His matter reads as well as it sounds, thus demonstrating his ability as a rhetorician, his manner is graceful and forceful, and the general feeling, after listening to one of his addresses, is that a master has spoken. The author has heard Mr. Roosevelt many times during the past twenty years, and the improvement in his delivery is marked. There was a time when everything was sacrificed to force, he would snap his jaws and try to drive the voice through his clenched teeth, but now his enunciation is clear, and his entire delivery delightful. This shows the good that is to be derived from a speaker considering his manner as well as his matter.

Joseph H. Choate and W. Bourke Cockran are excellent examples of effective speakers of a decade or so ago, the former having been the most alluring and convincing in both his matter and his manner, and the latter entrancing and powerful in diction and delivery.

Forensic oratory has almost ceased to exist, while pulpit oratory is rarely to be found. This is a sad state of affairs, and requires immediate attention if the art of all arts is to be saved from extinction. The two essentials most missing in our public speakers are constructive skill and effective delivery—some lacking in one and some in the other—and the author asserts that great orators will not arise until both these essentials are found in the one man. Two thousand years ago Cicero, discoursing on oratory, said:

And why need I add any remarks of delivery itself, which is to be ordered by action of body, by gesture, by look, and by modulation and variation of the voice, the great power of which, alone and in itself, the comparatively trivial art of actors and the stage proves; on which though all bestow their utmost labor to form their look, voice, and gesture, who knows not how few there are, and have ever been, to whom we can attend with patience? . . . In those arts in which it is not indispensable usefulness that is sought, but liberal amusement for the mind, how nicely, how almost fastidiously, do we judge? For there are no suits or controversies which can force men, though they may tolerate indifferent orators in the forum, to endure also bad actors upon the stage. The orator, therefore, must take the most studious precaution not merely to satisfy those whom he necessarily must

186

satisfy, but to seem worthy of admiration to those who are at liberty to judge disinterestedly.

How many modern orators measure up to this standard set by the ancient master? The author knows of none.

How is one to obtain an effective delivery?

By close observation, hard study, and diligent practice. The student should observe his delivery, note the defects in breathing, voice production, articulation, inflection, and emphasis, and correct them; he should be sure to understand all he aims to explain, see all he desires others to see, and believe all he aims to make others believe. No speaker whose delivery is poor will be able to hold, convince, and persuade an audience, and unless he can do these three things he should refrain from speaking, as no man possesses a valid commission publicly to address his fellows unless he has a message to communicate and knows how to deliver it.

EXAMPLES OF MODERN ORATORY

PATRICK HENRY

LIBERTY OR DEATH[26] (1775)

No man thinks more highly than I do of patriotism, as well as abilities, of the very worthy gentlemen who have just addressed the house. But different men often see the same subject in different lights; and, therefore, I hope it will not be thought disrespectful of those gentlemen, if, entertaining as I do, opinions of a character very opposite to theirs, I shall speak forth my sentiments freely and without reserve. This is no time for ceremony. The question before the house is one of awful moment to this country. For my own part, I consider it as nothing less than the question offreedom or slavery; and in proportion to the magnitude of the subject ought to be the freedom of the debate. It is only in this way that we can hope to arrive at truth, and fulfil the great responsibility which we hold to God and our country. Should I keep back my opinions at such a time, through fear of giving offence, I should consider myself as guilty of treason toward my country, and of an act of disloyalty toward the Majesty of Heaven, which I revere above all earthly kings.

Mr. President, it is natural to man to indulge in the illusions of hope. We are apt to shut our eyes against a painful truth, and listen to the song of that siren, till she transforms us into beasts. Is this the part of wise men, engaged in a great and arduous struggle for liberty? Are we disposed to be of the number of those, who, having eyes, see not,

---

[26] Delivered in the Virginia Convention, on a resolution to put the commonwealth into a state of defense, March 23, 1775.

187

and having ears, hear not, the things which so nearly concern their temporal salvation? For my part, whatever anguish of spirit it may cost, I am willing to know the whole truth; to know the worst, and to provide for it.

I have but one lamp by which my feet are guided, and that is the lamp of experience. I know of no way of judging of the future but by the past. And judging by the past, I wish to know what there has been in the conduct of the British Ministry for the last ten years to justify those hopes with which gentlemen have been pleased to solace themselves and the House. Is it that insidious smile with which our petition has been lately received? Trust it not, sir; it will prove a snare to your feet. Suffer not yourselves to be betrayed with a kiss. Ask yourselves how this gracious reception of our petition comports with those warlike preparations which cover our waters and darken our land. Are fleets and armies necessary to a work of love and reconciliation? Have we shown ourselves so unwilling to be reconciled that force must be called in to win back ourlove? Let us not deceive ourselves, sir. These are the implements of war and subjugation; the last arguments to which kings resort. I ask gentlemen, sir, What means this martial array, if its purpose be not to force us to submission? Can gentlemen assign any other possible motive for it? Has Great Britain any enemy, in this quarter of the world, to call for all this accumulation of navies and armies? No, sir, she has none. They are meant for us; they can be meant for no other. They are sent over to bind and rivet upon us those chains which the British Ministry have been so long forging. And, what have we to oppose to them? Shall we try argument? Sir, we have been trying that for the last ten years. Have we anything new to offer upon the subject? Nothing. We have held the subject up in every light of which it is capable; but it has been all in vain. Shall we resort to entreaty and humble supplication? What terms shall we find, which have not already been exhausted? Let us not, I beseech you, sir, deceive ourselves longer. Sir, we have done everything that could be done to avert the storm which is now coming on. We have petitioned; we have remonstrated; we have supplicated; we have prostrated ourselves before the throne, and have implored its interposition to arrest the tyrannical hands of the Ministry and Parliament. Our petitions have been slighted: our remonstrances have produced additional violence and insult; our supplications have been disregarded; and we have been spurned, with contempt, from the foot of the throne! In vain, after these things, may we indulge the fond hope of peace and reconciliation. There is no longer any room for hope. If we wish to be free—if we mean to preserve inviolate those inestimable privileges for which we have been so long contending—if we mean not basely to abandon the noble struggle in which we have been so long engaged, and which we have pledged ourselves never to abandon, until the gloriousobject of our contest shall be obtained—we must fight! I repeat it, sir, we must fight! An appeal to arms and to the God of Hosts is all that is left us!

They tell us, sir, that we are weak; unable to cope with so formidable an adversary. But when shall we be stronger? Will it be the next week, or the next year? Will it be when we are totally disarmed, and when a British guard shall be stationed in every home? Shall we gather strength by irresolution and inaction? Shall we acquire the means of effectual resistance by lying supinely on our backs and hugging the delusive phantom of hope, until our enemies shall have bound us hand and foot? Sir, we are not weak, if we make a proper use of those means which the God of nature hath placed in our power. Three millions of people armed in the holy cause of liberty, and in such a country as that which we possess, are invincible by any force which our enemy can send against us. Besides, sir, we shall not fight our battles alone. There is a just God who presides over the destinies of nations, and who will raise up friends to fight our battles for us. The battle, sir, is not to the strong alone, it is to the vigilant, the active, the brave. Besides, sir, we have no election. If we were base enough to desire it, it is now too late to retire from the contest. There is no retreat, but in submission and slavery! Our chains are forged! Their clanking may be heard on the plains of Boston! The war is inevitable—and let it come! I repeat it, sir, let it come.

It is in vain, sir, to extenuate the matter. Gentlemen may cry, peace, peace—but there is no peace. The war is actually begun! The next gale that sweeps from the north will bring to our ears the clash of resounding arms! Our brethren are already in the field! Why stand we here idle? What is it that gentlemen wish? What would they have? Is life so dear, or peace so sweet, as to be purchased at the price of chains and slavery? Forbid it, Almighty God! I know not what course others may take; but as for me, give me liberty or give me death!

DANIEL WEBSTER

ON THE CLAY COMPROMISE[27]

(Known as "The Seventh of March Speech," 1850)

Slavery did exist in the states before the adoption of this Constitution, and at that time. Let us, therefore, consider for a moment what was the state of sentiment, North and South, in regard to slavery—in regard to slavery at the time this Constitution was adopted. A remarkable change has taken place since; but what did the wise and great men of all parts of the country think of slavery then? In what

---

[27] Delivered in the United States Senate, March 7, 1850, in support of Clay's compromise resolutions. Abridged.

estimation did they hold it at the time when this Constitution was adopted? It will be found, sir, if we will carry ourselves by historical research back to that day, and ascertain men's opinions by authentic records still existing among us, that there was no diversity of opinion between the North and the South upon the subject of slavery. It will be found that both parts of the country held it equally an evil, a moral and political evil. It will not be found that, either at the North or at the South, there was much, though there was some, invective against slavery as inhuman and cruel.

The great ground of objection to it was political; that it weakened the social fabric; that, taking the place of free labor, society became less strong and labor less productive; and therefore we find from all the eminent men of the time and clearest expression of their opinion that slavery is an evil. They ascribed its existence here, not without truth, and not without some acerbity of temper and force of language, to the injurious policy of the mother country, who, to favor the navigator, had entailed these evils upon the Colonies.

The whole interest of the South became connected, more or less, with the extension of slavery. If we look back to the history of the commerce of this country in the early years of this government, what were our exports? Cotton was hardly, or but to a very limited extent, known. In 1791 the first parcel of cotton of the growth of the United States was exported, and amounted only to 19,200 pounds. It has gone on increasing rapidly, until the whole crop may now, perhaps, in a season of great product and high prices, amount to a hundred millions of dollars. In the years I have mentioned, there was more of wax, more of indigo, more of rice, more of almost every article of export from the South, than of cotton. When Mr. Jay negotiated the treaty of 1794 with England, it is evident from the Twelfth Article of the Treaty, which was suspended by the Senate, that he did not know that cotton was exported at all from the United States.

Mr. President, in the excited times in which we live, there is found to exist a state of crimination and recrimination between the North and the South. There are lists of grievances produced by each; and these grievances, real or supposed, alienate the minds of one portion of the country from the other, exasperate the feelings, and subdue the sense of fraternal affection, patriotic love, and mutual regard. I shall bestow a little attention, sir, upon those various grievances existing on the one side and on the other. I begin with complaints of the South. I will not answer, further than I have, the general statements of the honorable senator from South Carolina, that the North has prospered at the expense of the South in consequence of the manner of administering the government, in the collection of its revenues,and so forth. These are disputed topics, and I have no inclination to enter into them.

But I will allude to other complaints of the South, and especially to one which has, in my opinion, just foundation, and that is, that there has been found at the North, among individuals and among legislators, a disinclination to perform fully their constitutional duties in regard to the return of persons bound to service who have escaped into the free States. In that respect, the South, in my judgment, is right, and the North is wrong. Every member of every Northern Legislature is bound by oath, like every other officer in the country, to support the Constitution of the United States; and the article of the Constitution which says to these states that they shall deliver up fugitives from service, is as binding in honor and conscience as any other article. No man fulfils his duty in any legislature who sets himself to find excuses, evasions, escapes from this constitutional obligation. I have always thought that the Constitution addressed itself to the legislatures of the states or the states themselves. It says that those persons escaping to other states "shall be delivered up," and I confess I have always been of the opinion that it was an injunction upon the states themselves. When it is said that a person escaping into another state, and coming therefore within the jurisdiction of that state, shall be delivered up, it seems to me the import of the clause is, that the state itself, in obedience to the Constitution, shall cause him to be delivered up. That is my judgment. I have always entertained that opinion, and I entertain it now.

Then, sir, there are abolition societies, of which I am unwilling to speak, but in regard to which I have very clear notions and opinions. I do not think them useful. I think their operations for the last twenty years have produced nothing good or valuable. At the same time, I believe thousands of their members to be honest and good men, perfectlywell-meaning men. They have excited feelings; they think they must do something for the cause of liberty; and, in their sphere of action, they do not see what else they can do than to contribute to an abolition press, or an abolition society, or to pay an abolition lecturer.

I do not mean to impute gross motives even to the leaders of these societies, but I am not blind to the consequences of their proceedings. I can not but see what mischief their interference with the South has produced. And is it not plain to every man? Let any gentleman who entertains doubts on this point, recur to the debates in the Virginia House of Delegates in 1832, and he will see with what freedom a proposition made by Mr. Jefferson Randolph, for the gradual abolition of slavery was discussed in that body. Every one spoke of slavery, as he thought; very ignominious and disparaging names and epithets were applied to it. The debates in the House of Delegates on that occasion, I believe were all published. They were read by every colored man who could read, and to those who could not read, those debates were read by others. At that time Virginia was not unwilling or afraid to discuss this question, and to let that part of her population know as much of the discussion as they could learn.

That was in 1832. As has been said by the honorable member from South Carolina, these abolition societies commenced their course of action in 1835. It is said, I do not know how true it may be, that they sent incendiary publications into the slave states; at any rate, they attempted to arouse, and did arouse, a very strong feeling; in other words, they created great agitation in the North against southern slavery. Well, what was the result? The bonds of the slaves were bound more firmly than before; their rivets were more strongly fastened. Public opinion, which in Virginia had begun to be exhibited against slavery, and was opening out for thediscussion of the question, drew back and shut itself up in its castle. I wish to know whether anybody in Virginia can now talk openly, as Mr. Randolph, Governor McDowell, and others talked in 1832, and sent their remarks to the press. We all know the fact, and we all know the cause; and everything that these agitating people have done has been, not to enlarge, but to restrain, not to act free, but to bind faster, the slave population of the South.

Mr. President, I should much prefer to have heard from every member on this floor declarations of opinion that this Union could never be dissolved, than the declaration of opinion by anybody, that in any case, under the pressure of any circumstances, such a dissolution was possible. I hear with distress and anguish the word "secession" especially when it falls from the lips of those who are patriotic, and known to the country, and known all over the world for their political services. Secession! peaceable secession! Sir, your eyes and mine are never destined to see that miracle. The dismemberment of this vast country without convulsion! The breaking up of the foundations of the great deep without ruffling the surface! Who is so foolish—I beg everybody's pardon—as to expect to see any such thing?

Sir, he who sees these states now revolving in harmony around a common center, and expects to see them quit their places and fly off without convulsion, may look the next hour to see the heavenly bodies rush from their spheres, and jostle against each other in the realms of space, without causing the crush of the universe. There can be no such thing as a peaceable secession. Peaceable secession is an utter impossibility. Is the great Constitution under which we live, covering this whole country, is it to be thawed and melted away by secession, as the snows on the mountains melt under the influence of a vernal sun, disappear almostunobserved, and run off? No, sir! No, sir! I will not state what might produce the disruption of the Union; but sir, I see, as plainly as I see the sun in heaven, what the disruption itself must produce; I see that it must produce war, and such a war as I will not describe, in its twofold character.

Peaceable secession! peaceable secession! The concurrent agreement of all the members of this great Republic to separate! A voluntary separation, with alimony on one side and on the other. Why, what would be the result? Where is the line to be drawn? What states are to secede? What is to remain American? What am I to be? An American no longer? Am I to become a sectional man, a local man, a separatist, with no country in common with the gentlemen who sit around me here, or who fill the other House of Congress? Heaven forbid! Where is the flag of the Republic to remain? Where is the eagle still to tower?—or is he to cower, and shrink, and fall to the ground?

Why, sir, our ancestors—our fathers and our grandfathers, those of them that are yet living among us, with prolonged lives—would rebuke and reproach us; and our children and our grandchildren would cry out shame upon us, if we, of this generation, would dishonor these ensigns of the power of the government and the harmony of that Union, which is every day felt among us with so much joy and gratitude. What is to become of the army? What is to become of the navy? What is to become of the public lands? How is any one of the thirty states to defend itself?

Sir, we could not sit down here today, and draw a line of separation that would satisfy any five men in the country. There are natural causes that would keep and tie us together; and there are social and domestic relations which we could not break if we would, and which we should not if we could.

Sir, nobody can look over the face of this country, at thepresent moment, nobody can see where its population is the most dense and growing, without being ready to admit, and compelled to admit, that ere long the strength of America will be in the valley of the Mississippi. Well, now, sir, I beg to inquire what the wildest enthusiast has to say on the possibility of cutting that river in two, and leaving free states at its source and on its branches, and slave states down near its mouth, each forming a separate government? Pray, sir, let me say to the people of this country, that these things are worthy of their pondering and of their consideration. Here, sir, are five millions of freemen in the free states north of the river Ohio.

Can anybody suppose that this population can be severed, by a line that divides them from the territory of a foreign and alien government, down somewhere, the Lord knows where, upon the lower banks of the Mississippi? What would become of Missouri? Will she join the arrondissement of the slave states? Shall the man from the Yellowstone and the Platte be connected, in the new Republic, with the man who lives on the southern extremity of the Cape of Florida? Sir, I am ashamed to pursue this line of remark. I dislike it; I have an utter disgust for it. I would rather hear of natural blasts and mildews, war, pestilence, and famine, than to hear gentlemen talk of secession. To break up this great government! to dismember this glorious country! to astonish Europe with an act of folly such as Europe for two centuries has never beheld in any government or any people! No, sir! no, sir! There will be no secession! Gentlemen are not serious when they talk of secession.

And now, Mr. President, instead of speaking of the possibility or utility of secession, instead of dwelling in these caverns of darkness, instead of groping with those ideasso full of all that is horrid and horrible, let us come out into the light of day; let us enjoy the fresh air of liberty and union; let us cherish those hopes which belong to us; let us devote ourselves to those great objects that are fit for our consideration and our action; let us raise our conceptions to the magnitude and the importance of the duties that devolve upon us; let our comprehension be as broad as the country for which we act, our aspirations as high as its certain destiny; let us not be pigmies in a case that calls for men. Never did there devolve on any generation of men higher trusts than now devolve upon us, for the preservation of this Constitution, and the harmony and peace of all who are destined to live under it. Let us make our generation one of the strongest and brightest links in that golden chain, which is destined, I fondly believe, to grapple the people of all the states to this Constitution for ages to come.

We have a great, popular, constitutional government, guarded by law and by judicature, and defended by the whole affections of the people. No monarchic throne presses these states together; no iron chain of military power encircles them; they live and stand upon a government popular in its form, representative in its character, founded upon principles of equality, and so constructed, we hope, as to last forever. In all its history it has been beneficent; it has trodden no man's liberty; it has crushed no state. Its daily respiration is liberty and patriotism; its yet youthful veins are full of enterprise, courage, and honorable love of glory and renown. Large before, the country has now, by recent events, become vastly larger. This Republic now extends, with a vast breadth, across the whole continent. The two great seas of the world wash the one and the other shore. We realize, on a mighty scale, the beautiful description of the ornamental edging of the buckler of Achilles—

> Now the broad shield complete, the artist crowned
> With his last hand, and poured the ocean round:
> In living silver seemed the waves to roll,
> And beat the buckler's verge, and bound the whole.

ROBERT YOUNG HAYNE
ON THE FOOTE REVOLUTION[28] (1830)

When the gentleman from Massachusetts adopts and reiterates the old charge of weakness as resulting from slavery, I must be permitted to call for the proof of those blighting effects which he

---

[28] Delivered in the Senate of the United States, January 21, 1830. Abridged.

ascribes to its influence. I suspect that when the subject is closely examined, it will be found that there is not much force even in the plausible objection of the want of physical power in slave-holding states. The power of a country is compounded of its population and its wealth, and in modern times, where, from the very form and structure of society, by far the greater portion of the people must, even during the continuance of the most desolating wars, be employed in the cultivation of the soil and other peaceful pursuits, it may be well doubted whether slave-holding states, by reason of the superior value of their productions, are not able to maintain a number of troops in the field fully equal to what could be supported by states with a larger white population, but not possessed of equal resources.

There is a spirit which, like the father of evil, is constantly "walking to and fro." It is the spirit of false philanthropy. The persons whom it possesses do not indeed throw themselves into the flames, but they are employed in lighting up the torches of discord throughout the community. Their first principle of action is to leave their own affairs,and neglect their own duties, to regulate the affairs and duties of others. Theirs is the task to feed the hungry and clothe the naked of other lands, while they thrust the naked, famished, and shivering beggar from their own doors—to instruct the heathen while their own children want the bread of life.

When this spirit infuses itself into the bosom of a statesman (if one so possessed can be called a statesman), it converts him at once into a visionary enthusiast. Then it is that he indulges in golden dreams of national greatness and prosperity. He discovers that "liberty is power," and, not content with vast schemes of improvement at home which it would bankrupt the treasury of the world to execute, he flies to foreign lands to fulfil obligations to "the human race," by inculcating the principles of "political and religious liberty," and promoting the "general welfare" of the whole human race. It is a spirit which has long been busy with the slaves of the South and is even now displaying itself in vain efforts to drive the government from its wise policy in relation to the Indians. It is this spirit which has filled the land with thousands of wild and visionary projects which can have no effect but to waste the energies and dissipate the resources of the country. It is the spirit of which the aspiring politician dexterously avails himself when, by inscribing on his banner the magical words, Liberty and Philanthropy, he draws to his support that class of persons who are ready to bow down at the very name of their idols.

But, sir, whatever difference of opinion may exist as to the effect of slavery on national wealth and prosperity, if we may trust to experience, there can be no doubt that it has never yet produced any injurious effect on individual or national character. Look through the whole history of the country from the commencement of the Revolution down to the present hour; where are there to be found brighter examples of intellectual and moral greatness than have been exhibited by the sons of the South? From the Father of his Country down to the distinguished chieftain who has been elevated by a grateful people to the highest office in their gift, the interval is filled up by a long line of orators, of statesmen, and of heroes, justly entitled to rank among the ornaments of their country, and the benefactors of mankind. Look at "the Old Dominion," great and magnanimous Virginia, "whose jewels are her sons." Is there any State in this Union which has contributed so much to the honor and welfare of the country? Sir, I will yield the whole question—I will acknowledge the fatal effects of slavery upon character, if any one can say that for noble disinterestedness, ardent love of country, exalted virtue, and a pure and holy devotion to liberty, the people of the southern states have ever been surpassed by any in the world.

The senator from Massachusetts tells us that the tariff is not an eastern measure, and treats it as if the East had no interest in it. The senator from Missouri insists it is not a western measure, and that it has done no good to the West. The South comes in, and in the most earnest manner represents to you that this measure, which we are told "is of no value to the East or the West" is "utterly destructive of our interests." We represent to you that it has spread ruin and devastation through the land and prostrated our hopes in the dust. We solemnly declare that we believe the system to be wholly unconstitutional and a violation of the compact between the states and the Union; and our brethren turn a deaf ear to our complaints, and refuse to relieve us from a system "which not enriches them, but makes us poor indeed." Good God! Mr. President, has it come to this? Do gentlemen hold the feelings and wishes of their brethren at so cheap a rate that they refuse to gratify them at so small a price? Do gentlemen value so lightly the peace and harmony of the country that they will not yield a measure of this description to the affectionate entreaties and earnest remonstrances of their friends? Do gentlemen estimate the value of the Union at so low a price that they will not even make one effort to bind the states together with the cords of affection? And has it come to this? Is this the spirit in which this government is to be administered? If so, let me tell, gentlemen, the seeds of dissolution are already sown, and our children will reap the bitter fruit.

What, sir, was the conduct of the South during the Revolution? Sir, I honor New England for her conduct in that glorious struggle. But great as is the praise which belongs to her I think at least equal honor is due to the South. They espoused the quarrel of their brethren with a generous zeal which did not suffer them to stop to calculate their interest in the dispute. Favorites of the mother country, possessed of neither ships nor seamen to create a commercial rivalship, they might have found in their situation a guaranty that their trade would be forever fostered and protected by Great Britain. But trampling on all consideration either of interest or of safety, they rushed into the conflict and fighting for principle, periled all in the sacred cause of freedom. Never was there exhibited in the history of the world higher examples of noble daring, dreadful suffering, and heroic endurance than by the Whigs of Carolina during the Revolution. The whole state, from the mountains to the sea, was overrun by an overwhelming force of the enemy. The fruits of industry perished on the spot where they were produced, or were consumed by the foe. The "plains of Carolina" drank up the most precious blood of her citizens! Black and smoking ruins marked the places which had been the habitations of her children! Driven from their homes into the gloomy and almost impenetrable swamps, even therethe spirit of liberty survived, and South Carolina (sustained by the example of her Sumpters and her Marions) proved by her conduct that though the soil might be overrun, the spirit of her people was invincible.

ABRAHAM LINCOLN

THE "HOUSE DIVIDED AGAINST ITSELF" SPEECH[29]
(1858)

If we could first know where we are, and whither we are tending, we could better judge what to do, and how to do it, we are now far into the fifth year since a policy was initiated with the avowed object, and confident promise, of putting an end to slavery agitation. Under the operation of that policy, that agitation not only has not ceased, but has constantly augmented. In my opinion, it will not cease until a crisis shall have been reached and passed. "A house divided against itself can not stand." I believe this government can not endure permanently half slave and half free. I do not expect the Union to be dissolved; I do not expect the house to fall; but I do expect that it will cease to be divided. It will become all one thing, or all the other. Either the opponents of slavery will arrest the further spread of it, and place it where the public mind shall rest in the belief that it is in the course of ultimate extinction; or its advocates will push it forward till it shall become alike lawful in all the states, old as well as new, North as well as South. Have we no tendency to the latter condition? Let any one who doubts carefully contemplate that now almost complete legal combination-piece of machinery, so to speak—compounded of the Nebraska doctrine and the Dred Scott decision.

Put this and that together, and we have another nicelittle niche, which we may, ere long, see filled with another Supreme Court

---

[29] Delivered at the Illinois Republican State Convention at Springfield, June 16, 1858.

decision, declaring that the Constitution of the United States does not permit a state to exclude slavery from its limits. And this may especially be expected if the doctrine of "care not whether slavery be voted down or voted up," shall gain upon the public mind sufficiently to give promise that such a decision can be maintained when made.

Such a decision is all that slavery now lacks of being alike lawful in all the states. Welcome or unwelcome, such decision is probably coming, and will soon be upon us, unless the power of the present political dynasty shall be met and overthrown. We shall lie down pleasantly dreaming that the people of Missouri are on the verge of making their state free, and we shall awake to the reality, instead, that the Supreme Court has made Illinois a slave state. To meet and overthrow that dynasty is the work before all those who would prevent that consummation. That is what we have to do. How can we best do it?

There are those who denounce us openly to their own friends and yet whisper to us softly that Senator Douglas is the aptest instrument there is with which to effect that object. They wish us to infer all, from the fact that he now has a little quarrel with the present head of the dynasty; and that he has regularly voted with us on a single point, upon which he and we have never differed. They remind us that he is a great man and that the largest of us are very small ones. Let this be granted. "But a living dog is better than a dead lion." Judge Douglas, if not a dead lion, for this work, is at least a caged and toothless one.

How can he oppose the advance of slavery? He does not care anything about it. His avowed mission is impressing the "public heart" to care nothing about it. A leading Douglas Democratic newspaper thinks Douglas's superior talent will be needed to resist the revival of the African slave-trade.Does Douglas believe an effort to revive that trade is approaching? He has not said so. Does he really think so? But if it is, how can he resist it? For years he has labored to prove it is a sacred right of white men to take negro slaves into the new territories. Can he possibly show that it is less a sacred right to buy them where they can be bought cheapest? And unquestionably they can be bought cheaper in Africa than in Virginia.

He has done all in his power to reduce the whole question of slavery to one of a mere right of property; and as such, how can he oppose the foreign slave-trade? How can he refuse that trade in that "property" shall be "perfectly free," unless he does it as a protection to the home production? And as the home producers will probably ask the protection, he will be wholly without a ground of opposition.

Senator Douglas holds, we know, that a man may rightfully be wiser today than he was yesterday—that he may rightfully change when he finds himself wrong. But can we, for that reason run ahead, and infer that he will make any particular change, of which he himself has given no intimation? Can we safely base our action upon any such vague inference? Now, as ever, I wish not to misrepresent Judge

Douglas's position, question his motives, or do aught that can be personally offensive to him. Whenever, if ever, he and we can come together on principle, so that our cause may have assistance from his great ability, I hope to have interposed no adventitious obstacle. But, clearly, he is not now with us—he does not pretend to be, he does not promise ever to be.

Our cause, then, must be entrusted to, and conducted by, its own undoubted friends—those whose hands are free, whose hearts are in the work—who do care for the result. Two years ago the Republicans of the nation mustered over thirteen hundred thousand strong. We did this under thesingle impulse of resistance to a common danger. With every external circumstance against us, of strange, discordant, and even hostile elements, we gathered from the four winds, and formed and fought the battle through, under the constant hot fire of a disciplined, proud, and pampered enemy. Did we brave all then, to falter now?—now, when that same energy is wavering, dissevered, and belligerent! The result is not doubtful. We shall not fail—if we stand firm, we shall not fail. Wise counsels may accelerate, or mistakes delay it; but, sooner or later, the victory is sure to come.

ON LEAVING SPRINGFIELD[30]

My friends, no one, not in my situation, can appreciate my feeling of sadness at this parting. To this place and the kindness of this people I owe everything. Here I have lived a quarter of a century and have passed from a young to an old man. Here my children have been born and one is buried.

I now leave, not knowing when or whether ever I may return, with a task before me greater than that which rested upon Washington. Without the assistance of that Divine Being who ever attended him I can not succeed. With that assistance I can not fail.

Trusting in Him who can go with me and remain with you and be everywhere for good, let us confidently hope that all will yet be well. To His care commending you, as I hope in your prayers you will commend me, I bid you an affectionate farewell.

WENDELL PHILLIPS

ON THE MURDER OF LOVEJOY[31] (1837)

A comparison has been drawn between the events of the Revolution and the tragedy at Alton. We have heard itstated here in

---

[30] Delivered on February 11, 1861.
[31] Delivered in Faneuil Hall, Boston, December 8, 1837.

Faneuil Hall, that Great Britain had a right to tax the Colonies; and we have heard the mob at Alton, the drunken murderers of Lovejoy, compared to those patriot fathers who threw the tea overboard! Fellow citizens, is this Faneuil Hall doctrine? The mob at Alton were met to wrest from a citizen his just rights—met to resist the laws. We have been told that our fathers did the same; and the glorious mantle of Revolutionary precedent has been thrown over the mobs of our day. To make out their title to such defense the gentleman says that the British Parliament had a right to tax these Colonies.

It is manifest that, without this, his parallel falls to the ground; for Lovejoy had stationed himself within constitutional bulwarks. He was not only defending the freedom of the press, but he was under his own roof, in arms with the sanction of the civil authority. The men who assailed him went against and over the laws. The mob, as the gentleman terms it—mob, forsooth! certainly we sons of the tea-spillers are a marvelously patient generation!—the "orderly mob" which assembled in the Old South to destroy the tea were met to resist, not the laws, but illegal exactions! Shame on the American who calls the tea tax and Stamp Act laws! Our fathers resisted not the king's prerogative, but the king's usurpation. To find any other account, you must read our Revolutionary history upside down. Our state archives are loaded with arguments of John Adams to prove the taxes laid by the British Parliament unconstitutional—beyond its power. It was not till this was made out that the men of New England rushed to arms. The arguments of the Council-chamber and the House of Representatives preceded and sanctioned the contest.

To draw the conduct of our ancestors into a precedent for mobs, for a right to resist laws we ourselves have enacted,is an insult to their memory. The difference between the excitements of those days and our own, which the gentleman in kindness to the latter has overlooked, is simply this: the men of that day went for the right, as secured by the laws. They were the people rising to sustain the laws and Constitution of the province. The rioters of our day go for their own wills, right or wrong. Sir, when I heard the gentleman lay down principles which place the murderers of Alton side by side with Otis and Hancock, with Quincy and Adams, I thought those pictured lips [pointing to the portraits in the hall] would have broken into voice to rebuke the recreant American the slanderer of the dead. The gentleman said that he should sink into insignificance if he dared not gainsay the principles of these resolutions. Sir, for the sentiments he has uttered, on soil consecrated by the prayers of Puritans and the blood of patriots, the earth should have yawned and swallowed him up.

Fellow citizens, I can not take back my words. Surely, the attorney-general, so long and well known here, needs not the aid of your hisses against one so young as I am—my voice never before heard within these walls!

200

Another ground has been taken to excuse the mob, and throw doubt and discredit on the conduct of Lovejoy and his associates. Allusion has been made to what lawyers understand very well—the "conduct of laws." We are told that nothing but the Mississippi River rolls between St. Louis and Alton; and the conflict of laws somehow or other give the citizens of the former a right to find fault with the defender of the press for publishing his opinions so near their limits. Will the gentleman venture that argument before lawyers? How the laws of the two states could be said to come into conflict in such circumstances I question whether any lawyer in this audience can explain or understand. No matter whether the line that divides one sovereignstate from another be an imaginary one or ocean-wide, the moment you cross it, the state you leave is blotted out of existence, so far as you are concerned. The Czar might as well claim to control the deliberations of Faneuil Hall, as the laws of Missouri demand reverence, or the shadow of obedience, from an inhabitant of Illinois.

I must find some fault with the statement which has been made of the events at Alton. It has been asked why Lovejoy and his friends did not appeal to the executive—trust their defenses to the police of the city. It has been hinted that, from hasty and ill-judged excitement, the men within the building provoked a quarrel, and that he fell in the course of it—one mob resisting another. Recollect, sir, that they did act with approbation and sanction of the mayor. In strict truth there was no executive to appeal to for protection. The mayor acknowledged that he could not protect them. They asked him if it was lawful for them to defend themselves. He told them it was, and sanctioned their assembling in arms to do so. They were not, then, a mob, they were not merely citizens defending their own property; they were in some sense the posse comitatus, adopted for the occasion into the police of the city, acting under the order of a magistrate. It was civil authority resisting lawless violence. Where, then, was the imprudence? Is the doctrine to be sustained here that it is imprudent for men to aid magistrates in executing the laws?

Men are continually asking each other, had Lovejoy a right to resist? Sir, I protest against the question instead of answering it. Lovejoy did not resist, in the sense they mean. He did not throw himself back on the natural right of self-defense. He did not cry anarchy, and let slip the dogs of civil war, careless of the horrors which would follow.

Sir, as I understand this affair, it was not an individual protecting his property; it was not one body of armed menresisting another, and making the streets of a peaceful city run blood with their contentions. It did not bring back the scenes to old Indian cities, where family met family, and faction met faction, and mutually trampled the laws under foot. No! the men in that house were regularly enrolled under the sanction of the mayor. There being no militia in Alton, about seventy

201

men were enrolled, with the approbation of the mayor. These relieved each other every other night. About thirty men were in arms on the night of the sixth, when the press was landed. The next evening it was not thought necessary to summon more than half that number; among these was Lovejoy. It was, therefore, you perceive, sir, the police of the city resisting rioters—civil government breasting itself to the shock of lawless men.

Here is no question about the right of self-defense. It is in fact simply this: Has the civil magistrate a right to put down a riot?

It has been stated, perhaps inadvertently, that Lovejoy or his comrades fired first. This is denied by those who have the best means of knowing. Guns were first fired by the mob. After being twice fired on, those within the building consulted together and deliberately returned the fire. But suppose they did fire first. They had a right so to do—not only the right which every citizen has to defend himself, but the further right which every civil officer has to resist violence. Even if Lovejoy fired the first gun, it would not lessen his claim to our sympathy or destroy his title to be considered a martyr in defense of a free press. The question now is, did he act within the Constitution and the laws? The men who fell in State Street on the 5th of March, 1770, did more than Lovejoy is charged with. They were the first assailants. Upon some slight quarrel they pelted the troops with every missile within reach. Did this bate one jot of the eulogy with which Hancock and Warren hallowed their memory, hailing them as the first martyrs in the cause of American liberty?

If, sir, I had adopted what are called peace principles, I might lament the circumstances of this case. But all you who believe, as I do, in the right and duty of magistrates to execute the laws, join with me and brand as base hypocrisy the conduct of those who assemble year after year on the Fourth of July to fight over the battles of the Revolution, and yet "damn with faint praise" or load with obloquy the memory of this man who shed his blood in defense of life, liberty, property, and the freedom of the press!

Imagine yourself present when the first news of Bunker Hill Battle reached a New England town. The tale would have run thus: "The patriots are routed—the redcoats victorious—Warren lies dead upon the field." With what scorn would that Tory have been received who should have charged Warren with imprudence! Who should have said that, bred a physician, he was "out of place" in that battle, and "died as a fool dieth!" How would the intimation have been received that Warren and his associations should have waited a better time? But, if success be indeed the only criterion of prudence, Respice finem—Wait till the end.

Mr. Chairman, from the bottom of my heart I thank that brave band at Alton for resisting. We must remember that Lovejoy had fled from city to city; suffered the destruction of three presses patiently. At length he took counsel with friends; men of character, of tried integrity, of wide views, of Christian principle. They thought the crisis had come. It was full time to assert the laws. They saw around them, not a community like our own, of fixed habits, of character molded and settled, but one "in the gristle, not yet hardened into the bone of manhood." The people there, children of our older states, seem to have forgotten the blood-tried principles of their fathers the moment they lost sight of our New England hills. Something was to be done to show them the priceless value of the freedom of the press, to bring back and set right their wandering and confused ideas. He and his advisers looked out on a community staggering like a drunken man, indifferent to their rights, and confused in their feelings. Deaf to argument, haply they might be stunned into sobriety. They saw that of which we can not judge: the necessity of resistance. Insulted law called for it. Public opinion, fast hastening on the downward course, must be arrested.

Does not the event show they judged rightly? Absorbed in a thousand trifles, how has the Nation all at once come to a stand! Men begin, as in 1779 and 1640, to discuss principles, to weigh characters, to find out where they are. Haply we may awake before we are borne over the precipice.

I am glad, sir, to see this crowded house. It is good for us to be here. When liberty is in danger, Faneuil Hall has the right, it is her duty, to strike the keynote for these United States. I am glad, for one reason, that remarks such as those to which I have alluded have been uttered here. The passage of these resolutions, in spite of this oppression, led by the attorney-general of the commonwealth, will show more clearly, more decisively, the deep indignation with which Boston regards this outrage.

JEFFERSON DAVIS

ON WITHDRAWING FROM THE UNION[32] (1861)

I rise, Mr. President, for the purpose of announcing to the Senate that I have satisfactory evidence that the State of Mississippi, by a solemn ordinance of her people in convention assembled, has declared her separation from the UnitedStates. Under these circumstances, of course, my functions are terminated here. It has seemed to me proper, however, that I should appear in the Senate to announce that fact to my associates, and I will say but very little more. The occasion does not invite me to go into argument, and my physical condition would not permit me to do so if it were otherwise; and yet it seems to become me to say something on the part of the state I here represent, on an occasion so solemn as this.

---

[32] Delivered in the United States Senate, January 21, 1861.

It is known to senators who have served with me here that I have for many years advocated, as an essential attribute of state sovereignty, the right of a state to secede from the Union. Therefore, if I had not believed there was justifiable cause; if I had thought that Mississippi was acting without sufficient provocation, or without an existing necessity, I should still, under my theory of the government, because of my allegiance to the state of which I am a citizen, have been bound by her action. I, however, may be permitted to say that I do think she has justifiable cause, and I approve of her act. I conferred with her people before the act was taken, counseled them then that if the state of things which they apprehended should exist when the convention met, they should take the action which they have now adopted.

I hope none who hear me will confound this expression of mine with the advocacy of the right of a state to remain in the Union, and to disregard the constitutional obligations by the nullification of the law. Such is not my theory. Nullification and secession, so often confounded, are indeed antagonistic principles. Nullification is a remedy which it is sought to apply within the Union, and against the agent of the states. It is only to be justified when the agent has violated his constitutional obligation, and a state, assuming to judge for itself, denies the right of the agent thus to act,and appeals to the other states of the Union for a decision; but when the states themselves, and when the people of the states, have so acted as to convince us that they will not regard our constitutional rights then, and then for the first time, arises the doctrine of secession in its practical application.

A great man who now reposes with his fathers, and who has been often arraigned for a want of fealty to the Union, advocated the doctrine of nullification because it preserved the Union. It was because of his deep seated attachment to the Union, his determination to find some remedy for existing ills short of a severance of the ties which bound South Carolina to the other states, that Mr. Calhoun advocated the doctrine of nullification, which he proclaimed to be peaceful, to be within the limits of state power, not to disturb the Union, but only to be a means of bringing the agent before the tribunal of the states for their judgment.

Secession belongs to a different class of remedies. It is to be justified upon the basis that the states are sovereign. There was a time when none denied it. I hope the time may come again when a better comprehension of the theory of our government, and the inalienable rights of the people of the states, will prevent any one from denying that each state is a sovereign, and thus may reclaim the grants which it has made to any agent whomsoever.

I therefore say I concur in the action of the people of Mississippi, believing it to be necessary and proper, and should have been bound by their action if my belief had been otherwise; and this brings me to the important point which I wish on this last occasion to present to the

Senate. It is by this confounding of nullification and secession that the name of the great man, whose ashes now mingle with his mother earth, has been invoked to justify coercion against a seceded state. The phrase "to execute the laws" was anexpression which General Jackson applied to the case of a state refusing to obey the laws while yet a member of the Union. That is not the case which is now presented. The laws are to be executed over the United States, and upon the people of the United States. They have no relation to any foreign country. It is a perversion of terms, at least it is a great misapprehension of the case, which cites that expression for application to a state which has withdrawn from the Union. You may make war on a foreign state. If it be the purpose of gentlemen, they may make war against a state which has withdrawn from the Union; but there are no laws of the United States to be executed within the limits of a seceded state. A state finding itself in the condition in which Mississippi has judged she is, in which her safety requires that she should provide for the maintenance of her rights out of the Union, surrenders all the benefits (and they are known to be many), deprives herself of the advantages (they are known to be great), severs all ties of affection (and they are close and enduring), which have bound her to the Union; and thus divesting herself of every benefit, taking upon herself every burden, she claims to be exempt from any power to execute the laws of the United States within her limits.

I well remember an occasion when Massachusetts was arraigned before the bar of the Senate, and when then the doctrine of coercion was rife and to be applied against her because of the rescue of a fugitive slave in Boston. My opinion then was the same that it is now. Not in a spirit of egotism, but to show that I am not influenced in my opinion because the case is my own, I refer to that time and that occasion as containing the opinion which I then entertained, and on which my present conduct is based. I then said, if Massachusetts, following her through a stated line of conduct, chooses to take the last step which separates her fromthe Union, it is her right to go, and I will neither vote one dollar nor one man to coerce her back; but will say to her, Godspeed, in memory of the kind associations which once existed between her and the other states.

It has been a conviction of pressing necessity, it has been a belief that we are to be deprived in the Union of the rights which our fathers bequeathed to us, which has brought Mississippi into her present decision. She has heard proclaimed the theory that all men are created free and equal, and this made the basis of an attack upon her social institutions; and the sacred Declaration of Independence has been invoked to maintain the position of the equality of the races. That Declaration of Independence is to be construed by the circumstances and purposes for which it was made. The communities were declaring their independence; the people of those communities were asserting that no man was born—to use the language of Mr. Jefferson—booted and spurred to ride over the rest of mankind; that men were created equal—meaning the men of the political community; that there was no divine right to rule; that no man inherited the right to govern; that there were no classes by which power and place descended to families, but that all stations were equally within the grasp of each member of the body politic. These were the great principles they announced; these were the purposes for which they made their declaration; these were the ends to which their enunciation was directed. They have no reference to the slave, else how happened it that among the items of arraignment made against George III was that he endeavored to do just what the North had been endeavoring of late to do—to stir up insurrection among our slaves? Had the Declaration announced that the negroes were free and equal, how was the prince to be arraigned for stirring up insurrection among them? And how was this to be enumerated among the high crimes which caused the Coloniesto sever their connection with the mother country? When our Constitution was formed the same idea was rendered more palpable, for there we find provisions made for that very class of persons as property; they were not put upon the footing of equality with white men—not even upon that of paupers and convicts; but, so far as representation was concerned, were discriminated against as a lower caste, only to be represented in the numerical proportion of three-fifths.

Then, senators, we recur to the compact which binds us together; we recur to the principles upon which our government was founded; and when you deny them, and when you deny us the right to withdraw from a government which, thus perverted, threatens to be destructive to our rights, we but tread in the path of our fathers when we proclaim our independence, and take the hazard.

I find in myself, perhaps, a type of the general feeling of my constituents toward yours, I am sure I feel no hostility to you, senators from the North. I am sure there is not one of you, whatever sharp discussion there may have been between us, to whom I can not now say, in the presence of my God, I wish you well; and such, I am sure, is the feeling of the people whom I represent toward those whom you represent. I therefore feel that I but express their desire when I say I hope, and they hope, for peaceful relations with you, though we must part. They may be mutually beneficial to use in the future as they have been in the past, if you so will it. The reverse may bring disaster on every portion of the country; and if you will have it thus, we will invoke the God of our fathers, who delivered them from the power of the lion, to protect us from the ravages of the bear; and thus, putting our trust in God, and in our firm hearts and strong arms, we will vindicate the rights as best we may.

In the course of my service here, associated at different times with a great variety of senators, I see now around me some with whom

I have served long; there have been points of collision; but whatever of offense there has been to me, I leave here; I carry with me no hostile remembrance. Whatever offense I have given which has not been redressed, or for which satisfaction has not been demanded, I have, senators, in this hour of our parting, to offer you my apology for any pain which, in the heat of discussion, I have inflicted. I go hence unencumbered of the remembrance of any injury received, and having discharged the duty of making the only reparation in my power for any injury offered.

Mr. President and senators, having made the announcement which the occasion seemed to me to require, it only remains for me to bid you a final adieu.

ROBERT TOOMBS

ON RESIGNING FROM THE SENATE[33] (1861)

The success of the Abolitionists and their allies, under the name of the Republican party, has produced its logical results already. They have for long years been sowing dragons' teeth and have finally got a crop of armed men. The Union, sir, is dissolved. That is an accomplished fact in the path of this discussion that men may as well heed. One of your confederates has already, wisely, bravely, boldly confronted public danger, she is only ahead of many of her sisters because of her greater facility for speedy action. The greater majority of those sister states, under the circumstances, consider her cause as their cause; and I charge you in their name today: "Touch not Saguntum."[34] It is not only theircause, but it is a cause which receives the sympathy and will receive the support of tens and hundreds of thousands of honest patriot men in the non-slaveholding states who have hitherto maintained constitutional rights, and who respect their oaths, abide by compacts, and love justice.

And while this Congress, this Senate, and this House of Representatives are debating the constitutionality and the expediency of seceding from the Union, and while the perfidious authors of this mischief are showering down denunciations upon a large portion of the patriotic men of this country, those brave men are coolly and calmly voting what you call revolution—aye, sir, doing better than that: arming to defend it. They appealed to the Constitution, they appealed to justice, they appealed to fraternity, until the Constitution, justice, and fraternity were no longer listened to in the legislative halls of their country, and then, sir, they prepared for the arbitrament of the sword;

---

[33] Delivered in the United States Senate, January 7, 1861.
[34] A city of Iberia (Spain). Captured by Hannibal in 219 b. c., in spite of Rome's warning. Hannibal's action caused the war between Rome and Carthage.

and now you see the glittering bayonet, and you hear the tramp of armed men from your capital to the Rio Grande. It is a sight that gladdens the eyes and cheers the hearts of other millions ready to second them. Inasmuch, sir, as I have labored earnestly, honestly, sincerely, with these men to avert this necessity so long as I deemed it possible, and inasmuch as I heartily approve their present conduct of resistance, I deem it my duty to state their case to the Senate, to the country, and to the civilized world.

Senators, my countrymen have demanded no new government; they have demanded no new Constitution. Look to their records at home and here from the beginning of this national strife until its consummation in the disruption of the empire, and they have not demanded a single thing except that you shall abide by the Constitution of the United States; that constitutional rights shall be respected, and that justice shall be done. Sirs, they have stood by your Constitution;they have stood by all its requirements, they have performed all its duties unselfishly, uncalculatingly, disinterestedly, until a party sprang up in this country which endangered their social system—a party which they arraign, and which they charge before the American people and all mankind with having made proclamation of outlawry against four thousand millions of their property in the Territories of the United States; with having put them under the ban of the empire in all the states in which their institutions exist outside the protection of federal laws; with having aided and abetted insurrection from within and invasion from without with the view of subverting their institutions, and desolating their homes and their firesides. For these causes they have taken up arms.

I have stated that the discontented states of this Union have demanded nothing by clear, distinct, unequivocal, well-acknowledged constitutional rights—rights affirmed by the highest judicial tribunals of their country; rights older than the Constitution; rights which are planted upon the immutable principles of natural justice; rights which have been affirmed by the good and the wise of all countries, and of all centuries. We demand no power to injure any man. We demand no right to injure our confederate states. We demand no right to interfere with their institutions, either by word or deed. We have no right to disturb their peace, their tranquility, their security. We have demanded of them simply, solely—nothing else—to give us equality, security and tranquility. Give us these, and peace restores itself. Refuse them, and take what you can get.

What do the rebels demand? First, "that the people of the United States shall have an equal right to emigrate and settle in the present and any future acquired territories, with whatever property they may possess (including slaves), and be securely protected in its peaceable enjoyment until such territory may be admitted as a state into the Union, with or without slavery, as she may determine, on an equality with all existing states." This is our territorial demand. We have fought for this territory when blood was its price. We have paid for it when gold was its price. We have not proposed to exclude you, though you have contributed very little of blood or money. I refer especially to New England. We demand only to go into those territories upon terms of equality with you, as equals in this great Confederacy, to enjoy the common property of the whole Union, and receive the protection of the common government, until the territory is capable of coming into the Union as a sovereign state, when it may fix its own institutions to suit itself.

The second proposition is, "that property in slaves shall be entitled to the same protection from the government of the United States, in all its departments, everywhere, which the Constitution confers the power upon it to extend to any other property, providing nothing herein contained shall be construed to limit or restrain the right now belonging to every state to prohibit, abolish, or establish and protect slavery within its limits." We demand of the common government to use its granted powers to protect our property as well as yours. For this protection we pay as much as you do. This very property is subject to taxation. It has been taxed by you and sold by you for taxes.

The title to thousands and tens of thousands of slaves is derived from the United States. We claim that the government, while the Constitution recognizes our property for the purposes of taxation, shall give it the same protection that it gives yours.

Ought it not to be so? You say no. Every one of you upon the committee said no. Your senators say no. Your House of Representatives says no. Throughout the length and breadth of your conspiracy against the Constitution there is but one shout of no! This recognition of this right is the price of my allegiance. Withhold it, and you do not get my obedience. This is the philosophy of the armed men who have sprung up in this country. Do you ask me to support a government that will tax my property; that will plunder me; that will demand my blood, and will not protect me? I would rather see the population of my native state laid six feet beneath her sod than they should support for one hour such a government. Protection is the price of obedience everywhere, in all countries. It is the only thing that makes government respectable. Deny it and you can not have free subjects or citizens; you may have slaves.

We demand, in the next place, "that persons committing crimes against slave property in one state, and fleeing to another, shall be delivered up in the same manner as persons committing crimes against other property, and that the laws of the state from which such persons flee shall be the test of criminality." That is another one of the demands of an extremist and rebel.

But the non-slaveholding states, treacherous to their oaths and compacts, have steadily refused, if the criminal only stole a negro and that negro was a slave, to deliver him up. It was refused twice on the requisition of my own state as long as twenty-two years ago. It was refused by Kent and by Fairfield, governors of Maine, and representing, I believe, each of the then friendly parties. We appealed then to fraternity, but we submitted; and this constitutional right has been practically a dead letter from that day to this. The next case came up between us and the state of New York, when the present senior senator (Mr. Seward) was the governor of that state; and he refused it. Why? He said it was not against the laws of New York to steal a negro, and therefore he would not comply with the demand. He made a similar refusal to Virginia. Yet these are our confederates;these are our sister states! There is the bargain; there is the compact. You have sworn to it. Both these governors swore to it. The senator from New York swore to it. The governor of Ohio swore to it when he was inaugurated. You can not bind them by oaths. Yet they talk to us of treason; and I suppose they expect to whip freemen into loving such brethren! They will have a good time in doing it!

It is natural we should want this provision of the Constitution carried out. The Constitution says slaves are property; the Supreme Court says so; the Constitution says so. The theft of slaves is a crime; they are a subject-matter of felonious asportation. By the text and letter of the Constitution you agreed to give them up. You have sworn to do it, and you have broken your oaths. Of course, those who have done so look out for pretexts. Nobody expected them to do otherwise. I do not think I ever saw a perjurer, however bald and naked, who could not invent some pretext to palliate his crime, or who could not, for fifteen shillings, hire an Old Bailey lawyer to invent some for him. Yet this requirement of the Constitution is another one of the extreme demands of an extremist and a rebel.

The next stipulation is that fugitive slaves shall be surrendered under the provisions of the Fugitive Slave Act of 1850, without being entitled either to a writ of habeas corpus, or trial by jury, or other similar obstructions of legislation, in the state to which he may flee: Here is the Constitution:

"No person held to service or labor in one State, under the laws thereof, escaping into another, shall, in consequence of any law or regulation therein, be discharged from such service or labor, but shall be delivered up on claim of the party to whom such services or labor may be due."

This language is plain, and everybody understood it the same way for the first forty years of your government. In1793, in Washington's time, an act was passed to carry out this provision. It was adopted unanimously in the Senate of the United States, and nearly so in the House of Representatives. Nobody then had invented pretexts to show that the Constitution did not mean a negro slave. It was clear; it

210

was plain. Not only the federal courts, but all the local courts in all the states, decided that it was a constitutional obligation. How is it now? The North sought to evade it; following the instincts of their natural character, they commenced with the fraudulent fiction that fugitives were entitled to habeas corpus, entitled to trial by jury in the state to which they fled. They pretended to believe that our fugitive slaves were entitled to more rights than their white citizens; perhaps they were right, they know one another better than I do. You may charge a white man with treason, or felony, or other crime, and you do not require any trial by jury before he is given up; there is nothing to determine but that he is legally charged with a crime and that he fled, and then he is to be delivered up upon demand. White people are delivered up every day in this way; but not slaves. Slaves, black people, you say, are entitled to trial by jury; and in this way schemes have been invented to defeat your plain constitutional obligations.

Senators, the Constitution is a compact. It contains all our obligations and the duties of the federal government. I am content and have ever been content to sustain it. While I doubt its perfection, while I do not believe it was a good compact, and while I never saw the day that I would have voted for it as a proposition de novo, yet I am bound to it by oath and by that common prudence which would induce men to abide by established forms rather than to rush into unknown dangers. I have given to it, and intend to give to it, unfaltering support and allegiance, but I choose to put that allegiance on the true ground, not on the false ideathat anybody's blood was shed for it. I say that the Constitution is the whole compact. All its obligations, all the chains that fetter the limbs of my people, are nominated in the bond, and they wisely excluded any conclusion against them, by declaring that "The powers not granted by the Constitution to the United States, or forbidden by it to the states, belong to the states respectively or the people."

Now I will try it by that standard; I will subject it to that test. The law of nature, the law of justice, would say—and it is so expounded by the publicists—that equal rights in the common property shall be enjoyed. Even in a monarchy the king can not prevent the subjects from enjoying equality in the disposition of the public property. Even in a despotic government this principle is recognized. It was the blood and the money of the whole people (says the learned Grotius, and say all the publicists) which acquired the public property, and therefore it is not the property of the sovereign. This right of equality being, then, according to justice and natural equity, a right belonging to all states, when did we give it up? You say Congress has a right to pass rules and regulations concerning the territory and other property of the United States. Very well. Does that exclude those whose blood and money paid for it? Does "dispose of" mean to rob the rightful owners? You must show a better title than that, or a better sword than we have.

What, then, will you take? You will take nothing but your own judgment; that is, you will not only judge for yourselves, not only discard the court, discard our construction, discard the practice of the government, but you will drive us out, simply because you will it. Come and do it! You have sapped the foundations of society; you have destroyed almost all hope of peace. In a compact where there is no common arbiter, where the parties finally decide for themselves, the sword alone at last becomes the real, if notthe constitutional, arbiter. Your party says that you will not take the decision of the Supreme Court. You said so at Chicago; you said so in committee; every man of you in both Houses says so. What are you going to do? You say we shall submit to your construction. We shall do it, if you can make us; but not otherwise, or in any other manner. That is settled. You may call it secession, or you may call it revolution; but there is a big fact standing before you—that fact is, freemen with arms in their hands.

RUFUS CHOATE

EULOGY OF WEBSTER[35] (1853)

Webster possessed the element of an impressive character, inspiring regard, trust and admiration, not unmingled with love. It had, I think, intrinsically a charm such as belongs only to a good, noble, and beautiful nature. In its combination with so much fame, so much force of will, and so much intellect, it filled and fascinated the imagination and heart. It was affectionate in childhood and youth, and it was more than ever so in the few last months of his long life. It is the universal testimony that he gave to his parents, in largest measure, honor, love, obedience; that he eagerly appropriated the first means which he could command to relieve the father from his debts contracted to educate his brother and himself; that he selected his first place of professional practice that he might soothe the coming on of his old age.

Equally beautiful was his love of all his kindred and of all his friends. When I hear him accused of selfishness, and a cold, bad nature, I recall him lying sleepless all night, not without tears of boyhood, conferring with Ezekiel how the darling desire of both hearts should be compassed, and he, too, admitted to the precious privileges of education; courageouslypleading the cause of both brothers in the morning; prevailing by the wise and discerning affection of the mother; suspending his studies of the law, and registering deeds and teaching school to earn the means, for both, of availing themselves of the opportunity which the parental self-sacrifice had placed within their reach; loving him through life, mourning him when dead, with a love and a sorrow very wonderful, passing the sorrow of woman; I recall the

---

[35] Delivered at Dartmouth College, July 27, 1853.

212

husband, the father of the living and of the early departed, the friend, the counselor of many years, and my heart grows too full and liquid for the refutation of words.

His affectionate nature, craving ever friendship, as well as the presence of kindred blood, diffused itself through all his private life, gave sincerity to all his hospitalities, kindness to his eye, warmth to the pressure of his hand, made his greatness and genius unbend themselves to the playfulness of childhood, flowed out in graceful memories indulged of the past or of the dead, of incidents when life was young and promised to be happy,—gave generous sketches of his rivals,—the high contention now hidden by the handful of earth,— hours passed fifty years ago with great authors, recalled for the vernal emotions which they then made to live and revel in the soul. And from these conversations of friendship, no man—no man, old or young— went away to remember one word of profaneness, one allusion of indelicacy, one impure thought, one unbelieving suggestion, one doubt cast on the reality of virtue, of patriotism, of enthusiasm, of the progress of man,—one doubt cast on righteousness, or temperance, or judgment to come.

I have learned by evidence the most direct and satisfactory that in the last months of his life, the whole affectionateness of his nature— his consideration of others, his gentleness, his desire to make them happy and to see them happy—seemed to come out in more and more beautiful and habitualexpressions than ever before. The long day's public tasks were felt to be done; the cares, the uncertainties, the mental conflicts of high place, were ended; and he came home to recover himself for the few years which he might still expect would be his before he should go hence to be here no more. And there, I am assured and duly believe, no unbecoming regrets pursued him; no discontent, as for injustice suffered or expectations unfulfilled; no self-reproach for anything done or anything omitted by himself; no irritation, no peevishness unworthy of his noble nature; but instead, love and hope for his country, when she became the subject of conversation, and for all around him, the dearest and most indifferent, for all breathing things about him, the overflow of the kindest heart growing in gentleness and benevolence—paternal, patriarchal affections, seeming to become more natural, warm, and communicative every hour. Softer and yet brighter grew the tints on the sky of parting day; and the last lingering rays, more even than the glories of noon, announced how divine was the source from which they proceeded; how incapable to be quenched; how certain to rise on a morning which no night should follow.

Such a character was made to be loved. It was loved. Those who know and saw it in its hour of calm—those who could repose on that soft grass—loved him. His plain neighbors loved him; and one said, when he was laid in his grave, "How lonesome the world seems!"

Educated young men loved him. The ministers of the gospel, the general intelligence of the country, the masses afar off, loved him. True, they had not found in his speeches, read by millions, so much adulation of the people; so much of the music which robs the public reason of itself; so many phrases of humanity and philanthropy; and some had told them he was lofty and cold—solitary in his greatness; but every year they came nearer and nearer to him, and as they camenearer, they loved him better; they heard how tender the son had been, the husband, the brother, the father, the friend, and neighbor; that he was plain, simple, natural, generous, hospitable—the heart larger than the brain; that he loved little children and reverenced God, the Scriptures, the Sabbath day, the Constitution, and the law—and their hearts clave unto him. More truly of him than even of the great naval darling of England might it be said that "his presence would set the church bells ringing, and give schoolboys a holiday, would bring children from school and old men from the chimney-corner, to gaze on him ere he died." The great and unavailing lamentations first revealed the deep place he had in the hearts of his countrymen.

You are now to add to his extraordinary power of influencing the convictions of others by speech, and you have completed the survey of the means of his greatness. And here, again, I begin, by admiring an aggregate made up of excellences and triumphs, ordinarily deemed incompatible. He spoke with consummate ability to the bench, and yet exactly as, according to every sound canon of taste and ethics, the bench ought to be addressed. He spoke with consummate ability to the jury, and yet exactly as, according to every sound canon, that totally different tribunal ought to be addressed. In the halls of Congress, before the people assembled for political discussion in masses, before audiences smaller and more select, assembled for some solemn commemoration of the past or of the dead—in each of these, again, his speech, of the first form of ability, was exactly adapted, also, to the critical proprieties of the place; each achieved, when delivered, the most instant and specific success of eloquence—some of them in a splendid and remarkable degree; and yet, stranger still, when reduced to writing, as they fell from his lips, they compose a body ofreading in many volumes—solid, clear, rich, and full of harmony—a classical and permanent political literature.

And yet all these modes of his eloquence, exactly adapted each to its stage and its end, were stamped with his image and superscription, identified by characteristics incapable to be counterfeited and impossible to be mistaken. The same high power of reason, intent in every one to explore and display some truth; some truth of judicial, or historical, or biographical fact; some truth of law, deducted by construction, perhaps, or by illation; some truth of policy, for want whereof a nation, generations, may be worse—reason seeking and unfolding truth; the same tone, in all, of deep earnestness, expressive

214

of strong desire that which he felt to be important should be accepted as true, and spring up to action; the same transparent, plain, forcible, and direct speech, conveying his exact thought to the mind—not something less or more; the same sovereignty of form, of brow, and eye, and tone, and manner—everywhere the intellectual king of men, standing before you—that same marvelousness of qualities and results, residing, I know not where, in words, in pictures, in the ordering of ideas, in felicities indescribable, by means whereof, coming from his tongue, all things seemed mended—truth seemed more true, probability more plausible, greatness more great, goodness more awful, every affection more tender than when coming from other tongues—these are, in all, his eloquence.

But sometimes it became individualized and discriminated even from itself; sometimes place and circumstance, great interests at stake, a stage, an audience fitted for the highest historic action, a crisis, personal or national, upon him, stirred the depths of that emotional nature, as the anger of the goddess stirs the sea on which the great epic is beginning; strong passions, themselves kindled to intensity, quickened every faculty to a new life; the stimulated associations of ideas brought all treasures of thought and knowledge within command; the spell, which often held his imagination fast, dissolved, and she arose and gave him to choose of her urn of gold; earnestness became vehemence, the simple, perspicuous, measured and direct language became a headlong, full, and burning tide of speech; the discourse of reason, wisdom, gravity, and beauty changed to that superhuman, that rarest consummate eloquence—grand, rapid, pathetic, terrible; the aliquid immensum infinitumque that Cicero might have recognized; the master triumph of man in the rarest opportunity of his noble power.

Such elevation above himself, in congressional debate, was most uncommon. Some such there were in the great discussions of executive power following the removal of the deposits, which they who heard them will never forget, and some which rest in the tradition of hearers only. But there were other fields of oratory on which, under the influence of more uncommon strings of inspiration, he exemplified, in still other forms, an eloquence in which I do not know that he has had a superior among men. Addressing masses by tens of thousands in the open air, on the urgent political questions of the day, or designed to lead the meditations of an hour devoted to the remembrance of some national era, or of some incident marking the progress of the nation, and lifting him up to a view of what is, and what is past, and some indistinct revelation of the glory that lies in the future, or of some great historical name, just borne by the nation to his tomb—we have learned that then and there, at the base of Bunker Hill, before the corner-stone was laid, and again when the finished column the centuries looked on him; in Faneuil Hall, mourning for those with whom spoken or written eloquence of freedom its arches had so often resounded; on the Rock of Plymouth; before the Capitol, of which there shall not be one stone left on another before his memory shall have ceased to live—in such scenes, unfettered by the laws of forensic or parliamentary debate, multitudes uncounted lifting up their eyes to him; some great historical scenes of America around; all symbols of her glory and art and power and fortune there; voices of the past, not unheard; shapes beckoning from the future, not unseen—sometimes that mighty intellect, borne upward to a height and kindled to an illumination which we shall see no more, wrought out, as it were, in an instant a picture of vision, warning, prediction; the progress of the nation; the contrasts of its eras; the heroic deaths; the motives to patriotism; the maxims and arts imperial by which the glory has been gathered and may be heightened—wrought out, in an instant, a picture to fade only when all record of our mind shall die.

In looking over the public remains of his oratory, it is striking to remark how, even in that most sober and massive understanding and nature, you see gathered and expressed the characteristic sentiments and the passing time of our America. It is the strong old oak which ascends before you; yet our soil, our heaven, are attested in it as perfectly as if it were a flower that could grow in no other climate and in no other hour of the year or day. Let me instance in one thing only. It is a peculiarity of some schools of eloquence that they embody and utter, not merely the individual genius and character of the speaker, but a national consciousness—a national era, a mood, a hope, a dread, a despair—in which you listen to the spoken history of the time. There is an eloquence of an expiring nation, such as seems to sadden the glorious speech of Demosthenes; such as breathes grand and gloomy from the visions of the prophets of the last days of Israel and Judah; such as gave a spell to the expression of Grattan and of Kossuth—the sweetest, most mournful, most awful of the words which man mayutter, or which man may hear—the eloquence of a perishing nation.

There is another eloquence, in which the national consciousness of a young or renewed and vast strength, of trust in a dazzling certain and limitless future, an inward glorying in victories yet to be won, sounds out as by voice of clarion, challenging to contest for the highest prize of earth; such as that in which the leader of Israel in the first days holds up to the new nation the Land of Promise; such as that which in the well-imagined speeches scattered by Livy over the history of the "majestic series of victories" speaks the Roman consciousness of growing aggrandizement which should subject the world; such as that through which, at the tribunes of her revolution, in the bulletins of her rising soldiers, France told the world her dream of glory.

And of this king somewhat is ours—cheerful, hopeful, trusting, as befits youth and spring; the eloquence of a state beginning to ascend to the first class of power, eminence, and consideration, and conscious of

216

itself. It is to no purpose that they tell you it is in bad taste; that it partakes of arrogance and vanity; that a true national good breeding would not know, or seem to know, whether the nation is old or young; whether the tides of being are in their flow or ebb; whether these coursers of the sun are sinking slowly to rest, wearied with a journey of a thousand years, or just bounding from the Orient unbreathed. Higher laws than those of taste determine the consciousness of nations. Higher laws than those of taste determine the general forms of the expression of that consciousness. Let the downward age of America find its orators and poets and artists to erect its spirit, or grace, and soothe its dying; be it ours to go up with Webster, to the Rock, the Monument, the Capitol, and bid "the distant generations hail!"

Until the seventh day of March, 1850, I think it wouldhave been accorded to him by an almost universal acclaim, as general and as expressive of profound and intelligent conviction and of enthusiasm, love, and trust, as ever saluted conspicuous statesmanship, tried by many crises of affairs in a great nation, agitated ever by parties, and wholly free.

JOHN BRIGHT

THE STRENGTH OF THE AMERICAN GOVERNMENT (1863)

Will anybody deny that the Government at Washington as regards its own people is the strongest Government in the world at this hour? And for this simple reason: because it is based on the will, and the good will, of an instructed people. Look at its power! I am not now discussing why it is, or the cause which is developing this power; but power is the thing which men regard in these old countries, and which they ascribe mainly to European institutions; but look at the power which the United States have developed! They have brought more men into the field, they have built more ships for their navy, they have shown greater resources, than any nation in Europe at this moment is capable of. Look at the order which has prevailed at their elections, at which, as you see by the papers, fifty thousand, or one hundred thousand, or two hundred and fifty thousand persons voting in a given state, with less disorder than you have seen lately in three of the smallest boroughs in England. Look at their industry. Notwithstanding this terrible struggle, their agriculture, their manufactures and commerce proceed with an uninterrupted success. They are ruled by a President, chosen, it is true, not from some worn-out royal or noble blood, but from the people, and the one whose truthfulness and spotless honor have claimed him universal praise; and now the country that has been vilified through half the organs of the press in England

217

during the last three years, and was pointed out, too, as an example to be shunned by many of your statesmen, that country, now in mortal strife, affords a haven and a home for multitudes flying from the burdens and the neglect of the old governments of Europe; and, when this mortal strife is over—when peace is restored, when slavery is destroyed, when the Union is cemented afresh—for I would say, in the language of one of our own poets addressing his country,

> The grave's not dug where traitor hands shall lay
> In fearful haste thy murdered corse away—

then Europe and England may learn that an instructed democracy is the surest foundation of government, and that education and freedom are the only sources of true greatness and true happiness among any people.

GEORGE WILLIAM CURTIS

ROBERT BURNS[36] (1880)

Burns died at the same age with Raphael; and Mozart, who was his contemporary, died only four years before him. Raphael and Mozart are the two men of lyrical genius in kindred arts who impress us and the most exquisitely refined by careful cultivation; and, although Burns was of all great poets the most unschooled, he belongs with Raphael in painting and Mozart in music, and there is no fourth. An indescribable richness and flower-like quality, a melodious grace and completeness and delicacy, belong to them all. Looking upon a beautiful human Madonna of Raphael, we seem to hear the rippling cadence of Mozart and the tender and true song of Burns. They are all voices of the whole worldspeaking in this accent of a native land. Here are Italy and Germany and Scotland, distinct, individual, perfectly recognizable, but the sun that reveals and illuminates their separate charms, that is not Italian or German or Scotch, it is the sun of universal nature. This is the singer whom this statue commemorates, the singer of songs immortal as love; pure as the dew of the morning, and sweet as its breath; songs with which the lover wooes his bride, and the mother soothes her child, and the heart of a people beats with patriotic exultation; songs that cheer human endeavors, and console human sorrow, and exalt human life. We cannot find out the secret of their power until we know why the rose is sweet, or the dew-drop pure, or the rainbow beautiful, we cannot know why the poet is the best benefactor of humanity. Whether because he reveals us to ourselves, or because he touches the soul with

---

[36] Extract from an address delivered at the unveiling of the Statue of the Poet, in Central Park, New York, October 2, 1880.

the fervor of divine aspiration, whether because in a world of sordid and restless anxiety he fills us with serene joy, or puts into rythmic and permanent form the best thoughts and hopes of man—who shall say? But none the less is the heart's instinctive loyalty to the poet the proof of its consciousness that he does all these things, that he is the harmonizer, strengthener, and consoler. How the faith of Christendom has been stayed for centuries upon the mighty words of the old Hebrew bards and prophets, and how the vast and inexpressible mystery of divine love and power and purpose has been breathed into parable and poem! If we were forced to surrender every expression of human genius but one, surely we should retain poetry; and if we were called upon to lose from the vast accumulation of literature all but a score of books, among that choice, and perfect remainder would be the songs of Burns.

How fitly, then, among the memorials of those who in different countries and times and ways have been leaders of mankind, we raise this statue of the poet whose geniusis an unconscious but sweet and elevating influence in our national life. It is not a power dramatic, obvious, imposing, immediate, like that of the statesman, the warrior, and the inventor, but it is as deep and strong and abiding. The soldier fights for his native land, but the poet touches that land with the charm that makes it worth fighting for, and fires the warrior's heart with the fierce energy that makes his blow invincible. The statesman enlarges and orders liberty in the state, but the poet fosters the love of liberty in the heart of the citizen. The inventor multiplies the facilities of life, but the poet makes life better worth living. Here, then, among trees and flowers and waters; here upon the greensward and under the open sky; here where birds carol, and children play, and lovers whisper, and the various stream of human life flows by—we raise the statue of Robert Burns. While the human heart beats, that name will be music in human ears. He knew better than we the pathos of human life. We know better than he the infinite pathos of his own. Ah! Robert Burns, Robert Burns! whoever lingers here as he passes and muses upon your statue will see in imagination a solitary mountain in your own beautiful Scotland, heaven-soaring, wrapped in impenetrable clouds. Suddenly the mists part, and there are the heather, the brier-rose, and the gowan fine; there are the

> Burnies, wimplin' down your glens
> Wi' toddling' din,
> Or foaming strang wi' hasty stens
> Frae lin to lin;[37]

the cushat is moaning; the curlew is calling; the plover is singing; the red dear is bounding; and look! the clouds roll utterly away, and the

---

[37] From Robert Burns' Elegy on Captain Matthew Henderson.

clear summit is touched with the tender glory of sunshine, heaven's own benediction!

L. Q. C. LAMAR

SUMNER AND THE SOUTH[38] (1874)

It was certainly a gracious act on the part of Charles Sumner toward the South, though unhappily it jarred on the sensibilities of the people at the other extreme of the Union, to propose to erase from the banners of the national army the mementos of the bloody internal struggle which might be regarded as assailing the pride or wounding the sensibilities of the Southern people. The proposal will never be forgotten by that people so long as the name of Charles Sumner lives in the memory of man.

But while it touched the heart and elicited her profound gratitude, her people would not have asked of the North such an act of self-renunciation. Conscious that they themselves were animated by devotion to constitutional liberty, and that the brightest pages of history are replete with evidences of the depth and sincerity of that devotion, they can but cherish the recollection of the battles fought and the victories won in defense of their hopeless cause; and respecting, as all true and brave men must respect, the martial spirit with which the men of the North vindicated the integrity of the Union, and their devotion to the principles of human freedom, they do not ask, they do not wish the North to strike the mementos of heroism and victory from either records or monuments or battle-flags. They would rather that both sections should gather up the glories won by each section, not envious, but proud of each other, and regard them as a common heritage of American valor. Let us hope that future generations, when they remember the deeds of heroism and devotion done on both sides, will speak, not of northern prowess or southern courage, but of theheroism, courage and fortitude of the Americans in a war of ideas—a war in which each section signalized its consecration to the principles, as each understood them, of American liberty and of the Constitution received from their fathers.

Charles Sumner in life believed that all occasion for strife and distrust between the North and South had passed away, and there no longer remained any cause for continued estrangement between these two sections of our common country. Are there not many of us who believe the same thing? Is not the common sentiment, or if not, ought it not to be, of the great mass of our people, North and South? Bound to each other by a common constitution, destined to life together under a

---

[38] Delivered in the House of Representatives, April 28, 1874. Extract.

common government, forming unitedly but a single member of a great family of nations, shall we not now at least endeavor to grow toward each other once more in heart, as we are indissolubly linked to each other in fortunes? Shall we not, while honoring the memory of this great champion of liberty, this feeling sympathizer with human sorrow, this earnest pleader for the exercise of human tenderness and heavenly charity, lay aside the concealments which serve only to perpetuate misunderstandings and distrust, and frankly confess that on both sides we most earnestly desire to be one—one not merely in political organization; one not merely in community of language, and literature, and traditions, and country; but more and better than all that, one also in feeling and in heart?

Am I mistaken in this? Do the concealments of which I speak still cover animosities, which neither time nor reflection nor the march of events have yet suffered to subdue? I can not believe it. Since I have been here I have scrutinized your sentiments, as expressed not merely in public debate, but in the abandon of personal confidence. I know well the sentiments of these by my southern friends, whose hearts areso infolded that the feeling of each is the feeling of all; and I am on both sides only the seeming of a constraint which each apparently hesitates to dismiss.

The South—prostrate, exhausted, drained of her life-blood as well as her material resources, yet still honorable and true—accepts the bitter award of the bloody arbitrament without reservation, resolutely determined to abide the result with chivalrous fidelity. Yet, as if struck dumb by the magnitude of her reverses, she suffers on in silence. The North, exultant in her triumph and elevated by success, still cherishes, as we are assured, a heart full of magnanimous emotions toward her disarmed and discomfited antagonist; and yet, as if under some mysterious spell, her words and acts are words and acts of suspicion and distrust. Would that the spirit of the illustrious dead, whom we lament today, could speak from the grave to both parties to this deplorable discord, in tones which would reach each and every heart throughout this broad territory: My country-men! know one another and you will love one another.

ROBERT INGERSOLL

AT HIS BROTHER'S GRAVE[39] (1879)

My Friends: I am going to do that which the dead oft promised he would do for me.

The loved and loving brother, husband, father, friend, dies where

---

[39] Delivered in Washington, D. C., June 3, 1879.

manhood's morning almost touches noon, and while the shadows were still falling toward the west.

He had not passed on life's highway the stone that marks the highest point, but, being weary for a moment, lay down by the wayside, and, using his burden for a pillow, fell into that dreamless sleep that kisses down his eyelids still. While yet in love with life and raptured with the world, he passed to silence and pathetic dust.

Yet, after all, it may be best, just in the happiest, sunniest hour of all the voyage, while eager winds are kissing every sail, to task against the unseen rock, and in an instant hear the billows roar above a sunken ship. For, whether in mid-sea or 'mong the breakers of the farther shore, a wreck at last must mark the end of each and all. And every life, no matter if its every house is rich with love and every moment jeweled with a joy, will, at its close, become a tragedy as sad and deep and dark as can be woven of the warp and woof of mystery and death.

This brave and tender man in every storm of life was oak and rock, but in the sunshine he was vine and flower. He was the friend of all heroic souls. He climbed the heights and left all superstitions far below, while on his forehead fell the golden dawning of the grander day.

He loved the beautiful, and was with color, form, and music touched to tears. He sided with the weak, and with a willing hand gave alms; with loyal heart and with purest hands he faithfully discharged all public trusts.

He was a worshiper of liberty, a friend of the oppressed. A thousand times I have heard him quite these words: "For justice, all place a temple; and all seasons, summer." He believed that happiness was the only good, reason the only torch, justice the only worship, humanity the only religion, and love the only priest. He added to the sum of human joy; and were every one to whom he did some loving service to bring a blossom to his grave, he would sleep tonight beneath a wilderness of flowers.

Life is a narrow vale between the cold and barren peaks of two eternities. We strive in vain to look beyond the heights. We cry aloud, and the only answer is the echo of our wailing cry. From the voiceless lips of the unreplying dead there comes no word; but in the night of death hope sees a star, and listening love can hear the rustle of a wing.

He who sleeps here, when dying, mistaking the approach of death for the return of health, whispered with his last breath: "I am better now." Let us believe, in spite of doubts and dogmas, and tears and fears, that these dear words are true of all the countless dead.

And now to you who have been chosen, from among the many men he loved, to do the last sad office for the dead, we give his sacred dust. Speech can not contain our love. There was, there is, no greater, stronger, manlier man.

WILLIAM GLADSTONE
AGAINST THE TORY GOVERNMENT[40] (1880)

To those gentlemen who talk of the great vigor and determination and success of the Tory government, I ask you to compare the case of Bulgaria and Turkey. Try them by principles, or try them by results, I care not which; we knew what we were about and what was to be done when we had integrity and independence to support. When they had integrity and independence to protect they talked indeed loud enough about supporting Turkey, and you would suppose they were prepared to spend their resources upon it; but all their measures have ended in nothing except that they have reduced Turkey to a state of greater weakness than at any portion of her history, whereas, on the other hand, in regard to the twelve or thirteen millions of Slavs and Roumanian population, they have made the name of England odious throughout the whole population, and done everything in their power to throw that population into the arms of Russia, to be the tool of Russia in its plans and schemes, unless, indeed, as I hope and am inclined to believe, thevirtue of free institutions that they have obtained will make them too wise to become the tools of any foreign power whatever, will make them intent upon maintaining their own liberties, as becomes a free people playing a noble part in the history of Europe.

I have detained you too long, and I will not, though I would, pursue this subject further. I have shown you what I think the miserable failure of the policy of the government. Remember, we have a fixed point from which to draw our measurements. Remember what in 1876 the proposal of those who approved of the Bulgarian agitation and who were denounced as the enemies of Turkey, remember what the proposal would have done. It would have given autonomy to Bulgaria, which has not got autonomy; but it would have saved all the remainder at less detriment to the rest of the Turkish Empire. Turkey would have had a fair chance. Turkey would not have suffered the territorial losses which she has elsewhere suffered, and which she has suffered, I must say, in consequence of her being betrayed into the false and mischievous, the tempting and seductive, but unreal and unwise policy of the present administration.

There are other matters which must be reserved for other times. We are told about the Crimean War. Sir Stafford Northcote tells us the Crimean War, made by the Liberal government, cost the country forty millions of debt, and an income tax of one shilling and four pence per pound. Now what is the use of telling us that? I will discuss the Crimean War on some future occasion, but not now. If the Liberal

---

40 Delivered in Edinburgh, Scotland, March 17, 1880.

government were so clever that they contrived to burden the country with forty millions of debt for this Crimean War, why does he not go back to the war before that and tell us what the Tory government did with the Revolutionary War, when they left a debt on the country of some nine hundred millions, of which six hundred andfifty millions then had made in the Revolutionary War, and not only so, but left the blessing and legacy of the corn laws, and of a high protective system, an impoverished country, and a discontented population—so much so that for years that followed the great Revolutionary War, no man could say whether the constitution of this country was or was not worth five years' purchase. They might even go further back than the Revolutionary War. They have been talking loudly of the colonies, and say that, forsooth, the Liberal party do nothing for the colonies. What did the Tory party do for the colonies? I can tell you. Go to the war that preceded the Revolutionary War. They made war against the American continent. They added to the debt of the country two hundred millions in order to destroy freedom in America. They alienated it and drove it from this country. They were compelled to bring this country to make an ignominious peace; and, as far as I know, that attempt to put down freedom in America, with its results to this country, is the only one great fact which has ever distinguished the relations between a Tory government and the colonies.

But gentlemen, these must be matters postponed for another occasion. I thank you very cordially, both friends and opponents, if opponents you be, for the extreme kindness with which you have heard me. I have spoken, and I must speak in very strong terms of the acts done by my opponents. I will never say that they did it from vindictiveness, I will never say that they did it from passion, I will never say that they did it from a sordid love of office; I have no right to use such words; I have no right to entertain such sentiments; I repudiate and abjure them. I give them credit for patriotic motives—I give them credit for those patriotic motives which are incessantly and gratuitously denied to us. I believe we are all united in a fond attachmentto the great country to which we belong, to the great empire which has committed to it a trust and function from Providence, as special and remarkable as was ever entrusted to any portion of the family of man. When I speak of that trust and that function I feel that words fail. I cannot tell you what I think of the nobleness of the inheritance which has descended upon us, of the sacredness of the duty of maintaining it. I will not condescend to make it a part of controversial politics. It is a part of my being, of my flesh and blood, of my heart and soul. For those ends I have labored through my youth and manhood, and, more than that, till my hairs are gray. In that faith and practice I have lived, and in that faith and practice I shall die.

JAMES G. BLAINE

EULOGY OF PRESIDENT GARFIELD[41] (1881)

His terrible fate was upon him in an instant. One moment he stood erect, strong, confident in the years stretching peacefully out before him. The next he lay wounded, bleeding, helpless; doomed to weary weeks of torture, to silence, and the grave.

Great in life, Garfield was surpassingly great in death. For no cause, in the very frenzy of wantonness, by the red hand of murder, he was thrust from the full tide of this world's interest, from its hopes, its aspirations, its victories, into the visible presence of Death—and he did not quail. Not alone for the one short moment in which, stunned and dazed, he could give up life, hardly aware of its relinquishment, but through days of deadly languor, through weeks of agony, that was not less agony because silently borne, with clear sight and calm courage, he looked into his opengrave. What blight and ruin met his anguished eyes, whose lips may tell—what brilliant broken plans, what baffled high ambitions, what sundering of warm, strong, manhood's friendships, what bitter rending of sweet household ties! behind him a proud, expectant nation, a great host of sustaining friends, a cherished and happy mother, wearing the full, rich honors of her early toil and tears; the wife of his youth, whose whole life lay in his; the little boys not yet emerged from childhood's days of frolic; the fair, young daughter; the sturdy sons just springing into closest companionship, claiming every day and every day rewarding a father's love and care, and in his heart the eager rejoicing power to meet all demands! Before him desolation and great darkness! And his soul was not shaken. His countrymen were thrilled with instant, profound, and universal sympathy. Masterful in his mortal weakness, he became the centre of a nation's love, enshrined in the prayers of a world; but all the love and all the sympathy could not share with him his suffering. He trod the wine-press alone. With unfaltering front he faced death. With unfailing tenderness he took leave of life. Above the demoniac hiss of the assassin's bullet, he heard the voice of God. With simple resignation, he bowed to the Divine decree.

As the end drew near his early craving for the sea returned. The stately mansion of power had been to him the wearisome hospital of pain, and he begged to be taken from its prison walls, from its oppressive, stifling air, from its homelessness and hopelessness. Gently, silently, the love of a great people bore the pale sufferer to the longed-for healing of the sea, to live or to die, as God should will, within sight of its heaving billows, within sound of its manifold voices.

---

[41] Extract from an oration delivered before the President and both Houses of Congress in the House of Representatives at Washington, D. C., February 27, 1882.

With wan, fevered face tenderly lifted to the cooling breeze, he looked out wistfully upon the ocean's changing wonders; on its far sails whitening in the morninglight; on its restless waves rolling shoreward to break and die beneath the noonday sun; on the red clouds of evening arching low to the horizon; on the serene and shining pathway of the stars. Let us think that his dying eyes read a mystic meaning which only the rapt and parting soul may know. Let us believe that in the silence of the receding world he heard the great waves breaking on a farther shore, and felt already upon his wasted brow the breath of the eternal morning.

WILLIAM J. BRYAN

"THE CROSS OF GOLD" SPEECH[42] (1896)

Mr. Chairman and Gentlemen of the Convention: I would be presumptuous indeed to present myself against the distinguished gentlemen to whom you have listened if this were a mere measuring of abilities; but this is not a contest between persons. The humblest citizen in all the land, when clad in the armor of a righteous cause, is stronger than all the hosts of error. I come to speak to you in defense of a cause as holy as the cause of liberty—the cause of humanity.

When this debate is concluded, a motion will be made to lay upon the table the resolution offered in commendation of the Administration, and also the resolution offered in condemnation of the Administration. We object to bringing this question down to the level of persons. The individual is but an atom; he is born, he acts, he dies; but principles are eternal; and this has been a contest over a principle.

Never before in the history of this country has there been witnessed such a contest as that through which we have just passed. Never before in the history of American politics has a great issue been fought out as this issue has been, by the voters of a great party. On the fourth of March, 1895, a few Democrats, most of them members of Congress, issued an address to the Democrats of the nation, asserting that the money question was the paramount issue of the hour; declaring that a majority of the Democratic party had the right to control the action of the party on this paramount issue; and concluding with the request that the believers in the free coinage of silver in the Democratic party should organize, take charge of, and control the policy of the Democratic party. Three months later, at Memphis, an organization was perfected, and the silver Democrats went forth openly and courageously proclaiming their belief, and declaring that, if successful, they would crystallize into a platform the declaration which

---

[42] Delivered in the National Democratic Convention at Chicago in 1896.

they had made. Then began the conflict. With a zeal approaching the zeal which inspired the crusaders who followed Peter the Hermit, our silver Democrats went forth from victory unto victory until they are now assembled, not to discuss, not to debate, but to enter up the judgment already rendered by the plain people of this country. In this contest brother has been arrayed against brother, father against son. The warmest ties of love, acquaintance, and association have been disregarded; old leaders have been cast aside when they refused to give expression unto the sentiments of those whom they would lead, and new leaders have sprung up to give direction to this cause of truth. Thus has the contest been waged, and we have assembled here under as binding and solemn instructions as were ever imposed upon representatives of the people.

We do not come as individuals. As individuals we might have been glad to compliment the gentleman from New York (Senator Hill), but we know that the people for whom we speak would never be willing to put him in a position where he could thwart the will of the Democratic party. I say it was not a question of persons; it was a question ofprinciple, and it is not with gladness, my friends, that we find ourselves brought into conflict with those who are now arrayed on the other side.

The gentleman who preceded me (ex-Governor Russell) spoke of the State of Massachusetts; let me assure him that not one present in all this Convention entertains the least hostility to the people of the state of Massachusetts, but we stand here representing the people who are the equals, before the law, of the greatest citizens in the state of Massachusetts. When you [turning to the gold delegates] come before us and tell us that we are about to disturb your business interests, we reply that you have disturbed our business interests by your course.

We say to you that you have made the definition of a business man too limited in its applications. The man who is employed for wages is as much a business man as his employer; the attorney in a country town is as much a business man as the corporation counsel in a great metropolis; the merchant at the cross-roads store is as much a business man as the merchant of New York; the farmer who goes forth in the morning and toils all day, who begins in spring and toils all summer, and who by the application of brains and muscle to the natural resources of the country creates wealth, is as much a business man as the man who goes upon the Board of Trade and bets upon the price of grain; the miners who go down a thousand feet into the earth, or climb two thousand feet upon the cliffs, and bring forth from their hiding places the precious metals to be poured into the channels of trade are as much business men as the few financial magnates who, in a back room, corner the money of the world. We come to speak of this broader class of business men.

Ah, my friends, we say not one word against those who live upon the Atlantic coast, but the hardy pioneers whohave braved all the dangers of the wilderness, who have made the desert to blossom as the rose—the pioneers away out there [pointing to the West], who rear their children near to Nature's heart, where they can mingle their voices with the voices of the birds—out there where they have erected schoolhouses for the education of their young, churches where they praise their Creator, and cemeteries where rest the ashes of their dead—these people, we say, are as deserving of the consideration of our party as any people in this country. It is for these that we speak. We do not come as aggressors. Our war is not a war of conquest; we are fighting in the defense of our homes, our families, and posterity. We have petitioned, and our petitions have been scorned; we have entreated, and our entreaties have been disregarded; we have begged, and they have mocked when our calamity came. We beg no longer; we entreat no more; we petition no more. We defy them!

The gentleman from Wisconsin has said that he fears a Robespierre. My friends, in this land of the free you need not fear that a tyrant will spring up from among the people. What we need is an Andrew Jackson to stand, as Jackson stood, against the encroachments of organized wealth.

They tell us that this platform was made to catch votes. We reply to them that changing conditions make new issues; that the principles upon which Democracy rests are as everlasting as the hills, but that they must be applied to new conditions as they arise. Conditions have arisen, and we are here to meet those conditions. They tell us that the income tax ought not to be brought in here; that it is a new idea. They criticize us for our criticism of the Supreme Court of the United States. My friends, we have not criticized; we have simply called attention to what you already know. If you want criticisms, read the dissenting opinions of the court. There you will find criticisms. They say that we passed an unconstitutional law; we deny it. The income tax law was not unconstitutional when it was passed; it was not unconstitutional when it went before the Supreme Court for the first time; it did not become unconstitutional until one of the judges changed his mind, and we cannot be expected to know when a judge will change his mind. The income tax is just. It simply intends to put the burdens of government justly upon the backs of the people. I am in favor of an income tax. When I find a man who is not willing to bear his share of the burdens of the government which protects him, I find a man who is unworthy to enjoy the blessings of a government like ours.

They say that we are opposing national bank currency; it is true. If you will read what Thomas Benton said, you will find he said that, in searching history, he could find but one parallel to Andrew Jackson; that was Cicero, who destroyed the conspiracy of Catiline and saved Rome. Benton said that Cicero only did for Rome what Jackson did for us when he destroyed the bank conspiracy and saved America. We say

228

in our platform that we believe that the right to coin and issue money is a function of government. We believe it. We believe that it is a part of sovereignty, and can no more with safety be delegated to private individuals than we could afford to delegate to private individuals the power to make penal statutes or levy taxes. Mr. Jefferson, who was once regarded as good Democratic authority, seems to have differed in opinion from the gentleman who has addressed us on the part of the minority. Those who are opposed to this proposition tell us that the issue of paper money is a function of the bank, and that the government ought to go out of the banking business. I stand with Jefferson rather than with them, and tell them, as he did, that the issue of money is a function of government, and that the banks ought to go out of the governing business.

They complain about the plank which declares against life tenure in office. They have tried to strain it to mean that which it does not mean. What we oppose by that plank is the life tenure which is built up in Washington, and which excludes from participation in official benefits the humble members of society.

Let me call your attention to two or three important things. The gentleman from New York says that he will propose an amendment to the platform providing that the proposed change in our monetary system shall not affect contracts already made. Let me remind you that there is no intention of affecting these contracts which, according to the present laws, are made payable in gold; but if he means to say that we cannot change our monetary system without protecting those who have loaned money before the change was made, I desire to ask him where, in law or in morals, he can find justification for not protecting the debtors when the act of 1873 was passed, if he now insists that we must protect the creditors.

He says he will also propose an amendment which will provide for the suspension of free coinage if we fail to maintain a parity within a year. We reply that when we advocate a policy which we believe will be successful, we are not compelled to raise a doubt as to our own sincerity by suggesting what we shall do if we fail. I ask him, if he would apply his logic to us, why he does not apply it to himself. He says he wants this country to try to secure an international agreement. Why does he not tell us what he is going to do if he fails to secure an international agreement? There is more reason for him to do that than there is for us to provide against the failure to maintain the parity. Our opponents have tried for twenty years to secure an international agreement, and those are waiting for it most patiently who do not want it at all.

And now, my friends, let me come to the paramount issue. If they ask us why it is that we say more on the money question than we say upon the tariff question, I reply that, if protection has slain its thousands, the gold standard has slain its tens of thousands. If they ask us why we do not embody in our platform all the things that we believe in, we reply that when we have restored the money of the Constitution all other necessary reforms will be possible; but that until this is done there is no other reform that can be accomplished.

Why is it that within three months such a change has come over the country? Three months ago, when it was confidently asserted that those who believe in the gold standard would frame our platform and nominate our candidates, even the advocates of the gold standard did not think that we could elect a President. And they had good reason for their doubt, because there is scarcely a state here today asking for the gold standard which is not in the absolute control of the Republican party. But note the change. Mr. McKinley was nominated at St. Louis upon a platform which declared for the maintenance of the gold standard until it can be changed into bimetallism by international agreement. Mr. McKinley was the most popular man among the Republicans, and three months ago everybody in the Republican party prophesied his election. How is it today? Why, the man who was once pleased to think that he looked like Napoleon—that man shudders today when he remembers that he was nominated on the anniversary of the battle of Waterloo. Not only that, but as he listens he can hear with ever-increasing distinctness the sound of the waves as they beat upon the lonely shores of St. Helena.

Why this change? Ah, my friends, is not the reason for the change evident to any one who will look at the matter? No private character, however, pure, no personalpopularity, however great, can protect from the avenging wrath of an indignant people a man who will declare that he is in favor of fastening the gold standard upon this country, or who is willing to surrender the right of self-government and place the legislative control of our affairs in the hands of foreign potentates and powers.

We go forth confident that we shall win. Why? Because upon the paramount issue of this campaign there is not a spot of ground upon which the enemy will dare to challenge battle. If they tell us that the gold standard is a good thing, we shall point to their platform and tell them that their platform pledges the party to get rid of the gold standard and substitute bimetallism. If the gold standard is a good thing, why try to get rid of it? I call your attention to the fact that some of the very people who are in this Convention today and who tell us that we ought to declare in favor of international bimetallism—thereby declaring that the gold standard is wrong and that the principle of bimetallism is better—these very people four months ago were open and avowed advocates of the gold standard, and were then telling us that we could not legislate two metals together, even with the aid of all the world. If the gold standard is a good thing we ought to declare in favor of its retention and not in favor of abandoning it; and if the gold standard is a bad thing why should we wait until other nations are willing to help us to let go? Here is the line of battle, and we care not upon which issue they force the fight; we are prepared to meet them on either side or on both. If they tell us that the gold standard is the standard of civilization, we reply to them that this, the most enlightened of all the nations of the earth, has never declared for a gold standard and that both the great parties this year are declaring against it. If the gold standard is the standard of civilization, why, my friends, should we not have it? If theycome to meet us on that issue we can present the history of our nation. More than that; we can tell them that they will search the pages of history in vain to find a single instance where the common people of any land have ever declared themselves in favor of the gold standard. They can find where the holders of fixed investments have declared for a gold standard, but not where the masses have. Mr. Carlisle said in 1878 that this was a struggle between "the idle holders of idle capital" and "the struggling masses, who produce the wealth and pay the taxes of the country"; and, my friends, the question we are to decide is: Upon which side will the Democratic party fight, upon the side of "the idle holders of idle capital" or upon the side of "the struggling masses"? That is the question which the party must answer first, and then it must be answered by each individual hereafter. The sympathies of the Democratic party, as shown by the platform, are on the side of the struggling masses who have ever been the foundation of the Democratic party. There are two ideas of government. There are those who believe that, if you will only legislate to make the well-to-do prosperous, their prosperity will leak through on those below. The Democratic idea, however, has been that if you legislate to make the masses prosperous, their prosperity will find its way up through ever class which rests upon them.

You come to us and tell us that the great cities are in favor of the gold standard; we reply that the great cities rest upon our broad and fertile prairies. Burn down your cities and leave our farms, and your cities will spring up again as if by magic; but destroy our farms and the grass will grow in the streets of every city in the country.

My friends, we declare that this nation is able to legislate for its own people on every question, without waiting for the aid and consent of any other nation on earth; andupon that issue we expect to carry every state in the Union. I shall not slander the inhabitants of the fair state of Massachusetts, nor the inhabitants of the state of New York, by saying that, when they are confronted with the proposition they will declare that this nation is not able to attend to its own business. It is the issue of 1776 over again. Our ancestors, when but three millions in number, had the courage to declare their political independence of every other nation; shall we, their descendants, when we have grown to seventy millions, declare that we are less independent than our forefathers?

No, my friends, that will never be the verdict of our people.

Therefore, we care not upon what lines the battle is fought. If they say bimetallism is good, but that we cannot have it until other nations help us, we reply that, instead of having a gold standard because England has, we will restore bimetallism, and then let England have bimetallism because the United States has it. If they dare to come out in the open field and defend the gold standard as a good thing, we will fight them to the uttermost. Having behind us the producing masses of this nation and the world, supported by the commercial interests, the laboring interests and the toilers everywhere, we will answer their demand for a gold standard by saying to them: You shall not press down upon the brow of labor this crown of thorns, you shall not crucify mankind upon a cross of gold.

JOHN HAYNES HOLMES

THE BIRTH OF AN ORATOR[43] (1912)

On the 9th day of December, 1837, there was held in Faneuil Hall, in the city of Boston, a great public meeting inprotest against the recent murder, in Alton, Illinois, of the Rev. Elijah P. Lovejoy. The historic old edifice was filled upon this momentous occasion to suffocation, as feeling was running very high upon both sides of the slavery question; and the audience was about equally divided between the friends and enemies of the cause. The meeting was opened with a brief and impressive address by Dr. Channing. Resolutions denouncing the murder of Lovejoy were then read and formally seconded. Everything seemed to be moving smoothly, when a man was seen making his way through the excited crowd to the great gilded eagle in the front of the gallery. He was instantly recognized as James T. Austin, a parishioner of Dr. Channing, a popular politician, and at that time the Attorney-General of the Commonwealth. Gaining his position, he began a harangue, calculated to fire the crowd and break up the meeting. He compared the slaves of the South to a menagerie, and likened Lovejoy to one who should "break the bars and let loose the caravan to prowl about the streets." He talked of the rioters of Alton as akin to the "orderly mob" which threw the tea into Boston Harbor in 1773; and, in direct allusion to his minister, Dr. Channing, he closed by asserting that a clergyman with a gun in his hand, or one "mingling in the debates of a popular assembly, was marvellously out of place."

No sooner were these words spoken than the chairman lost all control of the meeting. The Attorney-General had captured his audience, and friends and foes seemed to vie with one another in calling for the resolutions that they might vote them down, and then

---

[43] From a sermon delivered in the Church of the Messiah, New York City.

turn the protest of the occasion into an endorsement. At this wild moment, when all hope of saving the meeting seemed to be lost, a young man with pale face and close-pressed lips, was seen pushinghis way to the platform through the frenzied mob. A few persons recognized Wendell Phillips, a son of one of the richest and most conservative families of Boston, a graduate of Harvard College and Harvard Law School, and now just entered upon the practice of his profession. Leaping upon the stage, this unknown stripling faced the crowd, as tall and fair and beautiful as an Apollo, and, raising his hand, spoke two or three words in those marvellous silvery tones which were destined ultimately to chant their music in so many halls and before so many popular assemblies. Instantly the wild "tumult and shouting" was hushed, while men leaned forward curiously to hear what this foolish youth could find to say in answer to the Attorney-General. "Mr. Chairman," he began, "we are here met for the freest discussion of these resolutions, and the events which gave rise to them. I hope I shall be permitted to express my surprise as to the sentiments of the last speaker—surprise not only at such sentiments from such a man, but at the applause which they received within these walls. . . . Sir, when I heard the gentleman lay down principles which place the murders of Lovejoy side by side with Otis and Hancock, Quincy and Adams, I thought [pointing to the portraits of the revolutionary heroes in the hall] those pictured lips would have broken into voice to rebuke this recreant American—this slanderer of the dead." Instantly, with this utterance of magic eloquence, the tide of popular feeling was turned. Sentence after sentence fell from the speaker's lips like thunderbolts from the land of Jove, until at last his words were swept away in the wild tumult of applause; and with a mighty shout the resolutions were put and carried. Thus was the day unexpectedly saved, and from that moment on Faneuil Hall was identified with the name of Wendell Phillips as it had previously been identified withthe names of James Otis and Samuel Adams, and was dedicated to the cause of anti-slavery, as it had hitherto been dedicated to the cause of political independence.

PEACE BETWEEN LABOR AND CAPITAL44 (1912)

First of all, let me tell you that nothing will be gained by crushing unions and destroying organizations of labor. The time has passed by forever for that course of procedure. Labor is learning its power; and, what is more important still, society has itself learned the value of organized labor as a bulwark against the aggressions of militant capitalism. The man who thinks that labor can be permanently

---

44 From a sermon on "Capital vs. Labor," delivered in the Church of the Messiah, New York City.

repressed and exploited is mad, and his madness is a menace to the future peace of the country.

Neither can we solve this problem by talking about the interests of capital and labor being identical under the present system of industry, and by bringing capital and labor together into any such "moonshine" organization as the Civic Federation. We might as well recognize the fact once for all that, just as long as higher wages mean lower dividends, and shortened hours mean lessened output, the interests of capital and labor are not identical but opposite, not mutual but antagonistic.

The only way to bring peace into the present turmoil and confusion of industry is first, for the sake of ordinary decency and order, to make some laws to meet the situation—laws which will oblige two warring classes to bring their dispute before some impartial tribunal for peaceful settlement, as two warring individuals are obliged to do; and then, going straight to the heart of the matter, to recognize that our whole system of capital and labor, employer and employee, master and servant, is a form of feudalism, and that thisfeudalism must give way to democracy in the world of industry as it has long since given way to democracy in the world of politics. The social war will be over and peace established, when the man who invests his labor in an industry is given the same degree of ownership in that industry, as the man who invests his money—when the laborer with his hands, like the laborer with his brains, is given the full product of his labor—when the laborer becomes a capitalist and the capitalist becomes a laborer—when one man counts for one man in the organization of industry, whatever his class or station or wealth, just as one man is now counted for one man in the organization of government. In other words, when competition is succeeded by coöperation, private ownership and control by social ownership and control, feudalism by democracy, despotism by liberty, inequality by equality, antagonism by fraternity, hatred by good-will. And you and I can speed the coming of this happy day, by solemnly resolving in the sight of God, that, so far as we are concerned, we shall seek the enjoyment of no privilege which is not universal, demand the exercise of no right for ourselves which is denied to one of the least of these our brethren, and cherish no sentiment within our hearts save that of good-will for all the sons of men.

I have spoken upon this burning question this morning, my friends, with a freedom which makes misinterpretation inevitable and misquotation certain. I have spoken thus for two reasons! First, that you, as my people, may know, beyond all doubt, just where I, your minister, stand on this burning question. I want you to know that, in this present fight, I am on the side of labor. I excuse none of its crimes—I pardon none of its criminals; but no crime and no criminal can ever shake my faith in the justice of its cause. And, in the second place, I have thus spoken, that I may shake you out of that opinion which has been forced upon your minds by the public discussions of the last two weeks, and set your thinking upon this question all anew. If you go out of this place, and denounce me as a dynamiter, I shall have failed in my purpose; and the fault will be mine, that I cannot express clearly what I want to say. If you go out of this place, and, without accepting any of my opinions, think the whole problem through again, in prayer to God that you may find the truth and may do injustice to no living soul, I shall have succeeded; and the credit will be yours, that you have the open mind. But whether I succeed or fail, matters little, perhaps; for, in spite of you and in spite of me, "it is God who reigneth over all the earth—He will judge the world in righteousness and minister judgment to the people. He will not fail nor faint till He have set justice in the earth—till He have burst the yoke asunder and given liberty to all them that are oppressed."

RICHARD BRINSLEY SHERIDAN

THE PERFECT ORATOR

Imagine to yourself a Demosthenes, addressing the most illustrious assembly in the world, upon a point whereon the fate of the most illustrious of nations depended. How awful such a meeting! How fast the subject! Is man possessed of talents adequate to the great occasion? Adequate! Yes, superior. By the power of eloquence, the augustness of the assembly is lost in the dignity of the orator; and the importance of the subject, for a while superseded, by the admiration of his talents.

With what strength of argument, with what powers of the fancy, with what emotions of the heart, doth he assault and subjugate the whole man; and at once, captivate his reason, his imagination, and his passions. To effect this, must be the utmost effort of the most improved state of human nature. Not a faculty that he possesses is here unemployed; not a faculty that he possesses but is here exerted to its highest pitch. All his internal powers are at work; all his external, testify their energies.

Within, the memory, the fancy, the judgment, the passions, are all busy. Without, every muscle, every nerve, is exerted; not a feature, not a limb, but speaks. The organs of the body, attuned to the exertions of the mind, through the kindred organs of the hearers, instantaneously vibrate those energies from soul to soul.

Notwithstanding the diversity of minds in such a multitude, by the lightning of eloquence, they are melted into one mass; the whole assembly, actuated in one and the same way, become, as it were, but one man, and have but one voice. The universal cry is—"let us move against Philip—let us fight for our liberties—LET US CONQUER OR DIE!"

THEODORE ROOSEVELT
INAUGURAL ADDRESS[45] (1905)

My Fellow Citizens: No people on earth have more cause to be thankful than ours, and this is said reverently, in no spirit of boastfulness in our own strength, but with gratitude to the Giver of Good, who has blessed us with the conditions which have enabled us to achieve so large a measure of well-being and happiness.

To us as a people it has been granted to lay the foundations of our natural life in a new continent. We are the heirs of the ages, and yet we have had to pay few of the penalties which in old countries are exacted by the dead hand of a bygone civilization. We have not been obliged tofight for our existence against any alien race; and yet our life has called for the vigor and effort without which the manlier and hardier virtues wither away.

Under such conditions it would be our own fault if we failed, and the success which we have had in the past, the success which we confidently believe the future will bring, should cause in us no feeling of vainglory, but rather a deep and abiding realization of all that life has offered us; a full acknowledgment of the responsibility which is ours; and a fixed determination to show that under a free government a mighty people can thrive best, alike as regard the things of the body and the things of the soul. Much has been given us, and much will rightfully be expected from us. We have duties to others and duties to ourselves—and we can shirk neither. We have become a great nation, forced by the fact of its greatness into relation to the other nations of the earth, and we must behave as becomes a people with such responsibilities.

Toward all other nations, large and small, our attitude must be one of cordial and sincere friendship. We must show not only in our words but in our deeds that we are earnestly desirous of securing their good will by acting toward them in a spirit of just and generous recognition of all their rights.

But justice and generosity in a nation, as in an individual, count most when shown not by the weak but by the strong. While ever careful to refrain from wronging others, we must be no less insistent that we are not wronged ourselves. We wish peace; but we wish the peace of justice, the peace of righteousness. We wish it because we think it right, and not because we are afraid. No weak nation that acts rightly and justly should ever have cause to fear, and no strong power should ever be able to single us out as a subject for insolent aggression.

Our relations with the other powers of the world are important; but still more important are our relations among ourselves. Such

---

[45] Delivered at Washington, D. C., March 4, 1905.

growth in wealth, in population, and in power, as a nation has seen during a century and a quarter of its national life, is inevitably accompanied by a like growth in the problems which are ever before every nation that rises to greatness. Power invariably means both responsibility and danger. Our forefathers faced certain perils which we have outgrown. We now face other perils the very existence of which it was impossible that they should foresee.

Modern life is both complex and intense, and the tremendous changes wrought by the extraordinary industrial development of the half century are felt in every fiber of our social and political being. Never before have men tried so vast and formidable an experiment as that of administering the affairs of a continent under the forms of a democratic republic. The conditions which have told for our marvelous material well-being, which have developed to a very high degree our energy, self-reliance, and individual initiative, also have brought the care and anxiety inseparable from the accumulation of great wealth in industrial centers.

Upon the success of our experiment much depends—not only as regards our own welfare, but as regards the welfare of mankind. If we fail, the cause of free self-government throughout the world will rock to its foundations, and therefore our responsibility is heavy, to ourselves, to the world as it is today, and to the generations yet unborn.

There is no good reason why we should fear the future, but there is every reason why we should face it seriously, neither hiding from ourselves the gravity of the problems before us, nor fearing to approach these problems with the unbending, unflinching purpose to solve them aright.

Yet, after all, though the problems are new, though thetasks set before us differ from the tasks set before our fathers, who founded and preserved this Republic, the spirit in which these tasks must be undertaken and these problems faced, if our duty is to be well done, remains essentially unchanged. We know that self-government is difficult. We know that no people needs such high traits of character as that people which seeks to govern its affairs aright through the freely expressed will of the free men who compose it.

But we have faith that we shall not prove false to memories of the men of the mighty past. They did their work; they left us the splendid heritage we now enjoy. We in our turn have an assured confidence that we shall be able to leave this heritage unwasted and enlarged for our children's children.

To do so we must show, not merely in great crisis, but in every-day affairs of life, the qualities of practical intelligence, of course, of hardihood, and endurance, and, above all, the power of devotion to a lofty ideal, which made great the men who founded this Republic in the days of Washington; which made great the men who preserved this Republic in the days of Abraham Lincoln.

EDWIN G. LAWRENCE
OUR COUNTRY[46] (1912)

Mr. Toastmaster, Ladies and Gentlemen: In that long ago, that age just following the period when darkness covered the face of the earth, that age when God dispelled that darkness by issuing his fiat, "Let there be light," we are told in the Good Book that God followed the birth of the light with the creation of man, that He breathed the breath of life into his nostrils and that man became thereby a living soul.With the entrance of divine breath into the senseless clay, with the awakening of the soul of man, there came the realization of three spiritual facts: the belief in God, the love of home, and the devotion to country.

Nowhere in this vast universe does a conscious being exist who does not, in his heart, believe in God. Traverse the wilds of darkest Africa, enter the densest jungles of that great continent, and you will find that all its human inhabitants have some conception of God. In the remotest isles of the Pacific, among the cannibals who devour the flesh of their victims, is found evidence of the belief in the existence of God, although the evidence may be nothing more than the setting up of a symbol of wood or stone that typifies to the poor savage the Being he worships. Even the blasphemer, who, with the words of his mouth, denies the Almighty who created him, will, in his secret soul, hear the still small voice, the reflex of that great Creator, whisper unto him, "I am the Lord thy God."

The love of home is universal. Be that home a hovel or a palace, if the heart be there, happiness will be its companion. Love of home often exists where the home is only in the fancy, only in the heart that longs and hungers for its blessings. That sweet singer who sang of "Home, sweet home" was a wanderer on the face of the earth, and possessed that home only in his dreams. No matter how pomp and power may elevate us, no matter how our erring feet may carry us astray, still in our hearts will echo the refrain:

'Mid pleasures and palaces though we may roam,
Be it ever so humble, there's no place like home.

As we are gathered within this palatial building, around these well-laden tables, under the splendor of these electric lamps, how many of you at the sound of the word "Home" think of the little cottage perched upon the hill, or nestlingdown in the valley, where, seated at the plain wooden table, the room faintly lighted by a tallow candle, you have eaten your humble meal, blessed by the spirit that ever sanctifies

---

[46] Delivered at the Hotel Astor, New York City, on the occasion of the Eighth Annual Dinner of The Greene County Society, Jan. 30, 1912.

the home? How many of you at this moment are, in fancy, back in the dear old county of Greene? How many of you trace the winding brook climb the hills, till the fields, or sit within the holy confines of the House of God, humble in its man-made structure but magnificent with the glory of His presence?

Home is a thought, a dream, a wish, the longing of the soul for the attainment of the heaven upon earth; and because man keeps before him the vision of what he would have his home, and sees not the materiality of its reality, he conceives his home, no matter where it may be placed, to be the best on earth. That beautiful writer, weak man, and luckless wanderer, Oliver Goldsmith, thus expresses the idea I would convey to you:

> But where to find that happiest spot below
> Who can direct, when all pretend to know?
> The shudd'ring tenant of the frigid zone
> Boldly proclaims that happiest spot his own.
> Extols the treasures of his stormy seas,
> And his long nights of revelry and ease:
> The naked negro, panting at the Line,
> Boasts of his golden sands and palmy wine,
> Basks in their glare, or stems the tepid wave,
> And thanks his gods for all the good they gave.
> Such is the patriot's boast where'er he roam,
> His first, best country, ever is at home.

What does the word country signify? It means the same to the Russian on the frozen Volga; the German on the castled Rhine; the Irish on the shores of the River Lee, listening to "those bells of Shandon"; to the English onthe Thames, that little stream pregnant with the history of a world; and to the American by the shores of the Hudson, the Columbia or the Mississippi. To all men, in all climes, "my country" means the land of my fathers, or the land of my choice; the place of sacred memories, of strong endeavors and of fervent hopes. Be that country the rock-ribbed land of Scotland, the sands of Africa, the vine-clad hills of France, the plains, the valleys and the mountains of America, it is "my country" to her sons and daughters. No matter what may be the language spoken, no matter what may the natural formation of the landscape, be it Holland with her dykes and ditches or Switzerland with her home in the clouds, no matter what may be the color of her children, be they white, yellow, black or brown, to them she is their mother, and they adore her.

All this and more "our country" means to us Americans. She means more to us than most lands can mean to their children, because she offers us greater opportunities for advancement in education, more religious, social and political liberty, and instills into us an appreciation of the necessity of working for the uplifting of mankind.

While laboring to uplift ourselves and our fellows, we should keep ever in mind the first tenth of that Decalogue given to the children of Israel for their guidance and government, and which is as necessary to our national preservation as it was to their national formation. That commandment states "Thou shalt have no other gods before Me"; and wherever that divine order was broken, the peoples so breaking it, went down to destruction. When Athens turned from her high ideals of progress and liberty she became the vassal of Macedonia and passed out of existence as an independent state. When the Emperor Augustus mounted the throne of the world-power of Rome, the people of that vast empire were slaves to sensuality and luxury, and from that moment,when her greatness appeared fixed for all times, her decline began. Let America pause and ponder as she stands on the brink of that gulf wherein lie buried Israel, Assyria, Carthage, Greece, and Rome, for unless she turns from the false god Mammon, and returns to the worship of the Lord God, she will as surely be plunged into the bottomless pit as were the nations that preceded her in wealth and power and which she is imitating by bowing down to and worshiping the golden calf. Let us keep before our country the lights of truth and justice that they may guide her from this threatening peril on to that upward and onward path leading to the holy of holies wherein sits enthroned the one true God—the God of Equality and of Love.

It is well to blend God, Home and Country, because the belief in all three makes the believer, man or woman, the patriot and the child of God. Take God out of the home and what have we? A shelter for the body, perhaps, but a wilderness for the spirit. Take God out of the country and what have we? A ship of state without a compass whereby to direct its course. Therefore, if either love of God or love of home fails to exist in the hearts of the citizens of any land, that part of the earth's surface will be their habitation but it will fail to be their country. When the patriot thinks of the nation he loves he does not picture it as so much land, so much water, so many mountains or so many plains. No, he sees it as he sees his flag, symbolical of all that is dear, holy and true. It is the spirit of our flag that we love. It is the spirit of God and the spirit of Home that make us love our Country. Let us look to hear as our mother, let us be to her faithful and loving children, and may she be the better for having nurtured us in her arms.

Ladies and Gentlemen: Our Country. God grant she may always stand for the fulfillment of His word.

CHAPTER X

LESSON TALKS

These lesson talks will be of value to students only after they have diligently studied the contents of this book, particularly the first, second, and sixth chapters, which treat of the means of speech construction and the forms of delivery. It is absolutely necessary that students should have a thorough understanding of inflection, emphasis, apposition, opposition, and the series, in order that they may understand and appreciate the work of this chapter. These talks are intended to exemplify the application of the rules laid down in this book for the guidance of those who seek proficiency in the art of public speaking, but they will help little unless the student has prepared himself to receive them by thoroughly mastering the technique of the art as expounded in the different chapters.

It will be well for the student to mark the speeches given in this chapter according to the instructions given in the lesson talks, as then he will have an object lesson before him that will enable him more readily to grasp the written instructions regarding the series, emphasis, and inflection.

Cuba Must Be Free. On March 24, 1898, Senator John M. Thurston of Nebraska delivered a speech "On the Affairs of Cuba," from which this extract is taken. While it is but a portion of a speech, being the peroration only, still it is a complete speech in itself, as it conforms to all the requirements of speech construction. Its opening, or statement, consists of the laying down of the facts upon which the argument is to be based, these facts being the legal rights of individuals and states as opposed to the moral rights. The statement ends with the second paragraph. The body, or argument, closes with the fifth paragraph and consists in showing that nations, like individuals, should be governed by high moral motives and not shrink from obligations because they have the legal right to do so; and that in the performance of these obligations force is the only means that can bring about the desired end. The balance of the speech forms the conclusion, and it consists of a summing up of the great events of the world's history wherein progress was made in man's struggle for liberty only by the exercise of force.

The opening sentence states the claims of those who oppose intervention in behalf of Cuba by the United States, and sets forth their claims. This forms the base of Senator Thurston's argument. The second sentence is a qualified acknowledgment of the legal right of the United States to refrain from interfering. In other words, he frankly

241

confesses that there is no legal power that can compel the United States to interfere between Spain and her colony, but clearly shows that he intends to uphold the moral right of that country to intervene, the construction of this sentence, "It may be the naked legal right of the United States to stand thus idly by," plainly denoting the senator's opinion.

The second paragraph is devoted to illustrating the legal rights of the individual; the third paragraph, the effects that would flow from an exercise of those rights; the fourth paragraph, an application of the principle to nations that has previously been applied to individuals, and an explanation as to the senator's conception of the religious doctrine as taught by Christ; the fifth paragraph states the meaning of intervention, force, and war, defines the force that should be used, and makes two strong assertions in the form of indirect questions; the sixth paragraph is devoted to the production of cumulative evidence as to the efficacy of force, and a stirring appeal that this force be exercised. The quotation from "The Battle Hymn of the Republic" is used to emphasize this last point; the seventh paragraph states the position that the senator takes on the question.

"Cuba" and "United States" are contrasted, consequently both require emphasis as well as different inflections, and as the former is affirmative it should be given the falling inflection, and the latter, because it is negative, should be given the rising inflection. The balance of the sentence consists of a concluding series that is out of the ordinary for the reason that the last member of the series forms a series by itself, and it is therefore termed a series within a series. The last sentence of the openingparagraph requires the falling inflection because it is an affirmative statement.

The opening sentence of the second paragraph requires the falling inflection because it is a positive statement. The word "legal" should be emphasized for the reason that it qualifies the word "right," and by means of emphasis placed on the word "legal" a contrast is immediately suggested with the "moral" right. In the next sentence the word "my" is the important word because it qualifies the word "dog," and as it states that "it is not my dog," the word "my" should be given the rising inflection to show its negative quality. If the emphasis and inflection should be placed on the word "dog," it would then be indicated that the "dog" is not mine but the cat or the horse is. Care must be exercised to place properly both the inflection and the emphasis in order that a correct interpretation may be given. "Mine," in the next sentence, should be given the rising inflection for the same reason that governs the inflection on the word "dog," the meaning being that it may be the policeman's duty to interfere but it is not the speaker's. The word "my," in the next phrase, requires the rising inflection for the same reason, the occurrence taking place on premises

242

but not on "my" premises. The conclusion of the paragraph should be given the falling inflection because it is assertive.

"But if I do" is conditional and therefore requires the rising inflection; "I am a coward and a cur" being the concluding clause to the conditional, and being positive,it should have the falling inflection; "live" is contrasted with "die," and "God knows" is parenthetical. "Dog," "woman," and "force" all require the rising inflection because they are negatived, the statement being that "I cannot protect the dog," "I cannot save the woman," "without [not employing] force." The reverse of the form used in the speech, the positive, would be: I can protect the dog, I can save the woman, by exercising force.

"We cannot intervene and save Cuba without the exercise of force" requires the rising inflection because it is a negative statement, "and force means war; war means blood" requires the falling inflection because they are positive. The next sentence requires a like inflection for a like reason. "Liberty" and "humanity" are negatived, and therefore should be giving the rising inflection. The next sentence is a negative one, and all its members require the rising inflection. The sentence that follows is positive, and requires the falling inflection. The phrase "I believe in the doctrine of peace," is also positive, but as it is qualified by "men must have liberty before there can come abiding peace," it requires the rising inflection, the qualifying phrase taking the falling inflection because it is assertive.

The three short opening sentences of the fifth paragraph require the falling inflection because they are positive. "God's" requires emphasis for the reason that it qualifies "force." The two questions that follow, being indirect questions, should be given falling inflections.

The sixth paragraph represents a masterly arrangement of concluding series. The first series enumerates three great charters: Magna Carta, the Declaration of Independence, and the Emancipation Proclamation; the second, three instances where the people struggled against oppression: the storming of the Bastille, the battle of Bunker Hill, and the suffering of the American army at Valley Forge; the third, three battles of the war between the states; the fourth, three Federal generals; the fifth, the results that followed the Civil War. All these are concluding series; therefore, in each series, the first member should be given the falling inflection, the second member the rising inflection, and the third member the falling inflection. If these directions are not clear, review the section on series, in the second chapter. The two sentences that follow the series are positive and require falling inflections. In the first sentence the word "again" requires emphasis because it is important, while in the second, "once more" should be given emphasis for the same reason.

In the quotation, "you" and "me" are contrasted, and there is a double contrast between "He" and "us," "holy" and "free." "God," in the last line of the quotation, requires emphasis because of its importance.

In the last paragraph there is a double opposition between "others," each time the word is used, and "me," "hesitate," "procrastinate" and "negotiation" with "act now," while "which means delay" is parenthetical. The speech ends with a concluding series.

Transcriber's Note: The sixth paragraph of the following oration includes a term that many find offensive.

CUBA MUST BE FREE[47]

JOHN M. THURSTON

Mr. President, there are those who say that the affairs of Cuba are not the affairs of the United States, who insist that we can stand idly by and see that island devastated and depopulated, its business interests destroyed, its commercial intercourse with us cut off, its people starved, degraded, and enslaved. It may be the naked legal right of the United States to stand thus idly by.

I have the legal right to pass along the street and see a helpless dog stamped into the earth under the heels of a ruffian. I can pass by and say that is not my dog. I can sit in my comfortable parlor with my loved ones gathered about me, and through my plate glass window see a fiend outraging a helpless woman nearby, and I can legally say this is no affair of mine—it is not happening on my premises; and I can turn away and take my little ones in my arms, and, with the memory of their sainted mother in my heart, look up to the motto on the wall and read, "God bless our home."

But if I do, I am a coward and a cur unfit to live, and, God knows, unfit to die. And yet I cannot protect the dog nor save the woman without the exercise of force.

We cannot intervene and save Cuba without the exercise of force, and force means war; war means blood. The lowly Nazarene on the shores of Galilee preached the divine doctrine of love, "Peace on earth, good will toward men." Not peace on earth at the expense of liberty and humanity. Not good will toward men who despoil, enslave, degrade, and starve to death their fellow men. I believe in the doctrine of Christ. I believe in the doctrine of peace; but, Mr. President, men must have liberty before there can come abiding peace.

Intervention means force. Force means war. War means blood. But it will be God's force. When has a battle for humanity and liberty ever been won except by force? What barricade of wrong, injustice, and oppression has ever been carried except by force?

Force compelled the signature of unwilling royalty to the great Magna Carta; force put life into the Declaration of Independence and

---

[47] This extract is from a speech delivered in the United States Senate, March 21, 1898.

made effective the Emancipation Proclamation; force beat with naked hands upon the iron gateway of the Bastille and made reprisal in one awful hour for centuries of kingly crime; force waved the flag of revolution over Bunker Hill and marked the snows of Valley Forge with blood-stained feet; force held the broken line at Shiloh, climbed the flame-swept hill at Chattanooga, and stormed the clouds on Lookout Heights; force marched with Sherman to the sea, rode with Sheridan in the valley of the Shenandoah, and gave Grant victory at Appomattox; force saved the Union, kept the stars in the flag, made "niggers" men. The time for God's force has come again. Let the impassioned lips of American patriots once more take up the song:

> In the beauty of the lilies Christ was born across the sea,
> With a glory in His bosom that transfigured you and me;
> As He died to make men holy, let us die to make men free,
> For God is marching on.

Others may hesitate, others may procrastinate, others may plead for further diplomatic negotiation, which means delay, but for me, I am ready to act now, and for my action I am ready to answer to my conscience, my country, and my God.

Evidence and Precedents in Law. Here is an example of argumentative oratory, an extract from a speech by Thomas Erskine, that will repay careful consideration.

The opening statement, "Before you can adjudge a fact, you must believe it," is positive, and demands the falling inflection; "not suspect it, or imagine it, or fancy it" are all negatived and require the rising inflection; "but believe it" is positive and must be given the falling inflection, and the balance of the sentence is negative and requires the rising inflection throughout. The question that follows is an indirect one and should be given the falling inflection. "Neither more nor less" are negatived and therefore both "more" and "less" require the rising inflection; "justice" should be given the falling inflection because it completes a positive statement; the balance of the sentence should receive the same inflection for the same reason. "As they are settled by law, and adopted in its general administration" is parenthetical; the main idea, "the rules of evidence are not to be overruled or tampered with" is negative, consequently the negatived words "overruled" and "tampered" should receive the rising inflection. The passage that follows, ending with the word "life," is a concluding series of four members, and all members except the next to the last, "in the truth of history," receive the falling inflection, the exception requiring the rising inflection; "and whoever ventures rashly to depart from them" is, in its spirit, conditional, and for that reason should be given the rising inflection; the balance is assertive and requires the falling inflection; a contrast should be shown between "God" and "man."

Let the student work out the balance of the speech.

EVIDENCE AND PRECEDENTS IN LAW

THOMAS ERSKINE

Before you can adjudge a fact, you must believe it—not suspect it, or imagine it, or fancy it, but believe it—and it is impossible to impress the human mind with such a reasonable and certain belief, as is necessary to be impressed, before a Christian man can adjudge his neighbor to the smallest penalty, much less to the pains of death, without having such evidence as a reasonable mind will accept of as the infallible test of truth. And what is that evidence? Neither more nor less than that which the Constitution has established in the courts for the general administration of justice; namely, that the evidence convince the jury, beyond all reasonable doubt, that the criminal intention, constituting the crime, existed in the mind of the man upon trial, and was the mainspring of his conduct. The rules of evidence, as they are settled by law, and adopted in its general administration, are not to be overruled or tampered with. They are found in the charities of religion—in the philosophy of nature—in the truth of history—and in the experience of common life; and whoever ventures rashly to depart from them, let him remember that it will be meted to him in the same measure, and that both God and man will judge him according.

These are arguments addressed to your reasons and your consciences; not to be shaken in upright minds by any precedent—for no precedents can sanctify injustice; if they could, every human right would long ago have been extinct upon the earth. If the state trials in bad times are to be searched for precedents, what murders may you not commit—whatlaw of humanity may you not trample upon—what rule of justice may you not violate—and what maxim of wise policy may you not abrogate and confound? If precedents in bad times are to be implicitly followed, why should we have heard any evidence at all? You might have convicted without any evidence; for many have been so convicted—and, in this manner, murdered—even by acts of Parliament. If precedents in bad times are to be followed, why should the Lords and Commons have investigated these charges, and the Crown have put them into this course of judicial trial? since, without such a trial, and even after an acquittal upon me, they might have attained all the prisoners by act of Parliament: they did so in the case of Lord Strafford.

There are precedents, therefore, for all such things, but such precedents as could not for a moment survive the times of madness and distraction which gave them birth: but which, as soon as the spurs of the occasion were blunted, were repealed and execrated even by Parliaments which (little as I may think of the present) ought not be compared with it—Parliaments sitting in the darkness of former times—in the night of freedom—before the principles of government were developed, and before the constitution became fixed. The last of these precedents, and all the proceedings upon it, were ordered to be taken off the file and burnt, so the intent that the same might no longer be visible to after ages; an order dictated, no doubt, by a pious tenderness for national honor, and meant as a charitable covering for the crimes of our fathers. But it was a sin against posterity—it was a treason against society; for, instead of commanding them to be burnt, they should rather have directed them to be blazoned in large characters upon the walls of our Courts of Justice, that, like the characters deciphered by the prophet of God to the Eastern tyrant, they might enlarge and blacken in your sights, to terrify you from acts of injustice.

The Permanency of Empire. This extract opens with an earnest appeal which requires the falling inflection. The question that follows it is a direct one, consequently all its members require the rising inflection. From the exclamation "Alas" to the end of the sentence, all is positive, therefore the falling inflection should be used throughout. The next question is an indirect one and requires the falling inflection. "So thought the countries of Demosthenes and the Spartan" is a positive thought and should be given the falling inflection. Then comes a triple opposition, "Leonidas" being contrasted with "Athens," "trampled" with "insulted," and "slave" with "Ottoman." The three words qualifying "Ottoman" constitute a commencing series, and for this reason "servile" and "mindless" should be given the falling inflection, and "enervate" the rising. The next sentence is a positive one and the falling inflection should be given the word "footsteps," which closes it; "from the palace to the tomb" and "with their ruins" are both parenthetical, and there is a contrast between "palace" and "tomb." The phrase ending with "as if they had never been" is conditional and requires the rising inflection; the balance of the sentence contains a parenthetical clause, "rude and neglected in the barren ocean," and a double contrast, the last of the four members of which is a concluding series, the contrasts being "then" with "now," "speck" with the concluding series "the ubiquity of their commerce, the glory of their arms, the fame of their philosophy, the eloquence of their Senate and the inspiration of their bards." There is a double opposition between "England" and "America," and "Athens is" with "Athens was"; "contemplating the past," "proud and potent as she appears," "then," and "one day" are parenthetical; the conclusion of the extract consists of a parenthesis, "for its time," and a double contrast, "Europe" being contrasted with "that mighty continent" (America), and "shall have mouldered, and the night of barbarism obscured its very ruins" with "emerge from the horizon to rule sovereign of the ascendant."

247

THE PERMANENCY OF EMPIRE
WENDELL PHILLIPS

I appeal to history! Tell me, thou reverend chronicler of the grave, can all the wealth of a universal commerce, can all the achievements of successful heroisms, or all the establishments of this world's wisdom, secure to empire the permanency of its possessions? Alas! Troy thought so once; yet the land of Priam lives only in song! Thebes thought so once; yet her hundred gates have crumbled, and her very tombs are but as the dust they were vainly intended to commemorate. So thought Palmyra—where is she? So thought the countries of Demosthenes and the Spartan; yet Leonidas is trampled by the timid slave, and Athens insulted by the servile, mindless, and enervate Ottoman. In his hurried march, Time has but looked at their imagined immortality, and all its vanities, from the palace to the tomb, have, with their ruins, erased the very impression of his footsteps. The days of their glory are as if they had never been; and the island that was then a speck, rude and neglected in the barren ocean, now rivals the ubiquity of their commerce, the glory of their arms, the fame of their philosophy, the eloquence oftheir Senate, and the inspiration of their bards. Who shall say, then, contemplating the past, that England, proud and potent as she appears, may not, one day, be what Athens is, and the young America yet soar to be what Athens was! Who shall say that, when the European column shall have mouldered, and the night of barbarism obscured its very ruins, that mighty continent may not emerge from the horizon to rule, for its time, sovereign of the ascendant!

Judicial Injustices. The next extract, from a powerful speech delivered by Senator Charles Sumner in September, 1854, is an excellent example of cumulative oratory. He asserts that he has no superstitious reverence for judicial proceedings, and then states his reasons, which he piles one upon another until the sum reaches such proportions as to utterly disarm any successful opposition to his statement, or even an attempt at opposition. This form of delivery is wonderfully effective, just as the opinion of a counselor-at-law would be when re-enforced by numerous decisions of the highest courts in the land. Only two means of attacking this style of oratory remain to the opposition, one being to impeach the authorities, the other to attack the application of them. Both these modes, however, are exceedingly dangerous to the objector when his opponent is a keen lawyer, an able speaker, and a learned man, such as was Charles Sumner.

The word "judges" takes the rising inflection because of the incompleteness of the thought, "in much respect" being necessary to complete the sense, and this takes the falling inflection because of the completeness, and theintervening thought "and especially the Supreme

Court of the Country" must be given parenthetically on account of its being an interjected remark; the words "judicial proceedings" take the falling inflection because they finish a positive thought, and "superstitious reverence" the rising, as the Senator means to express this thought negatively, as he does not possess any superstitious reverence for judicial proceedings. "Judges" and "men" are in apposition and for that reason take the same inflection, and as the statement is positive, the falling inflection must be used. The "worst crimes" and "sanction" require emphasis because they are important, and the sentence takes the falling inflection because it is positive. "Martyrs" and "patriots" require the rising inflection because they depend on "summons them to judgment" to complete the sense, and "crying from the ground" must be given parenthetically for the reason that it is interjected.

"Judicial tribunal" being the thing arraigned, requires emphasis whenever used in the speech. "Socrates" requires emphasis, and "hemlock" takes the falling inflection on account of the completion of the thought, "Saviour" is emphatic, and "Jerusalem" and "cross" take the falling inflection on account of completion of thought. The next line commences a concluding series which continues to the end of the paragraph. "Against the testimony and entreaties of her father," "in the name of the Old Religion," "amidst the shrieks and agonies of its victims," "in solemn denial of the great truth hehad disclosed," are all interjected remarks and therefore must be rendered parenthetically. All these parenthetical thoughts are complete in themselves, and consequently require the falling inflection. "Not" is emphatic, and the falling inflection is given "sun" because it expresses a contradiction.

The first phrase of the next paragraph requires the falling inflection, and the words "hesitate" and "unpitying," being negatived, require the rising. The close of the paragraph requires the falling inflection.

The next paragraph is a concluding series. "Surrounded by all the forms of law," "after deliberate argument," "in defiance of justice and humanity," "with Jeffreys on the bench," are all interjected remarks, complete in themselves, and require the falling inflection and parenthetical expression to each. "Queen" and "Sir Thomas More" require opposite inflections for the reason they are used to mark two distinct points in the despotic career of Henry the Eighth, just as one would say "from the first to the last," "Latimer, Ridley, and John Rogers" constitute a concluding series. "Justice" and "humanity" in the parenthetical clause are contrasted, and consequently given the opposite inflections, and "even" and "innocent women" require emphasis on account of their importance.

The last paragraph is a concluding series, "surrounded by all the forms of law" is an interjected complete thought, and therefore must be expressed parenthetically and given the falling inflection, and "our," in both instanceswhen used in this paragraph, requires emphasis and the falling inflection; while "unutterable" should take the rising inflection on account of its negative quality; the voice falling in conclusion on "Fugitive Slave Bill," because the final thought is a positive one.

JUDICIAL INJUSTICES
CHARLES SUMNER

I hold judges, and especially the Supreme Court of the country, in much respect, but I am too familiar with the history of judicial proceedings to regard them with any superstitious reverence. Judges are but men, and in all ages have shown a full share of human frailty. Alas! alas! the worst crimes of history have been perpetrated under their sanction. The blood of martyrs and of patriots, crying from the ground, summons them to judgment.

It was a judicial tribunal which condemned Socrates to drink the fatal hemlock, and which pushed the Saviour barefoot over the pavements of Jerusalem, bending beneath his cross. It was a judicial tribunal which, against the testimony and entreaties of her father, surrendered the fair Virginia as a slave; which arrested the teachings of the great Apostle to the Gentiles and sent him in bonds from Judea to Rome; which, in the name of the Old Religion, adjudged the Saints and Fathers of the Christian Church to death in all its most dreadful forms; and which afterwards, in the name of the New Religion, enforced the tortures of the Inquisition, amidst the shrieks and agonies of its victims, while it compelled Galileo to declare, in solemn denial of the great truth he had disclosed, that the earth did not move round the sun.

It was a judicial tribunal which in France during the longreign of her monarchs lent itself to be the instrument of every tyranny, as during the brief Reign of Terror it did not hesitate to stand forth the unpitying accessory of the unpitying guillotine.

It was a judicial tribunal in England, surrounded by all the forms of law, which sanctioned every despotic caprice of Henry the Eighth, from the unjust divorce of his queen to the beheading of Sir Thomas More; which lighted the fires of persecution that glowed at Oxford and Smithfield over the cinders of Latimer, Ridley, and John Rogers; which, after deliberate argument, upheld the fatal tyranny of Ship-Money, against the patriot resistance of Hampden; which, in defiance of justice and humanity, sent Sidney and Russell to the block; which persistently enforced the laws of Conformity that our Puritan Fathers persistently refused to obey; and which afterwards, with Jeffreys on the bench, crimsoned the page of English history with massacre and murder—even with the blood of innocent women.

Ay, Sir, and it was a judicial tribunal, in our country, surrounded by all the forms of law, which hung the witches at Salem; which affirmed the constitutionality of the Stamp-Act which it admonished "jurors and the people" to obey; and which now in our day, lent its sanction to the unutterable atrocity of the Fugitive Slave Bill.

AFTERWORD

We have now reached the end of our journey; but before parting, let us discuss generally the course over which we have traveled in order that some necessary incidents that may not have impressed themselves strongly on our memories may be reënforced, lest they otherwise be lost.

The public speaker should leave nothing to chance. It is customary to speak of the spontaneous bursting forth of eloquence, but eloquence is not spontaneous—it is the culmination of stored-up knowledge which has reached the point when it is fully matured and ready to use, and its apparent bursting forth is nothing but the arrival of the opportunity for its making its presence known. It is the coming together of the fully prepared man and the occasion that produces the orator. It is an axiom that nothing comes of nothing, and unless the would-be orator is willing to give his best in the way of fitting himself by study, labor, reflection, and industry, in their highest and broadest sense, to be a medium through which eloquence may be conveyed, he will look in vain for its appearance—the seed must be planted before the fruit can be gathered.

In the first place, the vocal mechanism must be thoroughly trained to stand the strain that is to be placedupon it, and to execute properly the manifold duties it will be called upon to perform. This necessitates careful and systematic practice in breathing, voice production, tone coloring, inflection, emphasis, and the many other sections of the vocal work which, when combined, comprise the vehicle which is to convey the thought.

In the second place, the mind must be fed and cultivated so as to enable it to produce thought. It must be strengthened by exercise, fed by reading of good matter, and made active by use. Time must be devoted to meditation, to thinking over the expressions of the ideas of the master minds that have gone before—weighing, refuting, and combining them, as well as receiving them and being influenced thereby—and to keeping the light of our own mind burning by thinking matters out in our own way and giving our thoughts the impress of our individuality. Only by these means can we hope to be at the same time wise and original. Originality that is foolish is worse than useless, and wisdom that is borrowed shines only with a reflected light; but that which is both original and wise will live through many ages and act as a beacon to light others to the attainment of originality and wisdom.

In the third place, an effective delivery is absolutely essential. There can no more be such a thing as an orator without a delivery than there can be a newspaper without paper or some other substance on which to print the news. A publisher might as well print a newspaper and then indifferently circulate it as for a man to fill hismind with great thoughts and ineffectively deliver them. Delivery is the soul of oratory; without it, there can be nothing but the form of speech; with it, there is the spirit that gives life to the words. The matter is the product, the delivery is the mode of conveyance; and each is necessary to the other if either is to be of value to the speaker.

The only really effective form of delivery is the extempore; and, after once it has been acquired, it is the easiest of the many forms. In the opinion of the author, matter that is written out and then read, or matter that is written out, memorized, and then spoken, is in neither case a speech. Speaking is conveying thought by word of mouth, and not by word of pen. The matter that is to form the speech should be diligently gathered, fully digested, and carefully arranged, but the words that are to clothe the thought should be spontaneous. Unless the words are willing servants, well trained, springing instantly to the performance of their duty, coming, not through a conscious effort to recall what has been memorized, but in response to the sub-conscious action of the mind, the words will fail to possess that mentality that alone can give them the expression that is really their soul. Only when the mind is released from all care concerning words can it be placed adequately upon the thought, and only by fully placing it upon the thought can the mentality enter the voice, thereby making the words convey by tone and general expression what they really stand for, and carry to the mind of the listener the thought which is in the mind of the speaker. In this manner is a connection brought about between listener and speaker, and by these means is generated that force which is commonly called magnetism but which is, in reality, the active mind of the speaker getting into communication with the mind of the listener through the mediumship of the vitalized spoken word. The language is but the wire which carries the message, or the atmosphere on which the message is sent; the thought is the electricity which produces the message. The language is material, the mentality is spiritual; the one being the body of expression, the other being the soul.

Finally, why are there so few orators in the world today? Merely because there are so few persons who are willing to spend the time and employ the labor necessary to acquire the qualifications for the making of orators. No great achievement in any walk of life is accomplished without labor, no movement in behalf of man has ever progressed without labor, and nothing is worth having unless it is secured by labor. Run your eye over the pages of history and try to find instances where chance has knocked with its golden wand on the door of man's existence; and for every one so found, at least a dozen will be discovered where man has cut through the rock of difficulties with the iron tools of industry and forged those tools in the fires of determination. Not all men who achieved greatness were born poor in this world's goods. Many of them, men like Marcus Aurelius, Washington, Lafayette, and Roosevelt, won renown in spite of their wealth; while, on the other hand, men like Moses, Franklin, and Lincoln gained their great eminence in the face of poverty. It matters not whether man be rich or whether man be poor, so far as his success in living a useful life is concerned, but it does signify much whether he is an idler or a laborer. Make yourself worthy of success, and success— in its true and only valuable sense—will be yours. Remember, that labor—proud, independent labor—is noble, and that it leads, not only to the making of orators, but to the formation of characters—the building of souls.

A SYSTEMATIZED STUDY

OF

"HOW TO MASTER THE SPOKEN WORD"

A GUIDE TO TEACHERS AND STUDENTS

Students are advised to read the work as a book, commencing with the first page and continuing straight on to the end. They should skip nothing, not even the long speeches, as they are introduced for specific purposes; but they should also guard against tarrying on the way to study and particular passages that may strike their fancy. They are advised to first read the book carefully in order that they may the better understand its scope and purpose, and gain some idea regarding the general plan that underlies its construction.

It will be noted that the first chapter does not contain instructions as to how the student of oratory is to breathe, or how he is to use the many other functions of body, voice, and mind that are necessary to the correct production of the spoken word; but it shows how famous speakers produced their effects, and it reveals to the student the means he must adopt if he is to produce like results, leaving to later chapters the task of revealing how the means are to be applied. This manner of arranging thematter was adapted in order to insure the student's interest being aroused in the subject at the start, thereby preventing an extinguishing of his enthusiasm by initiating him into the dry mysteries of the technical parts of speech before he had gained a fair idea regarding the means to employ in qualifying himself to become a public speaker. When, however, it is intended to use the work as a textbook, it should not be studied as it is read, but the lesson should be taken up in a natural sequence, beginning with breath and continuing through to the production of the finished speech or oration.

www.ingramcontent.com/pod-product-compliance
Lightning Source LLC
Chambersburg PA
CBHW011342090426
42741CB00017B/3435